CIVIL AND CORRUPT ASIA

Ernst van den Boogaart

Civil and Corrupt Asia

Image and Text in the *Itinerario* and the *Icones* of Jan Huygen van Linschoten

THE UNIVERSITY OF CHICAGO PRESS

CHICAGO AND LONDON

The University of Chicago Press, Chicago 60637
The University of Chicago Press, Ltd., London
© 2003 by The University of Chicago
All rights reserved. Published 2003
12 11 10 09 08 07 06 05 04 03   1 2 3 4 5

ISBN: 0-226-84700-4 (cloth)

Originally published in Amsterdam under the title
Het verheven en verdorven Azië: Woord en beeld in het Itinerario
en de Icones *van Jan Huygen van Linschoten*, © 2000, Het Spinhuis Amsterdam.

LIBRARY OF CONGRESS CATALOGING-IN-PUBLICATION DATA
Boogaart, E. van den.
    [Verheven en verdorven Azië. English]
    Civil and corrupt Asia: images and text in the Itinerario and the Icones of Jan
Huygen van Linschoten / Ernst van den Boogaart.
        p. cm.
    Includes bibliographical references and index.
    ISBN 0-226-84700-4 (cloth : acid-free paper)
        1. Linschoten, Jan Huygen van, 1563–1611. Itinerario, voyage ofte schipvaert van
Jan Huygen van Linschoten naer Oost ofte Portugaels Indien. 2. Linschoten, Jan
Huygen van, 1563–1611—Journeys—East Asia. 3. East Asia—Description and travel.
4. East Asia—Pictorial works. I. Title.
DS411.1.B6613 2003
915.04'3—dc21

                                                            2002020401

Contents

Foreword

Jan Huygen van Linschoten owes his fame to the *Itinerario,* an account of his voyage to Portuguese Goa and a description of the Asian countries in which the Portuguese traded. Published in Dutch in Amsterdam in 1595-1596, his book coincided with the start of Dutch and British expansion in Asia. It was widely read in English, French, Latin, and German translations during the seventeenth century. It has since come to be regarded as a classic in the literature of the history of European expansion and has often been consulted and reissued. Linschoten's *Icones Habitus Gestusque Indorum* may have been popular in its day as well, but until recently, only a single—not even complete—copy in the Universiteitsbibliotheek Amsterdam was believed to have survived. The *Icones* is a series of thirty prints from the *Itinerario,* captioned with excerpts from the book's Latin translation, that the publisher issued in 1604 as an independent publication. Like the book from which it derives, the *Icones* consists of a combination of words and images.

This rare edition is reproduced here in its entirety, together with a translation of the Latin texts. The plate that is missing from the exemplar in the Universiteitsbibliotheek Amsterdam has been taken from the complete set of prints in the Herzog August Bibliothek in Wolfenbüttel. The title page, missing in both the Amsterdam and Wolfenbüttel copies, was found in the Atlas van Stolk in Rotterdam. An introductory essay discusses the character of the combination of word and image in the *Icones* and the *Itinerario.*

The text of the *Itinerario* repeatedly refers to the images as depictions 'from life'. At the time, this suggested that their value and importance lay in their realistic character. The printed images were supposed to derive from careful renderings of observed facts drawn on the spot by the observer himself. Some of the prints probably derive from drawings that Linschoten made in Asia. Closer examination, however, reveals that their verisimilitude is rather limited. They contain many stereotypical elements. Parts of some prints were invented on the basis of the text. In a few cases their relation to the historical reality is downright puzzling. These prints do not offer the reader a scrupulous representation of Asian dress, means of transport, landscapes, or flora and fauna at the end of the sixteenth century. Neither are they detailed imaginations of the text.

The prints have a different intention. They constitute a visual manual for analytically reading and methodically coming to terms with Linschoten's text. They seduce the viewer to compare carefully the images and the texts and by that means teach him how a reliable and orderly picture of the different customs in Asia can be constructed and what moral message can be derived from this exercise. The texts provide the data, the images offer a way to classify them. To that end, an artist in Holland adapted the original 'counterfeits from life' to form an 'edifying series'. On this interpretation, the images in necessary combination with the text form a deliberate and skilfully constructed instrument for teaching careful observation, systematic description, and moral evaluation. There is some indirect evidence to support the hypothesis that the painter and art historian Karel van Mander, the 'Dutch Vasari', may have provided the concept for the series.

The introduction to this book is a revised version of my introduction to the prints in *Jan Huygen van Linschoten and the Moral Map of Asia,* published by the Roxburghe Club, a British bibliophile association, in 1999. The essay was commissioned by the late Mr H. Oppenheimer. I am very grateful to him for having granted permission to make use of that text again in the present publication. I was fortunate in finding C. L. Heesakkers prepared to translate the Latin texts of the *Icones* into Dutch. Peter Mason deftly turned the Dutch into English. He also translated my introduction and assisted the research in all kinds of ways. I am grateful to H. J. Nalis for his kindness in sharing his knowledge of the *Icones* with me. Nicolas Barker, Arie Pos, and John Saumarez-Smith followed the unexpected course of the investigation in all its vagaries and gave me highly appreciated assistance. For information and encouragement at different stages of the research I would like to warmly thank Leonard Blussé, Florike Egmond, Pieter Emmer, Roelof van Gelder, José da Silva Horta, Justin Howes, Adam Jones, Marjolein Leesberg, Jan Storm van Leeuwen, Hessel Miedema, Nicolette Mout, Eco Haitsma Mulier, the late Heiko A. Oberman, Christiaan Schuckman, Ben Teensma, Ilja Veldman, Alain Wijffels, and Johan van der Zande.

Finally, I owe a debt of gratitude to several institutions for permission to reproduce works in their possession: to Atlas van Stolk, of the Historisch Museum Rotterdam, for the title page of the *Icones;* to Universiteitsbibliotheek Amsterdam, for plates 1 and 3–30 of the *Icones* and for the title page of the *Itinerario;* and to the Herzog August Bibliothek Wolfenbüttel for plate 2 of the *Icones.*

ITINERARIO,

Voyage ofte Schipvaert / van Jan Huygen van Linschoten naer Oost ofte Portugaels Indien

inhoudende een corte beschrijvinghe der selver Landen ende Zee-custen / met aenwijsinge van alle de voornaemde principale Havens / Revieren / hoecken ende plaetsen / tot noch toe vande Portugesen ontdeckt ende bekent: Waer by ghevoecht zijn / niet alleen die Conterfeytsels vande habyten / drachten ende wesen / so vande Portugesen aldaer residerende / als van de ingeboornen Indianen / ende huere Tempels / Afgoden / Huysinge / met die voornaemste Boomen / Vruchten / kruyden / Specerijen / ende diergelijcke materialen / als ooc die manieren des selfden Volckes / so in hunnen Godts-diensten / als in Politie en Huijs-houdinghe: maer ooc een corte verhalinge van de Coophandelingen / hoe en waer die ghedreven en ghevonden worden / met die ghedenckweerdichste geschiedenissen / voorghevallen den tijt zijnder residentie aldaer.

Alles beschreven ende by een vergadert, door den selfden, seer nut, oorbaer, ende oock vermakelijcken voor alle curieuse ende Liefhebbers van vreemdigheden.

t'AMSTELREDAM.

By Cornelis Claesz. op't VVater, in't Schrijf-boeck, by de oude Brugghe.

Anno CIƆ. IƆ. XCVI.

Introduction

The Credibility of the Curious Traveller

The *Itinerario* by Jan Huygen van Linschoten was a book that launched a thousand ships. It provided the Dutch, English, French, and Danish merchants who from 1595 on began to dispatch fleets via the Cape of Good Hope to Asia with information about the centres of maritime trade, and it afforded their captains sailing instructions for the main routes. In the case of the Dutch, there was a direct link between the book and the voyages. The Amsterdam publisher Cornelis Claesz rushed the quires with sailing instructions through the press in order to give them to the first Dutch fleet to sail to the East Indies in April 1595. The rest of the book was published the following year.[1] The Dutch trading expedition set the example for other countries in northwestern Europe. The English followed immediately and resolutely. Linschoten's book also stimulated their enterprise directly. In 1598 the London publisher John Wolfe issued an English translation at the instigation of Richard Hakluyt. This propagandist of English expansion referred to the *Itinerario* in his recommendations to the recently founded East India Company in October 1599 and January 1601.[2] The French and Danes were slower and more sporadic in following the Dutch example.[3] They will have been spurred on by the Latin translations of 1599, published in Frankfurt by the brothers Johann Theodor and Johann Israël de Bry and in The Hague by Claesz in cooperation with others. A French translation, probably printed in Frankfurt, appeared in 1610, followed by a printing in Amsterdam in 1619.[4] Within a few decades the merchants and navigators of the countries of northwestern Europe had managed once and for all to break the monopoly on sailing to Asia that the Portuguese had maintained for a century. They thereby dealt an indirect blow to the Spanish Habsburgs —kings of Portugal as well between 1580 and 1640—whose bid for supremacy in Europe they contested vigorously.

All the same, the *Itinerario* was not a blueprint for an attack on the Portuguese trading empire or for the construction of a competitive commercial network in Asia. The first part, the *Itinerario* proper, did contain a description of the area in which Asian maritime trade was carried out, but it also contained much information that was less immediately relevant to the merchant. The thick volume on Asia was followed by a second, more slender volume with descriptions of West Africa and America and a third with sailing instructions. The work is a hybrid: part travel account, part compendium. It afforded a summary of knowledge about the 'newly discovered territories' to whoever wanted to challenge the Hispano-Portuguese monarchy, but he had to develop his own plan.

The title page of the *Itinerario* proper announces that the hefty folio volume comprises text and plates. The text is said to recount 'The Voyage and travailes of John Hugen van Linschoten into the East or Portingales Indies: Setting downe a briefe discourse of the said Landes, and sea coastes' supplemented by a 'briefe discourse of . . . their trade, and traffique in Marchandise, how and from whence their wares are sold, and brought thether' and 'a collection of the most memorable and worthiest thinges happened in the time of his beeing in the same countries'.[5] This is a correct, albeit incomplete, description. The themes mentioned correspond to sections or chapters in the text. It should be noted that the emphasis is on Linschoten's voyage, the experience on which the accounts of Asia are based. The plates, as described on the title page, show 'the manner of apparrell of the Portingales' inhabiting Asia and the appearance of 'the naturall borne Indians, their Temples, Idols, houses, trees, Fruites, Hearbes, Spices, and such like: Together with the customes of those countries, as well for their manner of Idolatrous religion and worshipping of Images, as also for their policie and government of their houses'. Here too the description matches the content. The thirty-six engravings by Joannes van Doetecum and his sons Baptista and Joannes consist of twenty-six plates mainly depicting the appearance and practices of the inhabitants of India and the Far East, four plates with illustrations of Asian trees, plants, and fruits, and six topographical prints. These topics are also covered in the text, but only the plants are dealt with in separate, successive chapters. Dress and outward appearance, political regime and social order ('policie'), family and economy ('government of their houses'), and religion are treated at various points in the geographical survey of Asia and in chapters on the ethnic groups that populated western India. The topics, however, correspond to thematic subseries into which the plates can be divided for analysis.

The detailed announcement of the images on the title page was intended to draw attention to a remarkable feature of the book. This was certainly not the first time that images of ethnic types from Asia had been included in a sixteenth-century travel account, but the scale, variation, and scope of the *Itinerario*'s visual programme were indeed remarkable. Donald Lach called it 'a watershed in Europe's pictorial impression of Asia'.[6] All the same, neither Linschoten nor Claesz emphasised the novelty of the engravings. They merely served to back up the claim that the text was based on the author's own experience. Not only could Linschoten describe the remote world of Asia; he could also show what it looked like. This point is further emphasised by the portrait engraving of the author at the beginning of the book, where he is represented as a thirty-two-year-old scion of Haarlem amid views of Goa, Mozambique, and Saint Helena. The inscription proclaims the admirable service that he has rendered with his book: 'Linschoten here gives us the world of the East. By the hand of the artist, this engraving gives us Linschoten'. In other words: Here you see the man who has seen those distant worlds with his own eyes. Both presentations were gifts based on perception. Text and image reinforced one another's verisimilitude.[7] Linschoten's motto, 'Souffrir pour parvenir', indicated that the acquisition of true knowledge demanded resolution and determination.

The plates alone were attractive to buyers. In 1604 Claesz issued thirty of the thirty-six engravings of the *Itinerario* as a separate set with a new title page. This collection comprised the plates depicting plants and the peoples and customs of Asia but omitted the topographic plates.[8] It was given the title *Icones, habitus gestusque Indorum ac Lusitanorum per Indiam viventium etc.* (hereafter *Icones* for short), a more or less complete rendering of the title of the *Itinerario* proper.[9] The brief captions in Dutch and Latin that accompanied the original plates were now followed by lengthy excerpts from the Latin edition of the *Itinerario*. It is evident from the *Icones* that, if the plates were detached from the original book, they still required a degree of textual commentary. The text both promoted a proper understanding of the images and reinforced their claim to offer an authentic representation of an observed reality. Like the *Itinerario,* the *Icones* was intended to give the impression of being a dependable source of information about Asia.

Linschoten certainly went to Asia, although he saw considerably less of it with his own eyes than the caption to his portrait suggests.[10] He began his voyage on board a Portuguese vessel, the *S. Salvador,* part of the fleet that left Belem, near Lisbon, for the East Indies on Good Friday 1583. At the time Linschoten was in the employ of the recently appointed archbishop of Asia, Vicente da Fonseca. After an untroubled rounding of the Cape of Good Hope, the fleet stopped in Mozambique, as was customary, to take on provisions and to trade in gold, ivory, and slaves. On 21 September 1583 Linschoten reached the city of Goa on the west coast of India. He remained there until November 1588, serving the archbishop first as a clerk and then as a tax official. He went on short trips of no more than a few dozen kilometres from the island on which Goa was situated. He visited the neighbouring islands under Portuguese rule, Bardes and Salsette, and the coastal strip to the west of the Ghats range that belonged to the native state of Bijapur. On his return journey he spent ten days in Honor, one and a half days in Cananore, and almost a month in Cochin—all on the Malabar coast south of Goa. The fleet was replenished on Saint Helena. The geographical views in the cartouches surrounding his portrait refer to this and indicate what he had seen more precisely than the inscription under the portrait does. Linschoten's personal experience of Portuguese Asia, a far-flung network of trading posts extending from Mozambique and Hormuz in the west to the Moluccan islands, China, and Japan in the east, was thus extremely limited.

Goa was the residence of the viceroy, the archbishop, and the provincial of the Jesuits, which made it the administrative and religious centre of Portuguese Asia. It was the final destination of the European fleets, the point of departure for homebound vessels, and thus also the central transshipment port for Portuguese trade in Asia. It attracted a large and varied group of native merchants and mariners from the trading zones of the western Indian Ocean. Those who used their ears and eyes and had access to the far-reaching channels of information that intersected in Goa could learn a lot about the East. But what information interested Linschoten, and what was he in a position to collect?

It has been supposed that Linschoten was sent by Dutch merchants to reconnoitre the world of commerce in Asia, as Cornelis and Frederik de Houtman had gathered information in Lisbon in 1592 for the preparation of the first Dutch fleet to Asia.[11] Such a hypothesis is far-fetched and projects the author of the *Itinerario* of 1595 back onto the seventeen-year-old who followed his two elder brothers to Seville in 1579.[12] Upon his arrival, his brother Willem had already left for Madrid to join the court. What the other brother—whose name is unknown—did for a living in Seville is not indicated in the sources. Ensuing events suggest that none of the brothers was primarily interested in trade. They proved to be after positions in the employ of the administrative elite of the Spanish monarchy. They saw opportunities for themselves in the preparations by Philip II for his proclamation as king of Portugal. The brother in Seville left for the court when it was in Badajoz and was taken into service by a Spanish ambassador who left on a mission to Italy. Soon afterward he died of the plague in Salamanca. Jan had entered the employ of a German or Dutch nobleman whom he followed to Lisbon. There he met up with his brother Willem, who was also under aristocratic protection. The two brothers spent two and a half years in the Portuguese capital. Jan worked for a while for a merchant 'until something else turned up'.[13] Through the offices of Willem he secured a position with Bishop Vicente da Fonseca. His brother sailed with the same fleet on His Majesty's service but returned immediately. Jan stayed on in Goa. His departure for Asia seems to have been by chance, not part of a preconceived plan, and to have arisen from an interest in the world of government rather than commerce. He did not set out as an undercover agent for Protestant merchant capitalism. He travelled to satisfy his curiosity about the wider world, to learn new languages and customs, and for his personal education. His interest had many facets.

It was not unusual in the sixteenth century for young Dutch men to spend a few years in Spain and Portugal before moving on to America or Asia.[14] Most cases that are known concern trainees attached to merchants, young men who found employment as mariners or soldiers, and members of missionary orders. The position in which Linschoten voyaged to Asia seems unusual in this respect. In his case—as in that of the missionaries—his religious conviction must have been an object of scrutiny. It is unlikely that the archbishop would have employed Jan if his Catholicism had been in doubt. The older Dutch literature that liked to present Linschoten as an adherent of William of Orange, the leader of the national revolt against Spain, and as an early supporter of the Reformed Church, was perplexed by this element in his biography. Later historians have shown that by 1579, the year of Jan's departure, there were large and varied groups in the rebellious provinces that adopted positions between the extremes of the political and religious spectrum. The Linschoten brothers appear to have belonged to these intermediate groups. It is unlikely that at this point they felt particularly hostile towards the Catholic church or the ruling circles of Spain and Portugal. Jan managed to secure the confidence of the archbishop. Although he would not have been a member of his employer's inner circle, there would have been no reason to exclude him from matters of importance. So his position within one of the central organisations of Portuguese Asia must have offered him opportunities to find out about regions remote from Goa as well.

In the late sixteenth century the educational tour to learn about the ways of the world was considered by some to be a serious affair requiring advance instruction. They wrote the so-called apodemic manuals, secular versions of the manuals for pilgrims, setting out instructions for edifying travel and the acquisition of empirical knowledge.[15] Travellers were expected to keep diaries and where possible to organise the day's observations systematically in the evening in a summary. They were also to establish contacts with knowledgeable informants and collect objects that illustrated the products of the country and its customs and habits.

It is not known whether Linschoten was familiar with these new instructions for travel, but it is certain that he put a number of the apodemic recommendations into practice. He kept a diary, not to record his private emotions, but to provide as objective as possible an account of the course of the voyage and of political and military events during his stay in Goa. He described experiences that he shared with others and that could be confirmed or checked by others. In Goa he derived information from English merchants and from a Venetian about Hormuz, Persia, and the route by land to Asia via the Middle East.[16] Dirck Gerritszoon Pomp, a fellow citizen from Enkhuizen, whom Linschoten met in Goa, informed him about the journey to Macao, in China, and from there to Japan.[17] Linschoten corresponded with a native of Flanders from Sluis who lived on the Coromandel coast. A captain who had been imprisoned on Banda for two years told him about the Spice Islands; he discussed with a black slave from Mozambique the land route from southeastern Africa to Angola.[18] He must also have picked up a lot from the Portuguese in Goa, both inside the archbishop's palace and elsewhere, but he says nothing about those contacts.[19]

In addition to written and oral information he collected objects, including two birds of paradise from the Moluccas, Chinese paper with words written in Chinese characters, pens, ink, two chopsticks, South Indian texts written on palm leaves (olas), small bells that the men of Pegu (Burma) introduced between the foreskin and the glans penis, and the seed of the *arbore triste,* a remarkable tree from western India.[20] He acquired rare books, such as the Goan impression of *Colóquios dos simples e drogas e cousas mediçinais da India* by Garcia da Orta, an exemplary treatise on the Indian flora and materia medica.[21] He probably collected manuscripts with information about the major trading areas of Portuguese Asia and possibly also sailing instructions for the much-frequented routes. Furthermore, he sometimes sketched objects of particular interest. For instance, at the instigation of the archbishop he made a drawing of an unusual fish that had been caught, and he may also have executed the bird's-eye view of Goa for his employer. He may have collected images made by Asians as well.

In short, Linschoten behaved as the early-modern ideal type of the curious traveller, the man who journeyed through many different climes to see the diversity of the world with his own eyes, the man for whom curiosity was not a vice but a virtue. This was different from the pilgrim, who journeyed to the sacred centre of the world, the Holy Land, or to the tomb or relic of a favourite saint for the good of his soul.[22] Because he had been a curious traveller, Linschoten could later claim with some justification that the *Itinerario* was a work of empirical knowledge.

However, it took time, a familiar clime, and a new setting for the curious traveller to become an author. At the end of 1588 Linschoten decided to return to Europe. He had received news of the deaths of his father and his surviving brother Willem. He must have been concerned about his mother and the family's affairs. A career in Asia was insecure, because his patron Vicente da Fonseca had also passed away. Moreover, he had reached the age at which it was customary for Dutch men to marry and start to lead an adult life. A career outside government circles usually meant becoming a merchant (not Linschoten's preferred occupation) and marrying a woman from one of the Luso-Indian families of Goa. The *Itinerario* betrays Linschoten's repugnance to marriage with native women, whom he viewed in a very dim light. His views will have been influenced by the unfortunate plight of his Flemish friend in Goa, Frans Coningh, who was murdered by the paramour of his Luso-Asian wife in August 1588.[23] He appeared to have decided to start his adult life in Europe soon afterward.

The return journey proceeded much less smoothly than the outbound one. The flagship of the fleet sank in a storm near the Cape of Good Hope, and the other ships only just managed to reach Saint Helena. They were hit by another heavy storm in the Azores. One ship with a particularly precious cargo ran aground at Angra on Terceira. Linschoten and others attempted to save the cargo and to ensure that what remained was taken safely to Lisbon. This was no easy matter, as English buccaneers had almost sealed off the Azores. It took Linschoten more than two years to escape with a part of the cargo. During his stay on Terceira he witnessed several disasters that struck the Spanish fleets from America and Portuguese vessels from Asia, caused either by storms or by English pirates. He also received news of the repulse of the Armada sent against England. If he had toyed with the idea of settling the family affairs and then pursuing a career in Hispano-Portuguese service, he appears here to have decided to try his luck on the other side of the European political and religious divide. He returned to Enkhuizen, the town where he had grown up, in late 1592. His experiences abroad were attested by his own notes and the manuscripts, books, illustrations, and objects that he had acquired. He could present himself as someone who knew Asia, the type of man for whom there was at that time a great demand in the provinces of Holland and Zealand.

Linschoten's return coincided with the period in which rebellious groups in the Northern Netherlands succeeded in expelling the Spaniards from the northeastern and eastern parts of the country and laid the foundations for a new sovereign state, the privileged position of the Reformed Church, and the economic and cultural flowering of the seventeenth-century Republic of the United Netherlands. Euphoria over their military and economic successes was widespread. After the capitulation of Groningen in 1594, Prince Maurice of Nassau, the commander of the rebel army, passed in triumph through the country. The burgomasters of Amsterdam organised the performance of a play about the battle between David (Maurice) and Goliath (Philip II) in his honour in Dam Square, near the shop belonging to Cornelis Claesz.[24] Some of David's people felt that other glorious opportunities beckoned beyond the horizon. The ports of Holland and Zealand extended their trading activities to Brazil, the Caribbean, and West Africa and considered fitting out merchant fleets for China and the Spice Islands. Merchants and geographers deliberated on the best course: the tried and tested route via the Cape of Good Hope, or the shorter route via the north. Enkhuizen was one of the ports that explored the possibilities for extra-European trade.

Linschoten suggested in the foreword of the *Itinerario* that he had collected his information about Asia without the intention of publishing it. His collection was intended 'to show something new to my friends in particular'.[25] At the age of twenty-two, he had written to his parents from Goa to justify his distant voyage: 'It will give me something to tell when I am old'.[26] Such statements were quite conventional in an oral culture in which written information still served primarily to buttress oral communication within one's own circle and in a world where change was slow. Knowledge of new things acquired in one's youth could be expected to last a lifetime. Already in the first sentence of the *Itinerario* proper, however, Linschoten demonstrates that he is a child of the typographic culture. Ever since boyhood he had been 'applying my selfe to the reading of Histories, and straunge adventures, wherein I tooke no small delight'.[27] That was why he had started to travel. The typographic system of communication was organised to be fed with new discoveries, recorded in print once the curiosity aroused by the existing books was satisfied. The people to whom he showed his collection in Enkhuizen also proved to be indebted to print culture, as they pressed him incessantly to publish the account of his voyage.[28] Linschoten had not only to tell what he knew but to publish it. News had to be rushed in print to the reader as soon as possible. Change had become permanent and had to be reported continuously.

Linschoten does not name the people to whom he showed his collection and told his tales. It is likely that they included not only old friends like Dirck Gerritszoon Pomp, but also those who demonstrably contributed to the *Itinerario* and were of importance for his further career. In Enkhuizen they included Berent ten Broecke (1550–1633), better known by his Latin name Paludanus, the town physician and the owner of a collection of curiosities that enjoyed national and international fame;[29]

François Maelson (1538–1602), a former town physician, pensionary of Enkhuizen in 1572, and an influential figure in local and national political life; and Lucas Jansz Waghenaer (1533/34–1606), a leading figure of the North Holland cartographic school, whose work had been promoted by Maelson.[30] It was probably Waghenaer who introduced Linschoten to Cornelis Claesz (ca. 1551–1609) in Amsterdam, who had published his books of charts.[31] In March 1594 Linschoten concluded a contract with Claesz for the publication of a 'certain book of the navigations of the East Indies, including illustrations'.[32] It may have been Claesz who put him in contact with several townsmen of nearby Hoorn who were interested in distant lands: Cornelis Taemsz (1577–1600), scion of a family of city fathers who, with the aid of a local sinecure, devoted himself to letters and was engaged in 1594 on the task of translating the account of China by Juan Gonzalez de Mendoza for publication by Claesz;[33] the physician and neo-Latin poet Petrus Hoogerbeets (1542–1599);[34] and the town physician and historian Theodorus Velius (1572–1630).[35] All of these men had travelled, most of them in Europe, but Paludanus had also been to the Middle East. Paludanus, Velius, and Hoogerbeets were all graduates of the University of Padua, the centre of 'empirical humanism', and they were eager to promote the diffusion of new knowledge based on experience, as can be seen from their support of Linschoten.[36]

Maelson provided the most direct assistance to Linschoten. He was responsible for Linschoten's high position with the fleets that searched for a northeast passage to Asia in 1594 and 1595. The first of these fleets considered that they had discovered a route that had never been tried before, even though they had covered only a small part of it. The glory was reflected on Linschoten. His poet friends in Hoorn eulogised him as the Dutch Magellan. Linschoten was now, two years after his return from Asia, a man of standing, and thus a suitable husband for Reinu Meynertsdochter Semeyns, the widowed daughter of the burgomaster of Enkhuizen, who already had a child from her previous marriage. Linschoten must have seen himself now as a devoted protector of the Reformed Church. Soon after the wedding he left on his second voyage to the north. This time the fleet ran into heavy ice and had difficulty getting back, but no harm was done to Linschoten's reputation. He was admitted to the Enkhuizen magistracy. From 1597 on he was city treasurer, and in 1606 he was appointed guardian of the hospital. He lived in Enkhuizen without engaging in any other distant voyages until his death in 1611, famous as the author of the *Itinerario* instead of as the discoverer of the northeast passage.

Linschoten's ideas about what the book that established his reputation should contain changed repeatedly in the years 1594–1595, when,

between voyages to the north, he was busy putting it together. The contract of March 1594 mentioned only a text on the voyage to the East Indies with corresponding visual material. Soon afterward, however, Claesz and Linschoten must have decided to widen the geographic scope of the book. The licence granted by the States General on 8 October 1594 refers to a work in two parts. Part 1 would contain a description of the East Indies (the *Itinerario* proper), sailing instructions (the *Reys-Gheschrift*), and a survey of the revenue of the king of Spain including revenue from the overseas territories (the *Extract*).[37] This volume mainly comprised material that Linschoten had collected before his return to Enkhuizen. The incorporation of the *Extract* was Maelson's idea, to give the work a political angle. Part 2 would consist of a translation of José de Acosta's *Historia natural y moral de las Indias*. This would have been Linschoten's idea. He had already enthusiastically made a start on the translation, but for some unknown reason it was later decided not to publish it together with the *Itinerario*.[38] It was replaced by a shorter text on America, derived from various sources, and a brief text on West Africa (the *Beschrijvinghe*). The editions of the *Itinerario* published in 1595 and 1596 comprised three parts and an appendix, each with its own title page: the *Itinerario* proper, the *Beschrijvinghe*, and the *Reys-Gheschrift*, to which the *Extract* was added without a break in the page numbering.

It is above all the text of the *Itinerario* proper that shows the contributions of Linschoten's friends in Enkhuizen and Hoorn. The poets from the neighbouring town all wrote short eulogies to enhance Linschoten's reputation. That was the only contribution of Velius, but Hoogerbeets also supplied short Latin verses for some of the plates, and Taemsz the ode *Vaygats ofte de straet van Nassau*, the apotheosis of Linschoten as the Magellan of Holland, included in the preliminary pages of the *Reys-Gheschrift*. Taemsz was familiar with the poetry of Camões, and it is not improbable that he suggested the borrowings from the *Lusíadas* in the geographical descriptions of the *Itinerario*. The long passages on China are excerpts from his translation of the work of Gonzalez de Mendoza, which was issued shortly before the *Itinerario* and contains a reference to its imminent publication. (The *Itinerario* also refers to the complete text of Gonzalez de Mendoza. These cross-references may have been the work of Cornelis Claesz, who published both books.) Paludanus provided many annotations to the natural history chapters of the *Itinerario* proper, which consist of excerpts from the *Colóquios* of Garcia da Orta, probably translated by Linschoten himself. While Maelson had established the link with contemporary politics, the others gave a scholarly and literary veneer to a book by an author who had studied only at the university of life and who apologised in his foreword—though this was a topos—for the simplicity and clumsiness of his work.

Decisions regarding the format and presentation of the book will have been taken mainly by Cornelis Claesz. He published several works on America, Africa, and China during the years spent preparing the *Itinerario*. He issued them as small, relatively inexpensive editions for a Dutch public. His ambitions with the *Itinerario* and the *Icones* were clearly somewhat different. The *Itinerario* has a folio format, the text is longer, the prints are greater in number, and more work has been put into the publication. The Latin poems by Hoogerbeets suggest an intention to translate the work into Latin for a wider European public.[39] Claesz also had several exemplars of the *Itinerario* bound for display in his shop on the Damrak. This was unusual in the sixteenth century, when customers bought books in plane sheet form and decided themselves how they wanted the work to be bound.[40] Claesz wanted to draw attention to Linschoten's book in a special way. The title page specifies the public he had in mind: the 'curious and lovers of strange things'. This would certainly have included the merchants and mariners for whom Claesz's maps and specialised nautical publications were intended, but also the kinds of readers with whom Linschoten and his friends in Enkhuizen and Hoorn identified: the practitioners of empirical science and literature.

The *Itinerario*, and especially the *Icones*, provide a clue as to what Claesz hoped to achieve with this format. The presentation of the visual material in the *Icones* is strongly reminiscent of the works on America, the so-called 'Grands Voyages', published by Theodor de Bry and his sons in Frankfurt from 1590 on. Most of these publications were in two parts, one textual, the other made up of illustrations accompanied by extensive descriptive passages, usually taken from the main text. These large folio volumes, dedicated to sovereigns, catered to the growing interest in geography among the elites of Europe and to the important place given to 'methodical' travel in their education. Claesz seems to have wanted to vie with his Frankfurt colleagues.

There were other reasons to present Linschoten's work on a grand scale. Earlier works on America, Africa, and Asia that had appeared in the Netherlands were the work of Spaniards, Portuguese, Italians, French, and Germans. The *Itinerario* was the first work on the East Indies—in fact, on any of the newly discovered territories—to be written in Dutch by a native of Dutch soil, a Dutch Magellan. The work appeared at a time of euphoria caused by the military and economic successes of the United Provinces. The dedications of the various volumes bear witness to the valiant author's commitment to the state that was being created in the Northern Netherlands. The *Itinerario* proper is dedicated to the States General, the *Reys-Gheschrift* to the stadholder Prince Maurice and the Admiralty of Holland, Zeeland, and West Friesland, and the *Extract*

to the States of Holland and West Friesland (remarkably, the *Beschrijvinghe* does not contain a dedication).[41] The work was not a very explicit challenge to Philip II, king of Spain and Portugal, but any contemporary with his wits about him would have had little difficulty in grasping the connection with the major conflicts of the time. A prestigious presentation of the work, with stress on its reliability, was appropriate to the collective ambitions of leading groups in the new state to be.

The title page of the *Itinerario* proper was designed to create the impression that the work's authority derived not only from the text, presented as a true-to-life account of the author's experiences, but also from the plates. It became clear in the years immediately following the first impression that the text contained valuable and reliable information for European merchants and seamen, although only a small part of it was actually based on Linschoten's experience. The contribution of the plates to empirical knowledge of Asia has never before been investigated. That will be analysed in what follows. The six topographic prints, mainly concerned with Linschoten's voyage to Asia and the return journey, will not be taken into consideration here. The analysis is confined to the thirty plates, and accompanying texts, that Claesz issued as an independent set: the *Icones*. What has been said about the role of the plates so far is that they were considered to support the claim of the text to reliability because they purported to reproduce scenes that Linschoten himself had seen and depicted. We shall first examine the credibility of this claim and what the general intention of these supposedly realistic images may have been. This will lead to a detailed consideration of the meaning of the prints in their own right, independently of the text, and finally to a discussion of the nature of the relation between word and image in the *Icones*.

The *Icones* 'Drawn from Life'?

The title page of the *Itinerario* proper refers to the thirty-six engravings as *conterfeytsels*, literally 'counterfeits'. In the foreword to the reader, Linschoten warns him not to expect 'very great artistry and exceptional beauty' *(seer groote const ende sonderlinghe frayichheyt)* from the plates, but to count on 'natural and verisimilar illustration' *(natuerlicke en waarachtighe afbeeldinghe)*.[42] Elsewhere in the text, as well as in the inscription accompanying the scene of the market in Goa (pl. 5), he reiterates the point that the plates were made 'from life' *(naer 't leven)*, 'from nature' *(polo natural* in Portuguese), 'from reality' *(naer de warachtigheyt)*.[43] He thus describes the illustrations in the *Itinerario* as 'true-to-life counterfeits' *(conterfeytsels naer 't leven)*.

In the sixteenth century this was primarily the term for an illustration of something in the observable world that had been perceived by the illustrator himself and rendered by him in as realistic a manner as possible. Exactly what aspects of the perceived object were depicted and how this was done, however, depended on the illustrator's intentions and skill. Linschoten became aware of this when he showed his renderings of Oriental fruits, plants, and trees to his learned friends in Enkhuizen. They were familiar with the late-sixteenth-century herbals and voiced some criticisms. Nevertheless, Linschoten maintained that his illustrations were all 'set down according to the life, although the leaves are not altogether so proportionable with their strings and veynes, as they should be, or as the Physitions and Doctors in their Herbals have described them, having onely shewed the forme and growth of the fruites, as I have seene and used them'.[44] A 'counterfeit from life' presupposed disciplined observation and careful depiction according to rules set for the different kinds of representations 'from life'. Apparently Linschoten had not quite met the standards in this particular case.

To be seen as 'true to life' a representation was expected to mirror its original, to reproduce the specific, perceived character of a particular object. The term 'counterfeit' was applied, for example, to lifelike portraits of human individuals. But the object perceived could also be regarded as an example of a kind of phenomenon. A realistic representation would in that case record more general characteristics; such typological illustrations had become increasingly prevalent in herbals in the sixteenth century.[45] Visual idioms thus developed for both the individualising and the typological variants of representations from life, with rules that prescribed how the various parts of the perceptible world were to be represented. In the case of the typological variant at least, one needed to know before making an image which aspects of an object would be deemed necessary for it to be identified on the basis of its representation.[46] This was particularly important when the representation had a practical function, as in navigation or medicine.

This empirical content distinguished the illustration *naer 't leven* from images that, even if they contained realistic elements, were not intended to allow identification in the outside world on the basis of representation. 'Invention' played a greater role in the creation of, for example, biblical and mythological scenes, than in *naer 't leven* representations. The late-sixteenth-century Dutch art theoretician, poet, and painter Karel van Mander (1548–1606) referred to this other type of illustration as products of the spirit or imagination *(uyt de gheest)*. Each kind of representation appealed to the viewer in a particular way. The 'exceptional beauty' of products of the imagination might appeal more strongly to the emotions, while the role of the viewer of '*naer 't leven*' representations was primarily that of a detached observer.

This use of the terms contrasted representations from life with products of the spirit or imagination. However, they could also be used to refer to two stages in the genesis of a representation. A representation from life could be a preliminary study for a more complex composition that called for more invention. Whether the final representation was still true to life depended on what the artist and viewer identified as recognisable reality. This more complex composition was no longer mere representation of an observation conducted in a disciplined fashion, but the rendering of a perception that had been interpreted and explicitly endowed with meaning.

'Counterfeits from life' lent themselves to attempts to provide a documentary and systematic classification of the visible world, which was often linked to a form of geographical description. In this sense they were expressions of a mapping impulse.[47] This was not confined to the topography of a specific area but could also be directed at its flora and fauna, the characteristic aspect of its towns and villages, and the appearance of its inhabitants.[48] Thus books were issued in the sixteenth century with views of cities, from Europe and all other parts of the world. Costume books registered the dress of the different nations of Europe and gradually widened their range to include non-European peoples. The same mapping impulse reigned in the collections of curiosities, where natural and manufactured objects from around the world were brought together, arranged, and displayed. Components of the visible world were classified according to hierarchical taxonomies, and collections of representations complemented the collections of actual objects. Collections of this kind introduced order to a world that had become bewildering for Europeans as a result of the voyages of discovery and the intellectual, religious, and political turmoil in sixteenth-century Europe.

This mapping impulse was connected not only with empirical disciplines such as geography and botany, but also with the more practical interests of sovereigns and local magistrates. For instance, Philip II commissioned *'relaciones geográficas'* of Spain and the Spanish colonies in America to provide information on the natural and human resources of these territories. Practical interest in geography was also expressed in the decorative programmes of the palaces of princes and nobles and the city halls in the large trading centres. An allegory of the Four Continents or a series of painted wall maps informed the viewer about what the world was like, but at the same time it made clear how the masters of the house saw their place in the world.[49] The same applied to the cabinets of curiosities. Scholarly and political interest thus combined to stimulate the mapping of the local, regional, and 'national' scene. The enterprise of compiling collections could expand to reflect universal pretensions, a process paralleled in the making of the actual maps in Ortelius's first world atlas, the *Theatrum Orbis Terrarum* of 1570, which was dedicated to Philip II.

The growing interest in realistic renderings of directly observed local life was also made to serve religious instruction. This was particularly so in the Netherlands. Images from everyday life—cheerful companies at table, market scenes, children's games—contained admonitory messages about the sinfulness of earthly existence. They were often issued in print form—as individual images or edifying series—which served to propagate the moralising message more widely than paintings or drawings. They kept alive the idea that the struggle between God and the devil was fought out in the here and now and in the lives of all.

Counterfeits from life, as a means of recording and transmitting empirical knowledge and opinions about the visible world, were used to advance both profane and religious interests. These interests were often intertwined, but in the course of the sixteenth century many people began to draw a sharper distinction between matters concerning their relation with God and matters primarily connected with their relation with the natural world and their fellow beings. With regard to human customs and practices, the difference grew between Christian discourses and discourses couched in terms of civility. The prints under examination here will prove to contain a discourse on civility in line with profane theoretical and practical interests, not a discourse on Christian virtues and vices.

By characterising the plates in the *Itinerario* as counterfeits from life, Linschoten intended to stress their high empirical content. All the prints bear Linschoten's name as well as those of the engravers. This seems to imply that the illustrations were derived from his own representations of what he had seen with his own eyes. It is perhaps no accident that the word *invenit* is not used. He had not invented or conceived the illustration. He simply represented what already existed in reality. '*Naer 't leven*' means here, in the first instance, 'based on autopsy'. Linschoten claimed that the appearance and customs of the 'Indians' and of the Portuguese living in the East as illustrated in the *Itinerario* corresponded to what he had seen on the spot, and were not based on hearsay, on what he had read, or on representations made by someone else. But can we believe his claims to have seen with his own eyes what he portrayed and to be the author of the drawings on which the prints in the *Itinerario* are based?

There is no reason to doubt Linschoten's claim that he made drawings in Goa. His technical ability must have been reasonable since he won the praise of the archbishop. In Goa he could have seen and recorded the Indian fruits, boats, and utilities that appear in the plates of the *Icones*. The same is true of the external appearance of many of the ethnic types. He lived among the Portuguese and had every opportunity

to observe them and the native population of the region. As a trading depot, Goa attracted many foreigners who stayed there for shorter or longer periods. Rich merchants from Cambaia (northwest India) and neighbouring Bijapur traded there in diamonds and precious fabrics. Poor Arab and Abyssinian seamen spent their time off on land performing tricks to earn drinking money. A large proportion of the slave population in Goa was from Mozambique; moreover, Linschoten had made a brief stop in this country during his outward journey. His return journey afforded him a firsthand opportunity to see various ethnic and religious groups on the Malabar coast. We can conclude that Linschoten would have been in a position to have observed with his own eyes the majority of the ethnic types that appear in the engravings. Thus it is possible that these images in the *Icones* are derived from sketches drawn from life by Linschoten himself.

However, it is not likely that all of the Indian subjects in the *Icones* go back to personal observations and sketches by Linschoten. Although he claims to have set out to watch a suttee ceremony in the area near Goa that was not under Portuguese rule, there is no indication in his text that he actually attended one.[50] The engraving of the suttee ceremony in the *Icones* (pl. 17) looks as though it was conceived in Europe. The mosque in Malabar (pl. 26) is hardly more convincing; the source of this image remains a mystery. The image of the king of Cochin on an elephant (pl. 23) had appeared in early-sixteenth-century representations of Asians; the engraving in the *Icones* may be an adaptation of a traditional subject. Linschoten does not say anything about a visit by the ambassador of Ballagate to Goa. The engraving with that subject (pl. 18) seems to have been composed from ingredients borrowed from other plates, with ethnic types from Goa and environs.

Even when it is plausible that Linschoten may have illustrated a subject on the basis of his own observation, the question still remains as to whether the engravings can be regarded as accurate copies of Linschoten's work. There is evidence that even the representations of what he knew best were later supplemented with material that did not go back to his own observations. For example, some large scenes with many figures, such as the market in Goa (pl. 5), display, it may be argued, more compositional skill than Linschoten is likely to have had.[51] Indian houses and huts do not look authentic but seem to have been added to fill out compositions. The prints' backgrounds are also problematic. They look less like representations of observations made in India than like a type of landscape that was popular in sixteenth-century European art. Fourteen of the prints of ethnic types and processions have as their background a landscape with wide river valleys and towering chains of mountains, seen from above and from afar. In his Antwerp period Joannes van

Doetecum, the engraver of the plates in the *Icones,* had frequently engraved that landscape type for the printer Hieronymus Cock.[52] With a few modifications to take account of the Asian *couleur locale,* he could easily have added it to the material that he received from Linschoten. The landscapes in two of the plates illustrating fruits, plants, and trees also appear to have been added by the engraver. If one discounts the landscape backgrounds in the *Icones,* simpler images are left: images of ethnic types, represented *en face* and in detail, specimens of a type of tree, fruit, or vessel, the image of a Hindu idol, a few scenes with a couple of moving figures. These scenes come much closer to Linschoten's likely models— European books of costumes and herbals—and it is easier to imagine that he sketched them on the basis of his own perceptions.[53]

With the possible exception of the Mozambiquan plates, however, the images of non-Indian subjects are extremely unlikely to have their origin in observations rendered into sketches by Linschoten himself. As he never travelled further than western India, he could not have seen Chinese mandarins boating on a river. Neither did Chinese junks sail to the west coast of India in his day. It is not entirely impossible, but very unlikely, that he was able to observe Moluccans, Javanese, or Malays in Goa. The representations of these subjects in the *Icones* must therefore be derived from a source different from that of the majority of the engravings.[54]

If these images are not based on Linschoten's own perceptions, what could their source be? As far as we know, none of the prints in the *Itinerario* is derived from printed or unprinted images that had previously circulated in Europe, with the possible exception of the depiction of the king of Cochin.[55] The model for the representations of what Linschoten had not seen himself may well have been images that were produced in Portuguese Asia. A collection of about fifty ethnic types from Mozambique to the Moluccas and China, painted on paper by an Indian, Luso-Indian, or Portuguese craftsman around 1550 and now in the Biblioteca Casanatense in Rome, displays a number of parallels with the sequence in the *Icones.* Both series consist of representations of ethnic types, interspersed with a few scenes of ceremonies, work, or leisure activities.[56] Linschoten could have supplemented his own material with illustrations from or after a series of this kind while he was still in Goa. Other potential sources are the manuscripts and books with representations of Chinese that were on sale to Europeans in Manila and Macao.[57] This kind of material may also have found its way to Goa or Lisbon, where Linschoten could have purchased or copied it. He could claim that a scene that he had not seen with his own eyes was still a counterfeit from life, provided the model was what he regarded as a faithful representation of perceived reality. An accurate copy of a representation *ad vivum* was still regarded as a representation *ad vivum.*

It seems likely that the visual material with which Linschoten returned to Enkhuizen consisted of his own sketches based on personal observation and representations of a more or less realistic character that he had copied or bought. These would have included coastal profiles, bird's-eye views of cities, pairs of ethnic types, and smaller images of individual fruits, plants, trees, and boats. The *conterfeytsels* will have had a predominantly typological character. The engravings in the *Itinerario* and the *Icones* cannot, however, be regarded as faithful copies of this original material. Rather, the material was adapted and supplemented in the course of making the drawings for the engravings.

It will be argued below that the prints constitute a series with a coherent structure in terms of content and form. This implies that the original material was adapted in such a way that the resulting prints formed pairs, fitted into series of similar scenes and arrangements, and referred to one another to draw the theme connecting them to the attention of the viewer. It is also conceivable that entirely new compositions were made for prints that were necessary for the series but for which there was little or no original material. The designs for the series may still have been regarded by their makers as counterfeits from life, but in a metaphorical sense. The realism of the prints corresponded less to perceived reality than to the interpretation of that reality that the maker of the series wanted to convey. As we shall see, the author raised the typological approach, which was already present in the basic material, to a more abstract level of generality and comparability. On this interpretation, the series is largely based on representations 'from life', but is equally a product of the spirit or imagination.

The *Icones* as a Depiction of the Hierarchy of Civility in Asia

The plates of the *Icones et Habitus Indorum* can be broken down into four thematic subseries: ethnic couples; elite personages in processions and types of ships, a curious combination that will be explained below; large-scale compositions dealing with religions; and fruits, plants, and trees. These subjects correspond to the subjects listed on the title page of the *Itinerario* proper and repeated on the Latin title page of the *Icones.* The book, we are told, will cover not only the flora of the East but also the customs of the heathen, as expressed in their 'Idolatrous religion', their 'policie' (designating the political regime in its inward and outward manifestations and the social order with which it was intertwined), and their *huyshoudinghe,* which refers to the domestic and wider economy but also includes relations between husband and wife, parents and children, masters and servants. In the English edition of 1598 the last term was translated as 'government of their houses', which captures well the social connotation. But one should constantly keep in mind the economic connotation as well.[58] These terms—'policie' and 'government of their houses'—make it clear that the plates are not confined to externals such as clothing, means of transport, and the shapes of houses and temples but are also intended to say something about the relations between members of the household, the economy, the political regimes, the hierarchy of social groups, and religiously prescribed forms of behaviour among the Asians and Portuguese resident in Asia.

In this section three of these subseries will be examined to see whether this ulterior message can be distilled from the plates and to identify the visual resources used to convey this message. The larger compositions with religious subjects will be discussed in the next section, where the text and composition of the series as a whole come under scrutiny.

The Subseries of Ethnic Couples

The depictions of ethnic couples (pls. 1, 2, 7, 11, 15, 19, 21, 22, 24, 25) constitute the core subseries of the *Icones*. It introduces the nations of Asia deemed important enough to be presented to Europeans, and it deals with the themes that are also treated in the other subseries: most extensively with the 'government of their houses', more succinctly with 'policie', and very briefly with religion. It does so primarily through the variety of meanings attached to clothing; other attributes such as betel leaves and weapons assist in conveying the message. At first sight, the series seems designed to display the similarities and contrasts in dress between different peoples of Asia.[59] In fact, dress functions as a general, polysemic marker for the customs of Asians. It may indicate aspects of the 'government of their houses'; for example, the extent to which the body is covered is an index of the degree of restraint in sexual behaviour, of modesty. The way in which clothing is made is indicative of the degree of technical skill in a society, while its quantity and quality displays the degree of prosperity that technical skill helps to create. Dress may further disclose aspects of 'policie', such as the distribution of wealth and prestige within a society. It can be a mirror of the social hierarchy. In brief, costume in this series is custom, or in the words of Karel van Mander, *broeck oft bruyck*.[60]

The customs that are illustrated in the *Icones* can be broken down into morals and practices. Morality covered behaviour that could be characterised as good or evil in ethical or religious terms. This included sexual behaviour important for the survival of the species and the relations between adult men and women, but also important as a marker

of the transition from youth to maturity and of relations between parents and children, and between families, i.e., some of the matters that were summed up on the title page as 'government of their houses'. Practices referred to activities that depended on the craftsmanship and technical skill present in a social group; they were connected with survival but were not necessarily good or evil in a moral or religious sense—at least from a European point of view. These included customs of food and dress, housing, experience in trade, and expertise in navigation. Most of these could also be counted as aspects of 'government of their houses'. Finally, there are the concerns summed up on the title page under the word *policie*: protection against enemies, maintenance of the internal order, and proper forms of behaviour. Customs in these areas governed survival in larger groups and called for recognised leadership and a social hierarchy. Whether they fell under the heading of morals or practices was the subject of heated debate. The combination of morals and practices constituted society and civility, distinguishing human groups from animals, which lacked morals and tools, and also from one another.[61] Some morals and practices were better than others in terms of technology or religion. Not only were there differences in civility within and between societies, but there was a hierarchy of civility, differing degrees of socially enforced restraint of the passions and socially beneficial application of reason. This is what the subseries of ethnic couples sets out to convey.

Whose customs are represented by the ethnic types in the subseries? The brief texts below the figures indicate where they come from. A total of twelve different territories are represented.[62] In three cases (Pegu, Cambaia, the Moluccas) a territory is represented by a single man, in the nine other cases by one or more couples, usually consisting of a man and a woman.[63] China, Goa, Ballagate, Malabar, and Mozambique show up with more than one couple.[64] In these cases both a hierarchy of social groups and religious and ethnic divisions within a single region may be illustrated. The social groups that are distinguished may be magistrates and commoners, as in the plate dealing with China; strata within the elite, as among the Portuguese men in Goa; higher and lower castes, as among the representatives of Ballagate and Malabar; or ethnic and religious groups, as in the depictions of natives of Goa, Malabar, and Mozambique. The seven territories for which no social hierarchy or ethnic-religious division is shown by no means stand for societies that are homogeneous in all respects. In the vision of sixteenth-century Europe, such societies were to be found only among a few very 'primitive' peoples in America or Africa, not in the relatively civilised continent of Asia. At most, ethnic-religious homogeneity is implied, in the case of Abyssinia in contradiction to the text.[65] The reason these territories are represented by a single couple or a single man is that they play a minor role in the argument that the series wants to propose.

A combination of criteria seem to have been applied in selecting territories to be treated at greater or lesser length in the subseries. All were territories with which the Portuguese maintained commercial relations. Representatives of many of these territories could be found in Goa itself. Most attention is paid to what Linschoten knew best: Goa, Ballagate, and the Malabar coast. China, however, is also represented with a number of plates. Moreover, an attempt has been made to provide a grid in which the populations bordering on the Indian Ocean and in the Far East could be fitted. A three-tiered division held in India, with Cambaia in the north, Goa and Ballagate in the centre, and Malabar in the south. A similar division seems to have been applied to the selected areas west and east of Goa: the western area comprises Arabia, Abyssinia, and Mozambique, while the eastern one includes China in the north, Malacca in the centre, and Java in the south. The position of Pegu (Burma) and the Moluccas in this arrangement is not entirely clear. They are probably classified as belonging to the centre rather than the south.

In each of the four territories that are treated at greater length—China, Goa, Ballagate, and Malabar—the population is represented by multiple couples indicating the social hierarchy and the ethnic and religious composition. But there are a few complications in determining which groups constitute the social hierarchy in each of the territories. First, the figures who represent the different social strata in Ballagate in the subseries of ethnic types are also found in Goa and the surrounding regions. For a proper grasp of the social structure of Goa they must also be included in the analysis of that region. The same goes for the Arabs, Abyssinians, and Mozambiquans. Second, not all of the figures in the elite of Ballagate and Malabar are represented in the subseries of ethnic couples. One has to look for them in the subseries of elite processions as well. Once these peculiarities are taken into account, the following picture emerges.

In each of these four territories, representatives of the elite are opposed to representatives of the common people. Thus the armed *fidalgo* of Goa and the unarmed Brahman of Ballagate are both opposed to the extremely poor Canarim labourer in the coconut plantation, equipped with a knife for cutting down coconuts. The armed elite of Hindu Malabar (Cochin) are the Nayars depicted in the entourage of the king of Cochin. They are contrasted with the poor Polya man and his wife, probably agricultural labourers like the Canarim. Moorish Malabar (Cananor) also has its warrior elite, while the common people are represented by a banana grower. In China the unarmed mandarin is op-

posed to the simple Chinese, whose long stick may be a reference to animal husbandry or agriculture.

The visual representation of the social stratification of Ballagate and Goa goes beyond a mere division between elite and commoners. The great Asian merchants are shown as a recognisable and influential social group in both regions. It is unclear whether this is an implicit reference to a less prominent social position for merchants in Malabar and China. The armed nobles and mercenaries in the entourage of the ambassador of Ballagate make it clear that warriors as well as Brahmans belong to the elite. The mercenary is also portrayed separately in the same plate as the *balhadeira*, probably to give an impression of the entourage of the elite of Ballagate. Perhaps this was intended to point to a contrast with the entourage of native warriors of the king of Cochin, who are not hirelings.

Malabar and Goa are further characterised as ethnically and religiously divided societies. In Malabar the Nayars and Polyas belonged to the same ethnic group, as can be seen from their elongated earlobes. The same was true of the Thomas Christians, but they had embraced a different religion.[66] The Moors from Cananor lived in Malabar, but they originated outside the area and their religion was different from that of the native population. Ethnic and religious heterogeneity was even greater in Goa, where European Catholics and Abyssinian Christians lived alongside native Hindus, Muslim immigrants (the Arab sailors), and recently converted Mozambiquan slaves. The ethnic and religious division of Malabar and Goa contrasts with the societies of Ballagate and China, which are characterised as ethnically and religiously homogeneous.

The dress of each of these figures provides a very general indication of the degree of modesty prevalent among the residents of a territory. The northern groups—the Chinese, Cambaians, and Arabs—are the most fully dressed (pls. 2, 15, 21). Men wear long-sleeved cloaks that reach the ground or three-quarter cloaks on top of trousers. They cover their heads with hats or turbans and they have footwear. The mandarin even covers his hands by concealing them in his wide sleeves. Their facial covering consists of beard and moustache. The bodies of the Chinese and Arab women (there is no Cambaian woman) are also completely covered, in the case of the mandarin's wife, from head to toe. The Chinese commoner's wife is barefoot. This forms a contrast with the bound feet of her mandarin counterpart (mentioned in the text), which are hidden from view, and suggests a lack of modesty. The Arab woman is also barefoot; this is perhaps a reference to the poverty of Arabian sailors' families in Goa.[67]

The large cast of figures from the centre areas (Goa, Ballagate, Pegu, Malacca, the Moluccas, Abyssinia) are less fully dressed. Not all of the men have beards and moustaches, and a larger proportion of them than in the north have no footwear. Neither do they all have headgear. There are also discrepancies in the degree of nudity of men and women. The women are always more covered than their male counterparts. This is probably intended to indicate not a greater degree of modesty among the women, but the mixed character of the centre. The differences between the couples may be based to some extent on actual differences in dress, but they indicate above all differences in sexual morality between social strata or ethnic-religious groups.

The Portuguese are a special case in this centre group (pls. 7, 11). The men and women are distributed over two pages, and the group of women has one member more than the men's group.[68] This woman, dressed in a see-through blouse and sarong, is the key to the formally deviant presentation. Her provocative indoor costume is a reminder that the Portuguese men and women who in public dressed so modestly —like 'northerners'—indulged in more 'southern' dress and morals indoors. The distribution of the men and women over two pages indicates that men maintained a façade of decency in public and could impose it there on their womenfolk, while behind closed doors the women were in charge and played fast and loose with morals.[69]

The south (Malabar, Java, Mozambique) is the territory of scantily dressed peoples with little moral compunction. Some of the men are virtually naked, such as the Mozambiquans who are clad in nothing but a penis string. The women are dressed slightly more decently. None of the men has any facial hair, and only a few have headgear. Only one of the southerners has footwear: a man from Cananor, on the Malabar coast, who wears sandals and is somewhat more clothed, probably as a sign of greater modesty by comparison with his partner, as we shall see.

Information conveyed by the clothing concerning the sexual morality of the various ethnic groups in 'India' is further elaborated by means of other devices. The most common additional marker is the composition of the couple; some consist of a man and a woman, others of two men.[70] The depiction of a male-female couple indicates that heterosexuality was the accepted norm in the society that it represents. The three male couples, all from the centre and south (pls. 15, 24, 25), suggest a tolerance or greater frequency of sodomy (in this instance anal intercourse between males).[71] In the eyes of a European of the sixteenth century, this was not only criminal sexual behaviour but also antisocial and antireligious crime strongly associated with witchcraft and paganism.[72]

The man from Pegu is the only figure in the subseries to be depicted in a seated posture (pl. 25). His posterior rests demonstratively on a soft cushion. The text leaves no room for doubt regarding his sodomy. It unequivocally reports that this unnatural behaviour was rife among the

men of Burma.[73] The man from Cananor is the only one in the subseries depicted from the rear and with bare buttocks (pl. 24). The text does not offer any clues, but the departure from the conventional manner of portraiture suggests that he is a sexual deviant.[74] It is less certain whether the merchant from Ballagate (pl. 15) is marked as a sodomite. The extent to which his body is covered might suggest a high degree of modesty, and he is represented standing up and *en face* like most of the other ethnic types. A suggestion that he may be involved in unusual sexual practices, however, is provided by the betel leaves that he is holding in his right hand. Betel was considered to be good for the stomach and gums and it combated bad breath, but Linschoten added that it was also supposed to promote lust.[75] The leaves may thus evoke an addiction to aphrodisiacs. This attribute is found with several figures in the subseries, both male and female; the merchant from Ballagate, however, is the only one who offers the leaves to another man.[76] As in the case of the Portuguese men, the extent to which his body is covered might point to a sturdy façade of high moral norms, with unnatural practices allowed behind the scenes. Pegu, Cananor, and Ballagate are thus probably marked as societies with a high frequency or tolerance of sodomy.

Whether three variants of sodomy are illustrated here, and whether they are part of a hierarchy, is more difficult to determine. The fan (otherwise only an attribute of one of the Portuguese women) and the flower behind the ear and in the hand of the man from Pegu suggest effeminate and egocentric behaviour: a portrait of a narcissist who seduces himself with flowers. The standing position and robust lance of the man from Cananor seem to suggest a more virile form of sodomy.[77] The merchant from Ballagate is discreet regarding his sexual practices, but the betel leaves make it unlikely that he stands for a more elevated form of friendship between males. On the contrary, they suggest hidden vices. In each of these three couples, the second figure does not appear to be marked as a sodomite. Their attributes indicate a contrast, albeit not a sexual one. The fighting man from the Moluccas contrasts with the unarmed and effeminate man from Pegu, the industrious banana cultivator from Cananor with the dissolute warrior, and the professional merchant with pen and paper from Cambaia with his colleague from Ballagate, who seems to have other things up his sleeve. Still, a heterosexual orientation of the contrasting figures seems to be implied too. After all, they are not marked in any way as sexual deviants.

Flowers and betel leaves are also a specification of sexual behaviour among the couples consisting of a male and a female.[78] In the case of the Malays, unparalleled among the 'Indians' in 'courtesy and amorousness' (*courtoisije ende amoureusheyt*), as the caption puts it, the man and woman seduce one another with flowers, each displaying equal interest (pl. 1).

The Javanese woman in the same plate resorts to heavier ammunition in her use of the betel leaf, but her male counterpart's receptive gesture and attitude indicate his readiness to comply. In the plate depicting the Chinese, the female commoner offers the man a flower from the plentiful supply that she is carrying on a stick over her shoulder (pl. 2). She is the only woman in this subseries of couples to be standing to the left of the man: she is breaking the rules.[79] That the sensible Chinese man has his reservations can be deduced from his defensive gesture and averted attitude. These plates illustrate contrasts between refined and coarse forms of seduction, as well as different attitudes towards female advances in the north, centre, and south of the Far East. Flowers as an indicator of a refined art of seduction appear only in the north and in one territory of the centre. Betel leaves are further to be found only with the couples of a man and a woman from central and south India. The Portuguese woman from Goa in a see-through blouse seduces her husband at home with them (pl. 11). The Polya man from Malabar playfully holds the leaves out of the woman's reach, while the fact that she turns toward him with an open gesture betrays her positive interest (pl. 24). The theme of the means of seduction deployed is not followed through in the depiction of the other couples.[80] In their case other aspects of 'the government of their houses' are depicted by means of other attributes.

Children as an attribute are certainly used to convey a message about how the 'government of their houses' is arranged in the society in question, but the exact content of that message is difficult to determine.[81] In this subseries children accompany only the Canarim couple (simple agricultural labourers from Goa and from Ballagate), the Arab couple, and one of the Mozambiquan couples (pls. 19, 21, 22). The Canarim, with two young children (a boy and a girl, as can be seen from their hair and dress), contrast with the *lascaryn,* or hired soldier, and the *balhadeira,* or female dancer (pl. 19). The text accompanying the latter figure describes her as a 'prostitute who earns a living by dancing and singing'. She forms a counterpart to the respectable mother of two; likewise, the Canarim man with the curiously shaped small knife for cutting off coconuts is a poor and meek counterpart to the mercenary with his large raised sword. The warrior enjoys more prestige than the agriculturalist, but the shameless way he looks at the female dancer suggests that he also behaves immorally. The scanty clothing of the Canarim, however, indicates that they are not paragons of modesty either. Their daughter watches the dancer avidly, while the young boy gives his sister a corrective tap on the shoulder. His mother points to his father with her right hand, while her left index finger points toward her thigh. As for the father, he looks past his wife in the direction of the dancing woman.

These two couples should be compared to the couples from the same

territory on plate 15. The Canarim couple with children can then be seen not only as the representatives of a poorer and lower stratum in the societies of Goa and Ballagate, but also as a more decent alternative to the sodomy of the upper strata in Ballagate. Similarly, the completely covered Brahman woman is contrasted to the *balhadeira* with her see-through blouse, and the unarmed but well-respected Brahman ascetic stands in opposition to the sword-bearing *lascaryn*. Ballagate is marked by distinctions between the elite and the commoners, between rich and poor, between moral, civilised members and immoral, uncivilised ones, but the hierarchies are not as clean-cut as they might be. At the top and all other levels, virtues are mixed with vices in this society of the centre.

The significance of the children in plates 21 and 22 is even more difficult to determine. The dress of the Islamic Arab couple and the Christian Abyssinian couple suggests that they share the same level of morality. The same is true of the Christian and Islamic couples from Mozambique, though the level is considerably lower.[82] In both plates the childless Christians bear indelible marks on their skin—a cross on the faces of the Abyssinians, the traces of pagan tattoos on the Mozambiquans—while the physically intact Arab Muslims hold a naked young child of indeterminate gender between them, and the equally intact Mozambiquan Muslim carries a baby on her back. The markings on their skin indicate that they are a peculiar kind of Christian and that the 'government of their houses' may be peculiar too. But the nature of this aberration, which is not indicated in the text either, cannot be deduced from the engraving. Perhaps their gestures offer a clue—particularly that of the Abyssinian woman, whose left hand is clasped in front of her groin while she points upward with three fingers of her right hand—but this remains to be unravelled.[83] The relations between parents and children among the Muslims appear to be in order, though there are differences between the couples. The Arab mother holds her child by the hand. With its right hand, the child reaches for the arrow that the father is holding, point downward, in his right hand; the bow he holds behind him, in his left hand. Both parents are attending to the child, playing with it, raising and training it. The Muslim Mozambiquans behave differently. The mother shows no signs of interest in the baby that is drinking from her pendulous left breast.[84] Nor does the father seem interested in his progeny; instead he holds a small bowlike instrument in his mouth, the string of which he strikes with a small stick. The difference in the Muslim couples' attitude toward their children may be intended to make a point about different approaches to raising and training children, but the precise meaning remains unclear.

Dress is used to establish not only a scale of modesty, but also a scale of technical skill and wealth. These are aspects of the 'government of their houses', but are also connected to 'policie', since good government was believed to create prosperity and a proper division of wealth. The gradations in wealth between all the territories treated in the *Icones* are indicated in a very general manner. All of the northerners wear stitched garments and are elaborately dressed. The inhabitants of the centre wear clothes that wrap around them. Their items of clothing are also fewer in number. The scanty dress of the peoples of the south, again made up mostly of wraps, is an indicator not only of their loose morals but also of their limited technical skill and lack of wealth. In addition, a level of prosperity and an internal distribution of wealth are indicated for each of the four societies that are treated at greater length. The general prosperity of the Chinese can be inferred from the generous amount of clothing they wear. In the other three societies people wear less. These societies are poorer. Differences in the amount of clothing also serve to visualize different distributions of wealth within each society. The number of different items of clothing worn by the Chinese commoners indicates that they share in the general prosperity and that there are no huge social inequalities in that respect. In Muslim Malabar the warrior elite and the commoners wear very little clothing. What they share between them is the general poverty. A somewhat higher level of prosperity and a relatively equal distribution of wealth seem to be indicated for Moorish Malabar. In Goa the Portuguese elite are richly dressed while the Canarim are very poorly dressed. Here wealth is very unevenly distributed and the level of prosperity is not particularly high. In Ballagate the Brahmans cultivate an ascetic lifestyle, but nevertheless the same standard of living and social inequality seem to be shown as in Goa.

The most important general marker used in this subseries for the 'policie' aspect of the Asian societies is weaponry. The absence or presence of weapons indicates whether a political elite rules its subjects by threat of arms or by authority.[85] The weapon in the possession of the male representative of a territory (or the male of the couple representing the elite if there is more than one couple for a particular territory) indicates that in these territories armed warriors rule over unarmed subjects. In a few cases the elite is unarmed: the mandarin in China, the Brahman in Ballagate, and the merchant in Cambaia.[86] It was probably not the intention to claim that the ruling elite in those territories consisted only of these unarmed types. The purpose was more likely to show which members of the elite were dominant in the internal power relations. The distinctions then are between elites dominated by warriors in most territories and by learned magistrates, priests, and merchants in a few others. The attributes of the unarmed elites introduce further distinctions

within this group. The Brahman's cord, for instance, indicates that his power is vested in moral or religious authority rather than in riches, as it was in the case of the merchants. For the majority of the territories, this is all that is shown regarding customs connected with 'policie'.

To sum up: the polysemic marker of dress is used to construct a scale of civility as shown in the 'government of their houses' and 'policie'. Each of the figures in the subseries of ethnic types is allocated a position on this scale. The scale corresponds to a three-tiered north-centre-south division, replicated in eastern Africa, in India, and in the Far East. Dress serves as the general marker of degrees of modesty, wealth, and technical skill. In the north a high degree of sexual restraint, prosperity, and technical ability prevails, due to good government, social stability, and ethnic and religious homogeneity. The further south one moves, the less civil society becomes. For specific groups of figures, specific markers indicate different forms of behaviour that undermine the stable family, among adults as well as between adults and children. Male couples, as opposed to couples consisting of a male and a female, indicate where and among whom sodomy was more prevalent. Flowers and betel leaves are used in the plates of the Far East and India to show who practised more or less refined techniques of seduction, and who regarded this as immoral. Depictions of children are used to indicate something out of joint in the social order of Goa and Ballagate, some as yet unresolved distinction in the 'government of their houses' between Christians and Muslims in eastern Africa, and a distinction in child-rearing practices between Muslims from the north and the south. The specifications do not affect the position of a territory in the general hierarchy of civility, but they do show that absolute perfection is nowhere to be found.

The Subseries with Elite Processions and Ships

The illustrations of elite processions are an elaboration of the representations of armed and unarmed elites and of ethnic-religious homogeneity or heterogeneity in Goa, Malabar, China, and Ballagate. The plates show individuals who do not usually travel on foot in public but instead ride animals, which place them above the crowd, or are carried. The only plates to show both men and women are those of the Portuguese elite in Goa and the mandarin scene. The Portuguese men and women are distributed over different pages (pls. 8, 9, 12, 13), as they were in the subseries of ethnic couples.

According to the short accompanying texts, the armed Portuguese represent noblemen and the wealthy. Noblemen who were governors or councillors travelled on horseback, while lesser nobles or the wealthy were carried in a litter. Each of the two *fidalgos* is accompanied by an entourage of eight or nine African and Asian servants. The latter are well dressed in both Western and Eastern costume, and they are armed. The captions on the illustrations indicate the specialisations within the ranks of the servants. The Portuguese on horseback is attended by the 'boy' who holds the parasol aloft, while the young page (bicho) carries a sheet of paper, perhaps a proclamation. The negro do mandil in Eastern dress walks in front, leading two black men in Western dress and bearing swords.[87] Two Asian servants in Western dress bring up the rear, while the faraz walks to one side to chase flies away from his master.[88] The composition of the entourage of the Portuguese man in a litter is more or less the same. The captions in the engraving identify the servants in front as negros, and those in the rear as escravos (slaves).[89]

The procession scenes with prominent Portuguese women display both similarities to and differences from those of the men. In both cases the entourage is considerable, consisting of both Africans and Asians dressed in both Western and Eastern costume. While men of standing had to appear in public with a certain regularity, their female counterparts were expected to leave the house as little as possible. When they did appear in public they were expected to display their status, not themselves, except in church. The woman in an open litter is thus breaking the rules, which explains why this is the only procession in the subseries that proceeds from left to right. The woman in the closed litter behaves comme il faut. The women are accompanied by a mixed staff: besides six women, there are two male litter bearers and two armed guards. Their attendants' functions are not identified by captions except for the wet nurse (ama), who carries a baby on her arm (pl. 13).

These scenes illustrate gradations within the Portuguese elite as well as distinction between master and servant, free and unfree. The size of the entourages varies, as does their composition in terms of the servants' functions, origin, gender, and age. Moreover, the Western style of dress indicates that some of the servants were expected to behave in an assimilated way.

The entourage of the king of Cochin shows the armed elite of Malabar (pl. 23).[90] Here too we see a gradation within the elite. The king himself rides on an elephant, surrounded by a large group of noblemen on foot. His dress is virtually the same as that of his retinue; it differs in the greater size of his loincloth, his turban, and, according to the text, several armbands. Both the warriors and the king have elongated earlobes, an attribute shared with the poor Polyas and the Thomas Christians, probably to indicate that they belonged to the same 'people'. Departing from the practice followed for the Portuguese, the ethnic and religious heterogeneity of this region is indicated not in the procession scenes but in the plates of ethnic couples. The warriors have undergone

some assimilation to the West, as can be seen from the muskets several of them carry.[91] The head of the long arrow or lance that the king is holding points downward, as does that held by the Nayar wearing a hat on the left, perhaps a commander. This feature refers to the peaceful coexistence of these Malabars with the Portuguese.[92]

The depiction of the unarmed Chinese elite can hardly be called a procession scene, although the mandarin on a litter and the boating mandarin move from right to left (pl. 3). In terms of content, however, this is an equivalent to the elite processions from the other regions. The mandarin is carried upright. This probably does not conform to reality, but appears to be intended to contrast with the Portuguese fidalgo, who reclines on large cushions in his litter. The Chinese dignitary was prepared to put up with a measure of inconvenience for the sake of decorum. His entourage consists of only two Chinese litter bearers. Despite his simple presentation, the higher-ranking mandarin is treated with great respect by the lower-ranking one, who kneels to present him with a written or printed message on a sheet of paper. After fulfilling the duties of his office, the mandarin can enjoy himself by having a copious meal served to himself and his wife during a cruise on the river.[93] Perhaps a contrast is intended with the other unarmed elite representative, the ascetic Brahman from Ballagate, with his numerous food taboos. The scholarly Chinese elite are presented as highly respected dignitaries who combine their duties, carried out with modesty and decorum, with refined leisure activities in which their wives can also take part. This bipartition of the Chinese scene is a remarkable formal difference from the other procession scenes, which depict high-ranking males who display their status in public but whose pleasures are better kept from view.

The entourage of the ambassador of the king of Ballagate is formally in line with the rest of the subseries (pl. 18). The composition of the engraving corresponds closely to that of the Portuguese fidalgo in his litter. In terms of content, however, there are a few problems.[94] As an elaboration of the elite theme, one would expect a representation of the king himself, as was the case with the king of Cochin. Moreover, the accompanying text states that the scene is set in Goa. The image also appears to be at odds with the subseries of ethnic couples, in which the elite of Ballagate was represented by the Brahman couple. These problems are connected with the double status of the people of Ballagate. Like the Arabs, Abyssinians, and Mozambiquans, they belong both to Goa and to their country of origin. The intention is probably to make it clear that the elite of Ballagate consisted of armed noblemen as well as unarmed Brahmans. The inventor of the series may also have wanted to show the restrained aggressiveness of these warriors in comparison with the wild Nayars of Cochin. Hence, they appear as the peaceful attendants of the ambassador of the king of Ballagate. One of the figures in the centre carries his sword ungirdled while another directs the head of his arrow downward. Both of these features can be seen as signs of good relations with Goa. Two unarmed delegates in front of the procession carry gifts and betel leaves, a reminder of the dubious morality of the Ballagate elite. The *lascaryns,* at the rear with their swords raised, are probably there to show that the rulers of Ballagate had not banned the use of weapons when required.

The three plates depicting different types of boats (pls. 4, 10, and 20) form part of the subseries with elite processions, corresponding to plates 3, 18, and 23 (see the commentary in table 1). Read in combination the paired images convey in two cases a message concerning the exterior relations of the territory to which the vessels belong. The unarmed Chinese junk indicates the restrained foreign policy of the empire ruled by scholars, the commercial ship that could be turned into a warship the duplicity of the aggressive king of Cochin toward the outside world. At the same time, however, the images of boats provide information about the position of their territory within the Asian hierarchy of technical skill. In short, by means of the two very different components, this subseries shows two manifestations of a single activity: the exercise of power over people and over nature.

Each vessel is depicted in profile, as is the pleasure craft of the mandarin in plate 3. This gives the viewer an idea of the shape of the hull and sail, the position of the mast and rowers, and in the case of the Indian boat the position of the outrigger. It also shows whether the vessel is propelled with oars or paddles. The boat carrying the Portuguese party is shown from a slightly higher vantage point than the other boats, which enables the viewer to see that is a dugout. It is possible to relate the Indian vessels to boats of the period,[95] but that is not so easy in the case of the Chinese craft.[96] The aim of these plates, however, was not to provide information about shipbuilding. The significance of the craft lies primarily in the human skills that they embody and the purposes to which they are put.

The Chinese junk is a large sailing vessel constructed from planks. It is seaworthy, carries no arms, and was used for peaceful trade as far as Java. The fust from western India is a smaller planked vessel that can be rowed or sailed. It is more of a coastal vessel, is armed—it even has cannon—and serves both for war at sea and for trade. According to the short caption, both the Portuguese and their enemies in Malabar used this type of ship. The *almadias* and the *tonis* from Goa and Cochin are small dugouts. They are rowed or carry a small sail. They are coastal vessels with a limited range. The direction of all of the boats is from right to left except for the *almadia* with outrigger, which proceeds contrary to

the rules of the visual code. Though the text has nothing to say on this score, the implication is probably that this boat does not entirely comply with the rules of the art: a vessel is supposed to be stable by itself.[97] The *tonis* and *almadias* are not armed. They are used for local, peaceful voyages with a utilitarian purpose, such as carrying water to larger vessels, or as pleasure craft. The boats form a hierarchy of skill and proper use, extending down from the technically advanced Chinese junk with its peaceful and useful purpose to the less advanced Indian fust with its dual purpose and the Indian dugouts with their potentially inappropriate function as pleasure craft.[98]

The Subseries with Fruits, Plants, and Trees

At first sight the subseries of images of South Asian fruits, plants, and trees seems to deal with a completely different subject than the others.[99] Plate 27 presents trees and plants as botanical specimens, clearly showing the shape of the fruit, the texture of the skin, its internal appearance, and the place where it grows on the plant or tree. In plate 28 the trees, plants, and fruits are set in a landscape in which human activity is also evident. Plates 30 and 32 repeat this pattern. The subseries, we see, is intended to describe not just the properties of the plants but how they are used by the 'Indians'.[100] Like the other subseries, it is concerned with customs and practices.

The fruits are arranged and marked corresponding to the use that was made of them. The subseries begins with five fruits that were known for their delicious flavour: the pineapple, iambo, mango, cashew, and jackfruit. Ginger, also shown on the first plate, was held in less esteem but was widely applied to improve the taste of food. The following plate shows fruits that provided the basic necessities of life. The banana was common as everyday food. The coconut palm yielded 'sweet food and drink', as well as 'material for ships, sails and ropes'. Pepper was a spice in general use. Betel, too, was a part of the everyday diet. It was good for the stomach and the gums and counteracted bad breath but, as we have noted, was also supposed to quicken the sexual appetite, in contrast to the innocent pleasures of the fruits in the preceding plate.[101] This second group of plants is situated in a garden where people are at work. The *chauderim* climbs the palm tree to cut down the nuts. Others may be brewing palm wine from the juice that has been collected in the jar applied to the palm on the left. Others are simply enjoying themselves, walking or boating on the river. One boat has capsized, but the swimmers suffer no harm. The garden also contains a *bayleo* (pleasure house).[102] In South Asia, too, nature furnished people with their basic necessities and more.

That nature sometimes dispensed her bounty in a remarkable way can be seen from the strikingly unusual trees in plates 29 and 30. The *arbore de rais* with its aerial roots was extremely large and thick, but there was no use for its wood. All it provided was plenty of shadow. The same plate illustrates the bamboo, exotic to Europeans but with many uses, and the Malaccan durian, which bore a fruit with an unpleasant smell but a delicious flavour. The *arbore triste,* shown on the following plate, was also remarkable in that it only blossomed at night, when it spread a delightful aroma. In the daytime it shed its leaves. It is shown here in the courtyard of a large residence that is reminiscent of a villa.[103] The garden with coconut palms to the side of the courtyard indicates the source of revenue of this distinguished household. A man and a woman are collecting the fallen leaves of the blossom of the *arbore triste,* which were used like saffron in the preparation of food.[104] Others draw water from sacks borne on the back of a buffalo and carry it to the balcony of the house. The *arbore triste,* which was planted in courtyards because of the delightful scent of its nocturnal blossom, the monkey, and the exotic bird in a cage on the balcony are all signs of a more cultivated pleasure than simply walking through the palm garden or cruising down the river in a dugout. The betel offered by the woman sitting in the right-hand corner of the plate with one breast bare seems to refer to less civilised pleasures. The pepper and the two coconuts displayed in the foreground, together with the water, refer to necessary, simple fare with no ethical connotations.[105]

This subseries of trees, plants, and fruit is constructed around contrasts and hierarchies derived from their significance in Indian life and the uses to which they were put. The specimens are marked not only in terms of their botanical characteristics, but above all by the practices of the Asians. These displayed gradations of civility. The place of this subseries within the general series and its relation to the other subseries will be spelled out in more detail below. Here it may be concluded that, contrary to appearances, it is thematically related to the subseries discussed above.

So far the analysis has revealed a consistency in terms of content between three of the subseries. The subseries of ethnic couples forms the core of the complete set. It indicates the central theme: the hierarchy of civility among Asians as it manifests itself in 'policie' and the 'government of their houses'. It imposes a grid on Asia, a descending hierarchy of civility running from north to south,[106] indicating the level of civility of the inhabitants of twelve territories. This grid, which covers virtually the whole of Asia, also entails a more detailed comparison between China, Goa, Ballagate, and Malabar. The other subseries further develop aspects of the core series. The subseries with elite processions and boats elaborates the theme of technical skill for China, Goa, Ballagate, and Malabar

and suggests a hierarchy of civility among the elites in these same four regions. Moreover, it repeats or modifies the contrasts between armed and unarmed elites and indicates the presence of ethnic-religious homogeneity or heterogeneity. The subseries with fruits can be regarded for the time being as a further specification of the general pattern of civility. It provides additional information about civilised and less civilised use of edible substances in South Asia.

It has been stated that the six prints with large scenes constitutes a fourth subseries, but this has not yet been demonstrated. Nor has it been explained how this subseries fits into the series as a whole. The best place to start is with a more comprehensive analysis in which the combination of image and text and the formal relations between the prints are taken into account. This will also advance our understanding of the subseries discussed so far.

The *Icones* as a Series of Instructive and Edifying Images

The prints which contain information about the customs of the 'Indians' and of the Portuguese in India can only be regarded as a series in the strict sense of the word if coherence between all their components is established. Before this can be shown, it is first necessary to explain the formal means used to create that coherence, and why the plates are arranged in the sequence that they have been given. Second, a connection must be demonstrated between the subseries of the ethnic types and the elite processions and boats, on the one hand, and those of the fruits, plants, and trees and the large scenes dealing with religion, on the other. Finally, it is necessary to establish the precise relation between image and text. Do the images illustrate the text, and thereby support the verisimilitude of the interpretation of reality that is given there? Or is the relation of a different kind? These are the questions dealt with in the present section. By way of conclusion, some of the more remarkable characteristics of the series and the identity of its designer are discussed.

The Formal Construction of the Visual Series: Pairs and Clusters, Contrasts and Hierarchies

To understand the *conterfeytsels* as a sequence, it is important to be sure that they are in the correct order. The three aids to interpretation offered by the *Itinerario* do not agree with one another on all points, but when taken in combination they provide the means of determining a preferable order (see table 1 and explanatory comments). The largest part of the entire series of engravings—plates 1 through 26—appears to consist of an interweaving of three subseries. The core subseries of ethnic couples indicates the levels of civility in both 'policie' and the 'government of their houses'. The subseries with ships and elite processions specifies practices relating to 'policie'. And, as will be argued below, the subseries of large-scale scenes specifies the influence of the dominant religions on morality, especially family morals, an aspect of the 'government of their houses'. All three subseries contribute to the presentation of a hierarchy of civility in Asia running from north to south. The fourth, botanical subseries belongs at the end and can best be regarded as a coda, in which civilised behaviour is depicted and recommended yet again in a different manner.

Within the established sequence, the plates can be seen to be arranged in successive clusters. The first cluster consists of the prints with Chinese subjects (pls. 2–4). On grounds of both content and form, plate 1, which shows couples from Malacca and Java, can be included in this cluster. The second cluster focuses on the Portuguese in Goa (pls. 5–14). A pair of scenes, from the market in Goa and a nearby village, introduce this cluster, which is followed by groupings dealing with Ballagate (pls. 15–20) and eastern Africa (pls. 21, 22). These images provide information about the background of the non-Portuguese residents of Goa. For the inhabitants of Ballagate, to which Goa belonged before it was conquered by the Portuguese, this is done on such a large scale that their representations form a relatively independent cluster. The groups from eastern Africa are represented in such a summary fashion that, although plates 21 and 22 constitute a pair in formal terms, they should be regarded not as a separate cluster but as an excursus. What is shown of the Arabs, Abyssinians, and Mozambiquans is primarily of importance because of their position in Goa. The penultimate cluster covers the inhabitants of Malabar, including (for reasons that have yet to be explained) the man from Pegu and the Moluccan (pls. 23–26). Finally, there is the cluster of plates showing fruits, trees, and plants (pls. 27–30).

Each of the first four clusters (China, Goa, Ballagate, and Malabar) includes two prints of ethnic types, one or more processions, a representation of boats, and one or more large-scale scenes with a message about religion. The Goa cluster stands out for its three large-scale scenes, with the market scene in an even larger format to draw special attention to the centre of the Portuguese empire in Asia. The plate with boats seems to be lacking in the Malabar cluster, but that is not so; boats from Malabar are illustrated together with those of Goa in plates 10 and 20, in the Goa and Ballagate clusters. This strange arrangement is probably intended to indicate the close friend/foe relationship of Goa/Ballagate and Malabar in this field. The Chinese cluster lacks a large-scale religious scene. That is probably not fortuitous. Two pairs of plates (pls. 14 and 26, and 16 and 17) not only show religious practices but also have a polemi-cal purpose. As will be explained below, they show the hypocritical observation of Christian family values by the Portuguese, the idolatry and inhumanity even toward family members of the Hindus, and—as the brief caption shows—the heretical sectarianism of Islam with its tolerance of sodomy. No such polemical intention applied with regard to China, which was presented as a model society, albeit a pagan one.

The three interwoven subseries are not continued in the final cluster of fruits, trees, and plants. This cluster consists of a combination of its own, comprising two prints which are formally similar to the plates with ethnic types, and two prints which recall the subseries with large scenes. In these prints the plants, trees, and fruits are incorporated in a landscape and a courtyard. They connect the botanical illustrations with the practices of the Indians and Portuguese more explicitly than the other two do. The similar structure of each cluster shows that they are comparable.

The whole series of the *Icones* offers an implicit argument whose main thread runs from cluster to cluster. In the first instance, it is about a comparison between China, Goa, Ballagate, and Malabar. These four regions define the moral map of Asia. The classification of the other peoples is supplementary information, based to a large extent on extrapolation from the image provided by these four. The repetition of similar combinations of plates (ethnic types, elite processions and boats, large-scale scenes on religion) invites the viewer to make comparisons and sets the discourse in motion. This is also the result of the consistent representation of contrasts and hierarchies. The linking of plates within and between clusters is also an invitation to compare continuously and systematically, and thus to discover meanings. Much of the significance of the series can be understood from a mere comparison of the plates. The implicit argument does not follow the same sequence within each cluster, but the same themes recur: the general level of civility, sexual morality, wealth, and technical ability (all correlated to dress), the nature of the regime both domestically and abroad, and the presence of ethnic-religious homogeneity or heterogeneity. The comparative argument about the different societies comes to a halt at the cluster with fruits, plants, and trees. The notion of civility, it will be argued, is explained one last time in this coda: it consists of the ability to secure and sustain the requirements of human existence as skilfully and rationally as possible, of mastery of the instincts and a striving for the general well-being and refined pleasures. The final print is a warning against dissolution.

How is the text linked with this implicit argument? The best way to examine this is to paraphrase the visual series and the accompanying texts to demonstrate the interaction of word and image. In doing so, we will use mainly the texts in the *Icones,* derived from the Dutch edition of the *Itinerario* with Latin text (1599). Since the series was in the first

TABLE 1. **Sequence and Grouping of Plates in the *Icones et Habitus Indorum***

Plate Number and Description	Paired with		Plate Number and Description *(continued)*	Paired with
I. CHINA			18. The ambassador of the king of Ballagate in litter with servants	10
1. Malayan and Javanese couples	Plate 2		19. Peasant couple *(Canarim)* with children; Indian mercenary	
2. Chinese couples: commoners and mandarins	1		*(lascaryn)* and dancing girl *(balhadeira)*	15
3. Mandarins boating and carried by attendants	4		20. Dugout and planked craft from Goa and Cochin (Malabar)	23
4. Chinese junk	3			
			Arabs, Abyssinians, and Mozambiquans	
II. PORTUGUESE GOA			21. Arab Muslim couple with child and Abyssinian	
5. Marketplace of Goa	Plate 6		Christian couple	Plate 22
6. Village near Goa	5		22. Muslim and Christian couples from Mozambique	21
7. Portuguese widower, casado, and soldado	11			
8. Portuguese nobleman on horseback with servants	9		**IV. MALABAR**	
9. Rich or well-born Portuguese in litter with servants	8		23. The king of Cochin on an elephant with warriors	
10. Western Indian warship with Portuguese commander			(Nayars)	Plate 20
and helmsman and crew from Malabar	18		24. Two Muslim men from Cananor and a couple of	
11. Unmarried, married, and widowed Portuguese women in			agriculturalists (Polya) from the Malabar Coast	25
public dress; Portuguese or Luso-Asian woman in house dress	7		25. Sodomite from Pegu (Burma), warrior from the Moluccas, and	
12. Portuguese woman in uncovered litter with servants	13		a Saint Thomas Christian couple from the Malabar Coast	24
13. Portuguese woman in covered litter with servants and			26. Hindu temple and mosque	14
wet nurse	12			
14. Portuguese couple with servants in nocturnal procession	26		**V. FRUITS, PLANTS, AND TREES**	
			27. Iambo, pineapple, mango, cashew, and jackfruit trees	
III. BALLAGATE			and fruit; ginger plant and root	Plate 28
15. Merchants from Ballagate and Cambaia (Gujarat);			28. Coconut palms, banana plant, pepper plant, and	
Brahman couple	Plate 19		betelnut tree *(arequeira)*	27
16. Hindu wedding in Ballagate	17		29. Bamboo, banyan tree *(arbore de rais)*, and durian	30
17. Suttee in Ballagate	16		30. *Arbore triste* in yard of country house near Goa	29

Commentary

The Correct Sequence

The plates of the *Icones* were originally designed for the *Itinerario*. The correct sequence of the plates in that book then must also obtain for the *Icones*. The first Dutch edition of the *Itinerario* provides—in addition to the division by chapters—three aids in determining the order of the

plates: the 'Direction for the bookbinders' (*Waerschouwinge voor de Boeckbinders*); the 'Register of figures and maps' (*Register van figueren ende caerte*), forming part of the 'Content of the Book' (*Inhout des Boecks*); and the page numbers printed on every plate. Each of these aids has its limitations. The Direction omits one of the plates of Saint Helena, while the Register lacks the plate with the man from Pegu, the Moluccan, and the Saint Thomas Christians; each, that is, lists only thirty-five of the thirty-six plates that belong to the *Itinerario*. The text of the *Itinerario* mentions a plate depicting an Arab caravan of camels (1:37), but this is not found in any edition. The *Icones,* which omits the *Itinerario*'s six topographical plates, consists of thirty plates.

The page numbers on the plates often show that a number of plates were to be bound together between two pages of the *Itinerario,* but they do not indicate the sequence. This problem can be solved with the help of the Direction and the Register. A combination of these three aids results in only a few problems. The Direction and the Register place the scene of the village near Goa at the end of the group with Asians in Goa and Ballagate. This is quite possible, but according to the page number on the plate itself, it must be inserted much earlier, after the market in Goa. This is in fact more in line with the rhetorical contrast and hierarchy of the visual narrative. According to the page numbers, the Mozambiquans should precede the Arabs and Abyssinians. This appears to be a mistake, because it contradicts the sequence of the chapters, which is closely followed by the plates in this part of the sequence, as well as the Direction and the Register. According to the page numbers and the Direction, the plate with the coconut palms precedes the *arbore de rais,* which forms a couple with the *arbore triste,* the reverse of the order indicated in the Register. In view of the composition and rhetoric of the plates, this seems a preferable sequence.

The Arrangement of the Plates in Pairs, Subseries, and Clusters

The thirty plates of the *Icones* can be divided into five clusters and four thematic subseries—the ethnic types, the processions and ships, the large-scale scenes dealing with religion, and the fruits, plants, and trees. The themes of the subseries correspond to the subjects of the counterfeits mentioned on the title pages of the *Itinerario* and the *Icones:* the 'government of their houses', 'policie', religion, and fruits, trees, and spices. Four of the clusters represent geographical and societal units— China, Goa, Ballagate, and Malabar. The fifth cluster consists of the plates depicting useful plants and is at the same time a subseries. Each subseries can be further divided into pairs of plates. The above table sets out the fifteen pairs that make up the *Icones.* An interpretation that aims to provide a rationale for this construction can be found in the text.

The clusters are established by the page numbers that appear on the plates, which in most cases separate them into geographical units. The plates that appear to stand on their own have been assigned to the nearest geographical unit. Some of the subseries and pairs can be immediately recognised as such because they consist of similar images on a comparable subject. The plates of ethnic couples can be grouped in pairs without any difficulty: plates 1 and 2, 7 and 11, 15 and 19, 21 and 22, and 24 and 25. The same is true of the series with fruits, plants, and trees: plates 27 and 29 and 29 and 30. Other subseries are recognisable as such only when an attempt is made to arrange all the plates in pairs.

For instance, it is not immediately obvious that the six plates with large-scale scenes form a subseries. They do not contain scenes of the same type, and it is not easy to detect a thematic coherence. It is easier to identify pairs in this group: plates 5 and 6 (market of Goa and nearby village) and plates 16 and 17 (Hindu wedding and suttee) are unmistakable pairs, and the plates follow one another in immediate succession. The remaining plates, 14 and 26 (Portuguese couple and Hindu temple and mosque), are widely separated from one another and do not appear to be related in terms of either form or content. The connection seems to be that both plates make a statement about religion in their respective societies, as is the case with plates 16 and 17. This suggests that plates 5 and 6 also contain an allusion to religion and that all of the plates with large-scale scenes can be considered as a subseries on the basis of their content. This hypothesis is confirmed in the fourth section of the text.

More problems are raised by the series with boats and processions. The plates with boats (pls. 4, 10, 20) seem to form a self-contained subseries. This also appears to be the case with the plates showing processions (pls. 3, 8, 9, 12, 13, 18, 23). Four of these processions (pls. 8, 9, 12, 13: the Portuguese men and women with prominent means of transport) form two matching pairs. This leaves plates 3, 18, and 23 (the mandarins, the ambassador of Ballagate, and the king of Cochin). They yield their significance when they are linked with the three plates of boats. It is natural to link the junk with the mandarin boating (pls. 3 and 4), a link which emphasises the peaceful character of the Chinese and their external relations. Likewise, the link between the Goan/Malabar commercial/war ship and the ambassador of Ballagate (pls. 10 and 18) characterises the external relations of these two regions with one another: peaceful relations between Goa and Ballagate, duplicitous relations between Goa and Malabar. The link between the king of Cochin and the dugouts (pls. 20 and 23) does not refer to the external relations of Malabar, which have already been indicated by the pairing of plates 10 and 18. This pair refers to the difference in practical skills between Goa/Ballagate and Malabar. Dugouts and fusts were found in both regions, as the text accompanying the plates admits, but on closer inspection the fust belongs to the Goan cluster while the dugouts belong to Malabar, a region with a very low level of technical ability. The plates of processions and vessels thus form a single subseries.

instance designed as a complement to the full text of the *Itinerario* proper, it will also be necessary occasionally to draw on the text of the first Dutch-language edition of that work (1596).

The Relation between Visual Series and Text: A Systematic Comparison of Morals and Practices in Four Asian Societies

The visual narrative begins, remarkably enough, with the print of the Malays and Javanese, followed by three prints with Chinese subjects. This is not what one would expect from the *Itinerario*. Its first 'ethnographic' chapters deal with the Portuguese and the native population of Goa. Linschoten then moves on to describe the representatives of the Indian regions to the north and east, passes on to the Arabs, Abyssinians, and Mozambiquans, and concludes with the ethnic and religious groups of the Malabar coast.[107] The Javanese, Malays, and Chinese appeared earlier in the text but in a section on the maritime trade in Asia.[108] Goa was the centre of Asia for Linschoten. It would have been consonant with this view if the visual narrative had started there and had stuck to the sequence of the ethnographic chapters, as it does in the following twenty-two prints.

Are the Malays, Javanese, and Chinese given pride of place because of the fitting out of the first Dutch fleet to Asia? After all, the aim of the enterprise was to secure a base on Java and from there to get trade under way with China and thus undermine the position of Malacca as an emporium. In 1596, the readers at whom the *Itinerario* was aimed were specially interested in Southeast Asia and the Far East. A consideration of this kind may have played a role in determining the sequence of the plates, but it would have been independent of the content of the engravings. It does not explain how the first four prints are connected with the rest, nor what the exact relation is in the visual narrative between the Malays and Javanese, on the one hand, and the Chinese, on the other. The motivation for the sequence in terms of content only emerges when plates 1 and 2 are seen to constitute a pair and their mutual cross-references have been unravelled.

The Malays and Javanese form a moderate contrast with the Chinese: the less well covered as against the very decently dressed. The contrast is strongest between the Javanese and the Mandarins, the couples on the right in the two plates, while the Malays and the Chinese commoners occupy an intermediate position. The armed men in plate 1 are opposed to the two unarmed men in plate 2. In the first plate, each of the couples represents a distinct people, while in the second plate the two couples represent a single people. Similarities between the couples in the two plates, which tone down the contrast, are indicated chiastically. Both the

Javanese woman and the Chinese commoner attempt to seduce their male counterparts, one with betel leaves, the other with flowers. Among the Javanese, where the woman correctly stands to the left of the man, an overture of this kind is apparently not a breach of morals. In the case of the Chinese commoners, however, where the woman occupies the 'incorrect' position, the rule is contravened. As for the Malay couple and the Mandarins, both man and woman behave compatibly and in accordance with the rules of moral behaviour.

The hierarchy of civility between Chinese, Malays, and Javanese that is expressed in the visual code of the dress is specified in the range of forms of behaviour between the sexes: a large degree of control and decorum in the north, courtesy in the middle, and little control in the case of the gesticulating Javanese. Plate 3 shows the mandarins again, but this time the man is exercising his function as a magistrate; sober, unarmed, he rules by virtue of his authority and knows how to balance obligation with pleasure. Plate 4, the Chinese junk, repeats the theme of Chinese technological superiority and prosperity, indicated in plates 1 and 2 in the contrast between a wealth of stitched clothing, on the one hand, and scanty clothing consisting of wraps or drapes, on the other.

The plates in the first cluster introduce the theme of the whole series: a comparison of the morals and practices of the Asian peoples and of the Portuguese who live among them. They also show which markers are used to indicate the points of comparison. They make it clear that the results of the comparison are embodied in contrast, relative similarity, and a hierarchy that corresponds to a three-tiered north-centre-south division. The use of a reversal of conventional left-right orientation to indicate the breach of a rule is also indicated. These plates introduce both the codes and the content.

The text of the *Icones* on the Malays and Javanese is based on the contrast, derived from Camões, between *Malaios namorados* and *Jaus valentes*. The Malays are extremely amorous, but they also compose love poetry and are the creators of an international language and a trade emporium. This all qualifies them as reasonably civilised. The Javanese, on the other hand, are rather thinly characterised in the text as warlike. In the plate they are presented as amorous, but in a less courtly way than the Malays, as the hierarchy of civility would lead one to expect. The Malay man in the plate has been provided with a kris, the attribute of a warrior, but seems to be more interested in flowers. The text of the *Icones* and of the *Itinerario* proper have hardly anything to report on the technical skill, wealth, or social structure of Malacca and Java, a good reason to keep the comparison with China very general on these counts.

The text of the *Icones* has plenty to say about the superiority of the Chinese. They were extremely clever, had invented the firearm and the art of printing centuries earlier, and possessed an advanced technology, as could be seen from the throngs of junks plying their trade on the big rivers and oceans and from the land yacht. They cultivated scholarship in many universities. They were very prosperous and saw to it that wealth was appropriately distributed among the different population groups. The elite were dressed in multicoloured robes of silk, while the commoners were decently dressed in cotton and dull materials. They did not have woollen clothing—an opening for European traders, may have been the implication.

The emperor did not rule his empire with belligerent dukes and counts, but with unarmed men recruited from the ranks of scholars, who were held in high esteem by the people. The life of a mandarin consisted not only of serious study and just administration; he liked to pursue pleasure too. The Chinese were an exceptionally peace-loving nation. Although they were heathen, they believed in an immortal soul and in reward or punishment after death, as the Christians did. Unlike the paganism of the Indians, theirs did not lead to irrational economic behaviour or breaches of the law of nature. Their households were a paragon of decency. The weak spot was the general Asian—perhaps one should say general human—problem of the luxuriousness of their womenfolk.[109] They bound the feet of their women to prevent them from following the path of vice. These texts elaborate the general message contained in the plates in more detail: China was a society with a high level of civility. The Chinese were not only more civilised than the Javanese and Malays; as we shall see, they were more civilised than any other group of people represented in the visual narrative.

This paragon of a civilised and peace-loving, albeit heathen, society, plying a maritime trade with large unarmed vessels, is followed by Goa, the centre of seafaring and trading Portuguese Asia, with its western, eastern, and southern peripheries. The market in Goa (pl. 5) and the village scene near Goa (pl. 6) introduce this cluster.[110]

The exceptionally large format of the engraving of the market in Goa establishes its importance in the series. The theme and its combination with a village scene must have seemed familiar to any Dutch reader in the sixteenth century who was at all acquainted with the literature and painting of his day. He would have understood that the market could be looked upon as a theatre of social order and morality, not just as a place where food and other daily necessities changed hands. The urban market could be contrasted with the peasant fair to illustrate in all kinds of ways the superiority of urban civility to the crude manners of the peasants. It was also the setting for the public display of social status, where it was always possible that someone might not be as he seemed and where knavery and deceit could exist alongside honest trade, as the

quacks demonstrated. Moreover, market scenes were a way of taking stock of the advanced commercialisation in the Netherlands. They represented the commercialisation of goods by showing the great variety of products for sale and how they were displayed, and commented on the phenomenon.[111] The engraving of the market of Goa introduces the centre of Portuguese Asia as a preeminently commercial society.

The row of houses, most with more than one storey, numerous windows, balconies, and tiled roofs, provide the urban backdrop to the market. Some of the main scenes are arranged on an arch that runs from the lower left corner of the picture through the middle to the lower right corner, creating a division between foreground and background. In the lower left we see two *pingues*—Indian porters from the countryside—entering the market with an enormous pitcher filled with drinking water, enough to quench the thirst of the whole market.[112] They face a group of Portuguese men gathered around a crier with a chain who is auctioning a dark child, a scantily clad female slave, and perhaps also the bare-chested male.[113] The men protect themselves from the heat of the morning sun with large parasols. To the right, at the peak of the arch, is a scene centred around a large table. Three Portuguese men seated beneath parasols are supervising another crier who is selling goods from an open chest in front of the table. On either side stands an interested crowd, mainly Portuguese men but also including two Asian traders. In the lower right corner, a Portuguese nobleman on horseback and a Portuguese noblewoman in a closed litter leave the market, surrounded by Asian or African servants. They pass by the Misericordia, a hospital. In the foreground an Asian merchant is selling an Arabian horse. The Portuguese ostentatiously displaying a rosary appears to be a potential buyer. Next to this scene stands a wet nurse with a baby. She gestures toward the sale of the slave child with her right hand. To her left stands a scantily dressed woman with a jar on her head, who points to the baby the wet nurse is carrying. These two women are surrounded by puppies playing. In the background of the picture, on the left, a money changer *(xaroffo)* is seated at a table and four Asian women are offering goods for sale from the baskets on their laps. On the right, a Portuguese man seated on a chair is drinking from a pitcher without touching it with his lips. A well-dressed Asian woman leans toward him. In the distance we see a Portuguese man sitting beneath a parasol, while another holds a circular object (a mirror?) in front of him. Next to him is a figure who appears to be another *xaroffo*.

Goa owed its position as an emporium to precious stones, costly fabrics, and spices, but that is not what we see for sale at this market. The *xaroffo* in the background is the most explicit allusion to the international character of the market in Goa. The four women selling goods from their baskets provide a more local colour; they may be offering for sale the jams and conserves mentioned in the text. The three scenes of trade that dominate the middle all characterise, not the rich trades of the Goan emporium, but behaviours prevalent among the Portuguese, especially their sexual mores and the way they take care of their families.

The proximity of the slave woman with child and the Arabian horse illustrate what Linschoten wrote about the daily sale of slaves: young and old are auctioned 'as beast are sold with us'.[114] This plate may well be the earliest Western representation of the sale of a slave to a European buyer.[115] The transaction is presented as dehumanising and disrupting a slave family. It is also shown to disrupt the family life of the masters, the Portuguese. The two women in the foreground are a reference to this. The woman with a pitcher looks very much like the slave who is being sold and is most likely one herself.[116] The text mentions that masters sent their slave women out to earn a living for them. They did so by selling all kinds of wares, including their own bodies.[117] The task of the woman with a jar was to slake the men's thirst. Many Portuguese kept their families with what they earned from their slave prostitutes. The wet nurse next to the woman with the pitcher is another allusion to the looseness of family ties among the Portuguese. If the Portuguese married, it was commonly with Asian women. Linschoten regarded these daughters of the tropical sun as extremely licentious, more interested in lovers than in babies. They put their offspring out to a wet nurse, most often a slave woman. The child—a mestizo or 'half-breed'—thus imbibed the vices of a slave society with its milk.

The sale from a chest, the prominent scene in the middle of the plate, shows the consequences of a dissolute life. It is the sale of a dead person's possessions. Linschoten explains: 'for that there die many men within the Towne, by meanes of their disordered living, together with the hotenes of the country'.[118] The Misericordia, the hospital where Portuguese men prematurely ended their dissolute lives, also refers to the extremely high mortality rate.[119] The Portuguese in tropical Asia suffered from an unquenchable thirst. The men on the left are carrying large quantities of water to slake that thirst. The placement of this scene opposite the scene near the Misericordia suggests that the thirst is also of a sexual kind. The heat of the climate was considered to encourage sexual arousal. The print of the market of Goa presents the moral corruption of the Portuguese, particularly their corrupt domestic morals.

The text accompanying this plate in the *Icones* mentions several aspects of the Goan emporium as a moral community, some of which are depicted in the engraving. The text shows that Linschoten regarded the slave trade as a dehumanising practice but touches only indirectly on its consequences for family life. He mentions the high mortality rate

among the Portuguese resulting from their dissolute way of life. Other subjects that he broaches, but which do not appear in the engraving, present a more positive picture of Goa. For instance, foreign merchants were allowed freedom of religion 'within the limits of the natural law, which prohibited inhuman marriage and funeral practices'. The city was a concentration of human skill in action, particularly in the crafts and medicinal practice, often performed by Asians. The city also had an extensive hierarchy of high- and lower-ranking groups. Linschoten mentions the existence of professional castes among the Indians without giving any indication of whether he considers it preferable to the European system of rank. According to this text, the city of Goa was a reasonably ordered moral community, as cities were supposed to be. The text veils over what the engraving emphasises and what will be elaborated in later texts: the moral corruption—resulting from slavery and other causes—that eroded the social order.[120]

The village scene may be intended to form a contrast to city life, but the question is how. It depicts a village of the Canarim near Goa, as described in chapter 39 of the *Itinerario*, but the caption also connects the scene with the 'dwellings of the Decanijns' in chapter 38. The Decanijns lived farther to the east, in Ballagate. The plate represents peasants as they were to be found in the countryside near Goa and in the adjoining Hindu society. The small mud huts smeared with dung are shown in the print with straw roofs and without windows, but their generous proportions reduce the contrast found in the text with the multistorey city houses with their tiled roofs.[121] The main activity in the Canarim villages, the cultivation of coconut palms, has been relegated to the background in the plate. This work is given more prominence in plate 28.[122] Other village activities, such as crushing rice or drawing water from the well, are depicted not in the centre but in the background or to one side. In the foreground and at the centre of attention are a naked woman who is having water poured over her by a scantily clad woman from the village and a squatting woman who is scooping up water in her left hand to wash herself between her legs. Next to them a cow, a thick-tailed ram, and a piglet have been placed, perhaps a parallel to the Arabian horse placed next to the women in the foreground of the market scene. The poorly clad women, native to the village and engaged in what seem simple acts of personal hygiene, contrast with the well-dressed, cosmopolitan men trading at the city market. But the point of all this remains implicit.

The texts of the *Icones* and of the *Itinerario* itself offer a measure of clarification.[123] The three women in the foreground are a reasonably accurate illustration of a passage on the villagers: 'They are verie cleane on their bodies, for every day they wash themselves all their body over, as often as they ease themselves or make water, both men and women, like the Moores or Mahometans. They wash themselves with the left hand, because they eate with the right hand, and use no spoones'.[124] The regular bathing of the Canarim and the purification with the left hand are here related to their great poverty. The message seems to be: the villagers are exceptionally poor and have little clothing, but they still keep their bodies scrupulously clean. Their purity was one of the few qualities of these miserable and miserably dressed Canarim. The cow, the pig, and the ram could be another reference to the wretched material conditions of the Canarim. Linschoten emphasises how little the Canarim ate and how skinny they were, though this is not reflected in the print. They kept cattle, sheep, and pigs, but their religion prohibited them from eating the flesh of these animals.[125] The text of the *Icones* notes that most of the villagers had been converted to Christianity and had improved their habits—probably an allusion to abandoning food taboos. This civilising effect of Portuguese colonialism is absent from the plate, nor is it mentioned in the original Dutch text of the *Itinerario*.

At first sight, one might think that the contrast around which the two plates introducing the cluster on Goa and Ballagate were constructed is simply between the poverty of the peasants in the villages and the wealth of the cosmopolitan city dwellers. However, the exceptionally low standard of living of the Canarim is addressed in the text not merely as an economic matter. Rather, Linschoten used it to propound his view of the village as a moral community. He did not regard poverty as a virtue. Extreme poverty, he wrote, led to slavish behaviour. Other vices may be implied as well in the engraving. The prominent position of the naked woman bathing and the woman washing herself with her left hand may be a reference to shamelessness and dissolution, although there is nothing in the text to suggest this. Nor should we forget that the threshold of shame in relation to nude public bathing and natural bodily functions was lower in the sixteenth century than was later the case.[126] The women in the bathing scene display some affinity with the personifications of the virtues and vices that would have been familiar to a Dutch reader from other series of edifying prints.[127] This also suggests a moral rather than an economic message, as was the case in the market scene. Despite all the external purity, the moral status of the villagers represented by the women seems to be dubious. Although the plates present an external contrast between the city and the village, the message seems to be that they did have something in common: they were both morally corrupt communities.

The engravings of the market in Goa and the village near Goa are formally related to the group of large-scale scenes that deal with the connection between religion and civility. Could looking at the plates from this perspective improve our understanding of their meaning? According to the text, the daily washing of the whole body and the use of the left hand for cleansing oneself were among the fixed rituals of the villagers. The text does not state that these rituals were prescribed by native religion, but the plate, in which the acts of the women are associated with animals representing food taboos, suggests that the viewer should understand them as religious observances. These rituals of cleanliness made little sense to Europeans. Neither did the food taboos. But the native villagers observed these seemingly irrational rules punctiliously, in spite of their great poverty.

The city also had its rituals, but of a different nature, exemplified by the daily sale of the possessions of the dead. The Portuguese paid lip service to the Christian family ethic and the injunction to be charitable, but the prescriptions were only honoured in the breach. In practice, their urban religion allowed the sale of slaves and thus contributed to the dissolution of the family. The only rules that were punctiliously observed in the city were the rules of the market. Commercialisation had gone so far as to turn human beings into commodities. In this perspective the two plates represent the contrast between the strict compliance with heathen rules in the village, leading to poverty of the households and its attendant slavishness, and the neglect of Christian prescriptions in the city, where the dominance of the market created wealth but corrupted family life. Both city and village were morally corrupt communities, but in different ways and for different reasons.

After presenting and characterising the city and the rural hinterland, the different ethnic groups are treated individually. Each of the ethnic groups in Goa to which Linschoten devoted a chapter is represented in one way or another, starting with the Portuguese, the lords and masters of the country. The visual narrative presents them in two groups of four plates. First come the armed men with their African and Asian servants on foot, on horseback, in an open litter, and in command of a fust with a native crew (pls. 7–10). The second group comprises women, most attended by male and female servants, on foot, in an open litter, in a closed litter, and on the way to church at night (pls. 11–14).[128] The worlds of men and women are distinguished in terms of openness and closedness. The men spend most of their time away from home. The women rarely show themselves in public, except to go to church, and then only in a closed litter.

The prints of the Portuguese men distinguish between the married men *(casados)* and the unmarried soldiers *(soldados)*. Above them are high-ranking noblemen, who ride on horseback, and the wealthy or lower-ranking nobility, who are carried in litters. In no case is the profession of these men marked by an attribute. However, they all carry swords. Unlike the situation in China, the elite in Goa could not rule without a show of arms. Their main activities, which were commercial rather than military, are not shown. Even the *casados,* who were shown trading on the market, appear here as men of rank without pressing duties, and the same applies to the *soldados.* The text of the *Icones* describes the decorum and courtly forms of behaviour observed by men from this richly dressed elite when they met in public, but at the same time reveals that the poor *soldados* who emigrated to Asia walked into a poverty trap. They had few prospects of a career or of returning, and often resorted to being kept by an Asian mistress.

The *fidalgos* in the service of the king could only find their way to genuinely lucrative positions after prolonged bureaucratic intrigues, but they could then make a fortune from the state revenues in a short time, a procedure which the viceroy did not spurn either. If they sought marriage partners, however, the *fidalgos* generally had to fall back on Asian women, and their children were thus usually mestizos. An honest profession and domestic bliss were rare in this world. In Goa these successful and civilised-looking masters were dependent on the subservience of their servants, drawn from many different nationalities, and on the agricultural labourers in the surrounding countryside. At sea they were the prey of pirates from Malabar, who sailed in the same kind of fusts.[129] In the south the Portuguese were forced to ally themselves with the pagan Nayars, the warriors of the king of Cochin, whose exceptionally conspicuous lack of chastity is mentioned in the text of the *Icones* under the engraving of the fust. The public display of decorum by Portuguese men was a façade, behind which almost everyone lived a life of immorality and corruption, many lived in poverty, and the masters were slaves to the loose morals of their subordinates.

The wives of the Portuguese were rarely European, but were more commonly native or of mixed ancestry. The texts make this clear, but it is hardly discernible in the plates. Unlike the men, they are not distinguished in terms of wealth. The three women on the left in plate 11, dressed in decent European clothing appropriate for appearing in public, are identified as unmarried, married, and widowed; they stand in contrast to the fourth woman, who wears seductive Asian indoor clothes. As with the Portuguese men, the women's public display of respectability and decorum concealed a secret life of unfettered vice. The text of the *Icones* contains a large selection of Linschoten's sensational observations on this score, more inspired by Ovid's description of the Iron Age than by empirical observation.[130] Inside the home, the women behaved as Asians not only in their manner of dress, but also in their eating habits and in their uncontrolled concupiscence. They ate rice, drank from a pitcher without touching it with their lips, and made fun of the new ar-

rivals from Europe who could not do the same.[131] They washed regularly and scented their whole body. They sat at the window all day, hoping for an opportunity to make contact with a suitor, all the while chewing 'like cows' on the intoxicating and aphrodisiac betel leaves. Their husbands only allowed them out on rare occasions, and then under supervision to prevent them from indulging their desires. However, this did not put a stop to incestuous relations with male relatives. Powerful men were often misled or eliminated by crafty women. The women drugged or poisoned their husbands in order to sport with their lovers undisturbed. Male honour could often only be saved by drastic measures. Cuckolded husbands regularly put their unfaithful wives to death. If the women left this domestic hell for a nocturnal procession, their female servants slipped away under cover of darkness to join their lovers (pl. 14). Devotion was merely a pretext for these women. There were no nunneries in Goa because no woman was prepared to swear an oath of chastity. There could be no question of a proper bringing up of children in this situation. The Portuguese women put their children in the charge of Indian nurses, so they sucked in Asian vices at the breast. These scenes call for the skill of characterisation of a Hogarth. In the *Icones,* however, the relentless war between the sexes and cultures is merely indicated by the attributes of the see-through blouse and the betel leaves. Nevertheless, for readers familiar with the text, the blunt display of decorum in the illustrations acquires a satirical edge.

On the bird's-eye map of Goa in the *Itinerario* (not included in the *Icones),* the city was presented as a large tropical trading port under Portuguese control, with a prominent place for the palaces of the viceroy and the archbishop. The numerous churches, monasteries, and chapels were precisely indicated. Goa looked like an Asian Lisbon, a Christian beacon amid pagan darkness. The prints and the accompanying texts present a different picture. The fust placed Goa on a lower rung of technical skill than Europe. The level of prosperity was mediocre, and social inequality was extreme: masters were richly dressed, the indigenous population barely. The internal social order was complex and under threat from the multiethnic character of the emporium. The *fidalgos,* with their impressive swords, knew how to handle an external enemy and to master their servants and slaves, but they were regularly defeated by their wives on the domestic front. These literate warriors respected the natural law, but the public display of Catholic virtue was a sham. Behind the scenes, these Christian authorities indulged in pagan vices. Their households were chaotic and corrupt. The rosaries carried so ostentatiously by the *casado* in plate 5, the *soldado* in plate 7 and two women in plate 11 should perhaps be taken as a hint that the sacramentalism of the Catholics encouraged vice. The text, however, avoids explicit anti-Catholicism.

This Goa forms a contrast with China, where learned, unarmed magistrates were in control, technical skill produced general prosperity, wise administration guaranteed internal and external stability, and home life was virtuous. The implication seems to be that a higher level of civility was connected with ethnic-religious homogeneity and the dominant position of learned men in the administration. While Linschoten's bird's-eye view of Goa presented the city as the Portuguese liked it to be seen, the prints of the *Icones* recounted a black legend of Portuguese imperialism in Asia.[132]

The next group of plates (pls. 15–20) shows the Hindu society of Ballagate, to the east of Goa, although most of the figures could also be found in Goa itself. Let us first examine the picture that is presented of Ballagate as an independent community before proceeding to compare it to the community that had grown up in the territory that the Portuguese had taken away from it.

The first four plates deal with the elite: merchants, Brahmans, and the warrior nobility surrounding the king. The remaining two plates depict the lower castes: agriculturalists, fishermen, mercenaries, and female dancers. The ascetic Brahman couple, the most preeminent, are contrasted with the two wealthy male merchants. The Brahman is scantily clad, wears the Brahmanic cord over his naked chest, and holds an object resembling a book in his left hand. His female counterpart is covered with a single cloak from head to toe and is barefoot. They are contrasted with the richly dressed but possibly sodomite merchant from Ballagate, the man with the betel leaves, and his companion from Cambaia with the pen and paper, probably only included here to indicate the prestigious social position of great merchants in the coastal communities of central and northern India. The text of the *Icones* praises the merchants for their professional knowledge, especially in the diamond trade, and mentions their vegetarianism. The Brahman is described as a member of 'the honestest and most esteemed nation' among the heathen, a priest, a counsellor to rulers, and often a skilful herbal doctor. In the background, however, we see his baleful influence: two figures kneeling before an awesome idol.[133]

The following two plates dramatically show the devilish work of the Brahmans in the territory outside Portuguese rule. In plate 16, a bridal couple is on the way to the ceremony, preceded by musicians with a trumpet, tambourine, and drum and accompanied by relatives, including a Brahman couple. It looks like a festive occasion. As was conventional in this part of the world, the bride and groom belong to the same caste, a civil arrangement. This deceptively innocent scene, however, soon becomes more ominous. First, the text of the *Icones* mentions that the bride and groom are only twelve years old. Then the reader may ask himself

where the procession is going. Linschoten wrote that the wedding ceremony was performed indoors.[134] That is not what we see here. It is thus appropriate to connect this scene with another part of the description of marital practices in the *Itinerario*. The bride was taken to the temple 'with great triumph and Musicke' where she was forcibly deflowered on the ivory penis of an idol by her 'neerest friends and kinswomen'.[135] The next plate shows where the wedding will eventually lead: a widow leaps into the fire that is consuming the corpse of her husband, to a musical accompaniment provided by the same musicians who performed at her wedding.[136] The text of the *Icones* explains that this custom, sanctioned by the Brahmans, had its origins in a measure that was taken to put a stop to the poisoning of husbands by their adulterous wives. Brahmans led the faithful to engage in wedding and funeral practices that were prohibited in Goa because they were in conflict with 'the law of nature'.

As indicated above, the following print, showing the ambassador of Ballagate in a litter surrounded by his entourage of servants, is difficult to interpret. It was suggested there that the print was intended to show that the elite of Ballagate consisted not only of unarmed Brahmans but also of armed nobles. Moreover, it would indicate the ethnic homogeneity of the population and the existence of stable, friendly relations between Goa and Ballagate, in contrast to adversarial relations with Malabar. The text of the *Icones* only mentions that the ambassador came to Goa on behalf of the ruler of Bijapur, who had the port under his control until the Portuguese arrived on the scene. His former palace was now the seat of the Inquisition. The message of this plate has to be derived almost entirely from the visual code.

The plate with the two couples from the lowest social ranks of Ballagate, the Canarim couple and the *lascaryn* and *balhadeira,* are the counterpart to the plate with the merchants and the Brahman couple. Within the engraving the industrious Canarim and their two toddlers are contrasted with the *lascaryn,* a mercenary, and the female dancer, who both lived in an unwedded state. The dancer, according to the caption, was a prostitute. The text of the *Icones,* though, does not elaborate on the contrast between these couples. It conveys hardly any information about the sexual morals of the rural population. What is emphasised is the poverty of the agriculturalists, as in the village scene, and their large families, a consequence of the early age of marriage. The Canarim dugouts and the coastal boat with outrigger in the next plate show that these simple souls did possess some measure of technical skill, but the text of the *Icones* says virtually nothing on the subject and dwells again on the miserable living conditions of the dark-skinned Canarim, who allow themselves to be bullied by the Portuguese and seem 'born to slavery'. The elites in this society were certainly no moral example, as is indicated by the sodomite merchant, but the common people were lacking in virtue too, as was shown in the village scene.

Ballagate society as it is presented in the *Icones* displays some similarities to Chinese society: the elite was unarmed and literate, and there was religious and ethnic homogeneity. The differences, however, are more striking. The poverty among the common people was great, the differences between rich and poor considerable, and the level of technical skill limited. The Chinese imposed limits on the immorality of their women by binding their feet, while in Ballagate widows were cremated alive as a punishment for their immorality and murderous disposition. This practice was incompatible with the law of nature, no less than sodomy, but it was sanctioned by their priestly elite. This is more than a slight difference from virtuous China. The extremely early age of marriage and the widespread use of betel are indications that the instincts were barely under control in this hot climate, despite the excessive penalties. An unarmed and ascetic elite was no guarantee of good government. These blinded priests violated the law of nature by their recommendation of suttee and by their lax attitude towards sodomy. If a people was misled by its priests, religious and ethnic homogeneity were no longer benefits.

The society of Portuguese Goa likewise displays several similarities with that of Ballagate; after all, it was grafted onto it. The difference between rich and poor was considerable. Under Portuguese rule the Canarim had remained paupers. Immorality in Goa was rife among all the ethnic groups, just as in Ballagate it had permeated the whole social hierarchy. But the differences with Ballagate were mainly in favour of Goa. The 'policie', the regime of armed aristocrats, had serious weaknesses, but at least it observed the most elementary rules of law. The law of nature was respected, at least in public. The burning of widows alive was not allowed. If women survived their husbands, they were merely required to behave with modesty in public, as the Portuguese widow dressed as a nun shows. There were many Brahmans in the city, but their temples were in ruins and the idolatrous marriage ceremonies were prohibited. Catholicism did not lead to irrational economic behaviour. Rather, commercialisation had transgressed healthy limits. The destruction of the original ethnic homogeneity through the Portuguese conquest and the import of African slaves was worrisome. The following two plates refer to this.

The two plates showing the Arabs and Abyssinians (pl. 21) and the two Mozambiquan couples (pl. 22) transport the reader to eastern Africa, but the reason for doing so is that a considerable number of individuals from this region lived in Goa. As explained above, the plates reveal a contrast between the civilised north and the wild south, as well as between Muslims whose 'government of their houses' seems to be in

reasonable order and branded Christians who appear to fall short on this score. The text accompanying plate 21 is somewhat out of keeping with the image itself. The Arabs and Abyssinians wear a stitched costume that covers most of the body. This conveys an impression of prosperity, but the text of the *Icones* refers to their position as poor sailors on the ships to the Red Sea, their clowning in Goa, and their submissiveness, all of which seems to imply that they were 'born to be slaves'. There is a second discrepancy between text and image. The print suggests that the Arabs bring up their children in an exemplary fashion, while the text states that men, women, and children in Goa staggered along the quay in an inebriated state. Perhaps these striking discrepancies between text and image are to be explained by the geographical scheme that was used in the series of prints. It required that persons from the north should be depicted as well-dressed and civilised, while the text is about the position of people from Arabia and Abyssinian in Goa. There they occupied extremely humble positions or were slaves, even though the Abyssinians were Christians of a kind. Perhaps the contrast between the caring Arabian and indifferent Mozambiquan parents also alluded to the contrast between free and slave status. The text indicates that the Arabs in Goa were free, and the image suggests that they maintained family ties appropriate to that liberty. Slaves, by contrast, had often been sold into servitude as children by parents in extreme circumstances. The Mozambiquan couple's apparent indifference toward their baby might be an allusion to this.[137]

The Mozambiquans are depicted as they would have looked in their country of origin: very lightly clad, in contrast to the two couples on the previous plate. The brief caption indicates that most Mozambiquans were Muslims and that few were Christians. As in earlier examples, here too chiastic correspondences can be detected between the two contrasting plates. The couple on the left with the tattoos and the woman who has covered her breasts form the pendant to the branded Christians from Abyssinia. As for the other couple, the man has a bow and the woman a child. This corresponds to the attributes of the Islamic Arabs, although the significance of the Mozambiquan's bow is puzzling. In the case of the Mozambiquan Christians, the tattoos and the man's very scanty clothing suggest that these immigrants had brought many of their heathen practices with them. The combination of plates 21 and 22 may be intended to show that in east Africa Muslims turned Christians—even if of suspect quality—into slaves and went on to sell them to other Christians in Goa.

The text accompanying the engraving of the Mozambiquans underscores the brutality of these black Africans by going into detail about their practice of warfare. They cut off the penises and testicles of their prisoners of war and hung them out to dry. They then presented these spoils to their ruler, first putting them in their mouths in his presence and then spitting them out. The ruler knighted these warriors by returning the penises to them, and the new nobles sewed the genitals into necklaces for their brides. They also ate the flesh of their dead foes. Mutual solidarity was unknown among this people. As a result of their frequent internecine wars, many of them ended up as slaves in Goa. Before their conversion to Christianity or Islam, the Mozambiquans had forgotten any notion of divinity and had lapsed into atheism.[138]

After reading the comments on their customs in their land of origin, the reader takes a different view of the black slaves in Western dress who formed a part of the entourages of the rich Portuguese in Goa in the earlier plates. Plates 21 and 22 refer once again to the dangers of the multiethnic character of Goan society, an evil that was made worse by slavery.

The next four plates (pls. 23–26) bring the reader to the southern periphery of Goa, the Malabar coast. The presentation of the customs in Malabar gets off to a dramatic start with the illustration of the Hindu king of Cochin riding an enormous elephant, surrounded by his gesticulating warriors, the Nayars with their extremely elongated earlobes. It concludes with the print of the mosque and Hindu temple. In between are two prints depicting ethnic couples. Three of the couples belong to Malabar, including the two men from Cananor. The other male couple consists of the 'misplaced' man from Pegu and the Moluccan.

The scanty dress of most of the couples from Malabar indicates the low level of technical skill, prosperity, and decency of the inhabitants of this region. The extremely summary dress of the nobles makes it clear that poverty was a common condition here and carries a message about the moral practices of the warrior elite. The Polya man with the betel leaves suggests that things are no better at the bottom end of the social ladder, and not much can be expected of the scantily dressed, accursed Thomas Christians with their swollen legs either. One of the Moors from Cananor is better dressed, and his bananas point to his industriousness, but the other Moor is probably intended to represent a degenerate sodomite. The population is heterogeneous in religious and ethnic terms, a point emphasised by the concluding plate, which shows a Hindu temple on the left and a mosque and school of the Muslim 'sect' on the right. The Hindu temple demonstrates heathen idolatry. Calvin regarded this misplaced love of images instead of what they represented as the most degenerate form of adultery. Consideration of the heathen marriage practices of the Indians showed this in a very literal way. The Moor with the long spear, who is suspected of sodomy, reclines decoratively in front of the mosque, showing why this mosque and school, even though they lack idols, are still not respectable temples of God. Malabar is evidently

situated on a very low rung of civility.

The text of the *Icones* confirms what the prints show. The Malabar nobility, the Nayars, were extremely dissolute. They were completely promiscuous and could claim any woman they chose.[139] The Nayar women practised intracaste polygamy, but they also secretly consorted with the Portuguese. The Nayars demanded that people give way to them in the street so that not even the shadow of anyone belonging to a lower caste would fall upon them. Despite this extreme fear of contagion, they bathed in stagnant water. Their laws of inheritance were exclusively matrilineal. The text of the *Icones* makes no mention of the Polyas, and all it has to say on the Saint Thomas Christians with elephantiasis is that they bore the external sign of their curse. Cananor morals are not mentioned in the text either, though it has plenty to say about the big daily market where a lot of pepper and excellent bananas—as seen in the plate—were on sale. The Moors, however, were duplicitous. Though allied with the Portuguese, they secretly collaborated with their enemies on the Malabar coast.

The text accompanying plate 26 portrays the Hindu as an extremely gullible idolater with a penchant for relics. In that respect the behaviour of the Muslims, whose mosque contained no idols, was better, although they performed ridiculous gestures when they prayed. The religious instruction that they gave their children would have been praiseworthy if it had not been in a false faith. Finally, reference is made to the richly decorated Hindu temple in Elephanta, though this is accredited to the Chinese who used to trade there.[140] The natives of India could not be expected to display genuine artistry.

The man from Pegu and the Moluccan are indeed geographically misplaced in this cluster, but they could not be left out of a presentation of the peoples of Portuguese Asia. Besides, their presence makes it clearer than had the depiction of the Javanese that the Far East also had its moral south. This was true first and foremost of the sodomite from Pegu, whose vice is capped with other perversities in the text of the *Icones*: the men of Pegu are said to allow strangers to have intercourse with their wives for money; nobles and even the king allow third parties to deflower their wives; and some women have their vaginas almost sewn up so that their husbands could later create openings of their preferred size. As for the Moluccan warrior, the text of the *Icones* merely states that he lived in a very dry country that had to import all its food crops, and where the population wore clothes made of straw. It was the source of the clove, a spice that was good for many medicinal purposes, but it had other uses too: 'foure Drammes being drunke with Milke, doe procure lust'.[141]

Of the four societies characterised in clusters of prints, only Malabar lacks any sign that it possesses the art of writing. The Chinese mandarin is offered a written or printed piece of paper (pl. 3). The page accompanying the mounted Portuguese holds a piece of written paper in his hand (pl. 8; compare the young page in pl. 7). The morally dubious merchant from Ballagate has not been provided with an attribute of literacy, but his colleague from Cambaia is shown with pen and paper. In the same print, the Brahman from Ballagate carries an object in his left hand that may be a book (pl. 15). None of the figures from Malabar, however, is accompanied by such an attribute. The text of the *Icones,* however, mentions that the mosque contained tablets inscribed in Chaldean, and the text of the *Itinerario* refers to the *olas,* texts written on palm leaves that Linschoten presented as a gift to Paludanus. Word and image suggest at the least that literacy was a low priority in dissolute Malabar.

Malabar society was lower in the hierarchy of civility than that of Goa and Ballagate, though the latter were far from exemplary. Technical skill stood at the level of the dugout. The art of writing was practically unknown, and literacy was believed to be of no importance. There was general poverty despite the quantities of pepper the country produced. The warrior elite did not even maintain the appearance of respect for monogamy. There were no orderly families to be found here. The population was heterogeneous in ethnic and religious terms. The Hindu elite upheld its prestige in a ridiculously superstitious and extremely aggressive way. The Moors tolerated sodomy. Even the Christians were accursed.

The result of the comparison of the four Asian societies is thus unambiguous. Measured by the standards of European civility—a specifically Christian standard is not applied here—China comes out on top, followed by Goa and Ballagate. Malabar and Pegu stand for dark decay. China opens the series for expository reasons. The sequence in which the four Asian societies are compared is one of a progressively deeper descent into barbarism. The sturdy Dutch sailors of the first voyage had a lot coming to them in South Asia. At the same time, the moral map of Asia constructed by the prints shows where Asians successfully strove for genuine humanity, in other words, a civilised way of life. The fact that they were not Christians was not an obstacle. Civilised pagans and civilised Christians could both show that life on earth was not necessarily a vale of tears and a pit of perdition, no matter what some Christians might claim to the contrary.

The last four plates in the *Icones* (pls. 27–30), as we have seen, depict plants and fruits that are useful or pleasurable, and present a variation on the theme of controlled, legitimate pleasure versus unrestrained, corrupt lust. The text of the *Icones* also sets the illustrations primarily in the context of the customs of the inhabitants of western India, and hardly at all in that of botanical or medical science, although the latter formed their

context in the text of the *Itinerario* proper.

The texts accompanying plates 28 and 30 do not record anything specific about human activities either, although the Latin text on the coconut palm deals extensively with its many uses. The banana is praised for being an important food that is easy to cultivate. There was thus some measure of practical skill in India, though at a very low level. There are no moralising comments or horror stories relating to the use of betel leaves here. The tone is restrained. The medicinal as well as other uses of the bamboo and durian are indicated. The *arbore de rais* is characterised as an Asian curiosity: the tropical tree that serves no useful purpose other than to provide shade. The text on the *arbore triste* mentions both the legitimate pleasure that it affords and its emblematic significance in Indian mythology, where it stood for unfaithfulness in love.[142] The *arbore triste* was said to have sprung from the ashes of a young virgin who had committed suicide after being deceived in love by the sun. That was why it only blossomed at night. The tree symbolized the tragedy of faithless love.

This reference to the moral significance that the Indians gave to the tree invites the viewer to ask what message the plate showing the *arbore triste* might have for Europeans. The final illustration in the series can be read as an admonition to travellers to Asia. The woman with the betel in the foreground and the *arbore triste* with the bovine water carrier and the villalike building in the background could be meant to indicate a choice. The warning would then be: Know, traveller, that you will have to choose between the temptations of betel, offered you by scantily dressed women, and the modest pleasures of the scent of the *arbore triste.* Choose moderation. Slake your thirst with water. Do not be like the Malabars. Remember the Portuguese who leave the market via the Misericordia. Follow the example of the educated Chinese instead.

Some Characteristics of This Instructive and Edifying Series

Evaluative Rather Than Explanatory Comparisons

The *Icones* are here presented as a bimedial work, a series of instructive and edifying images with accompanying text. The main theme of the series is a comparison of the morals and practices of China, Goa, Ballagate, and Malabar. This comparison is connected with an evaluation of Asian morals and practices by the standards of European civility. The narrative is constructed around a spectrum that ranges from exemplarily civilised to repulsively barbarous behaviour. The same procedure is applied, though much more superficially, to the morals and practices of the peoples of the other Asian regions with whom the Portuguese were in contact. This results in a wider spectrum of civility stretching from north to south, an elementary systematisation with the characteristics of a didactic simplification of complex facts and a weak invitation to look for explanations. The series closes with an exhortation to civil behaviour on the part of the European merchants who want to compete with the Portuguese in Asia. Analytical description and systematic comparison are connected in this discourse with an impulse less to explain cultural differences than to evaluate them from a European point of view.

The categories and concepts by which the spectrum of the *Icones* is constructed (see table 2) display some affinity with other late-sixteenth-century classifications for ethnographic description and the explanation of the similarities and differences between ethnic groups. The three-tiered north-centre-south division recalls Bodin's theory of climate, which also situates licentiousness in the south and self-control in more northerly regions, and which also identifies zones where warriors, magistrates, or priests and philosophers predominate.[143] This division by climate along a north-south axis implies that neither the *Icones* nor Bodin propose an 'orientalist' construction of contrasts between East and West. Both bring out resemblances between the Chinese and the Europeans and contrast them with the southern Asians and Africans.

The differences between Bodin's scheme and that of the *Icones* are no less striking. Bodin and his followers view the centre as the zone in which the ideal combination of properties can best arise, while the ideal zone in the *Icones* is the north. That north, however, is Bodin's centre, that is, the temperate area between 30° and 60° north latitude. Centre and south in the *Icones* are thus gradations within Bodin's south. Its scheme could be compatible with that of Bodin. But other differences remain.

Do the *Icones* suggest that the loose morals of the south are to be explained by the heat of the tropics? Sometimes they do suggest that a traveller would be more likely to come across immorality in warm climes than in cold ones and that the heat is the very cause of sexual hyperactivity.[144] In the prints of the market in Goa and the Portuguese man in a litter the sun is shown shining with extraordinary force. But there is nothing striking about the sun in the engravings of the village near Goa, in the procession of the king of Cochin, or other plates where it would have been appropriate. There is no consistent representation of tropical heat in the plates, nor does the text contain any clear and general statements on climate and human behaviour. The *Icones* displays less of a need to explain the diversity of custom in terms of conditions beyond human control than did Bodin's theory of climate. The engravings and the text contained mere adumbrations of an explanation of this kind.

The same reluctance to rely on natural or inborn qualities for explanations creates the uncertainty over the related question of the extent to which the Asian hierarchy of civility coincides with a hierarchy based on skin pigmentation and other innate physical characteristics. References to such innate differences are less frequent in the prints than in the text of the *Itinerario*. This is partly due to the limitations of the graphic medium. Linschoten usually wrote precisely about the skin colour, type of hair, physiognomy, and stature of different ethnic groups, but in the prints it is only the African blacks whose stereotypical physical differences stand out. The blacks from Mozambique are represented with curly hair, flat noses, and thick lips. There is no attempt to use hatching to suggest a darker skin colour, though it is used to that end for two servants of the Portuguese woman in an open litter (pl. 12).[145]

While the prints of the *Itinerario* do distinguish between white Europeans and black Africans, they appear to neglect innate physical differences between different Asian groups, or between Asians and Portuguese.[146] It can be deduced from the text of the *Itinerario* that whites and blacks formed the extremes of a spectrum running from north to south, but Linschoten did not reserve whiteness exclusively for the Europeans. The majority of the Chinese were white too in his view. Moreover, Linschoten undermines the unthinking acceptance of the European somatic norm image by mentioning that the skin colour of the whites made them monsters in the eyes of the blacks. Although his stance is not narrowly Eurocentric, he does seem to have maintained a certain colour prejudice. He tended to associate civility with a light skin rather than a dark one. He did not comment on the causes of the difference in colour. It remains unclear whether he regarded a dark skin as a divine sign setting those so marked on a lower rung of humanity, or as due to specific climatic conditions without any moral and intellectual implications.[147] The Asian hierarchy of civility of the *Icones* is probably not intended as a demonstration of a racial hierarchy.

Another important difference between the system of classification in the *Icones* and theories of climate à la Bodin concerns the nature of the characteristics by which ethnic differences are defined. In the theories of climate it is mainly psychological characteristics that define types of character, while in the *Icones* it is mainly political or sociological differences—to use an anachronistic terminology—that are significant (see table 2).[148] Slight parallels to this approach can be found in the apodemic literature, e.g., in Edmond Tyllney and Nathan Chytraeus.[149] The author of this edifying series seems to have concerned himself not so much with innate differences in national characters as with the differences in social organisation devised and put into practice by the nations themselves.[150] He shared a typological approach with the theoreticians of na-

TABLE 2. **Classifications Suggested by the Plates**

Ruling elite	warriors	restrained aggressive
		unrestrained aggressive
	priests	learned mandarins
		ritualistic magicians
Social hierarchy	elite	warriors
		priests
		merchants
	commoners	agriculturalists
		slaves
Ethnic composition	homogeneous population	homogeneous families
	heterogeneous population	homogeneous families
		mixed families
Technology	developed	fairly distributed prosperity
		very unequally distributed prosperity
	underdeveloped	unequally distributed poverty
		shared poverty
Public religion	exclusive religions	Chinese paganism with ethical observance
		Portuguese Catholicism with ethical nonobservance
	tolerant religions	Indian idolatry with strict ethical observance but violation of the law of nature
		Muslim sectarianism with tolerance of sodomy
Sexual mores	monogamy	observance
		nonobservance
	polygamy	group polygamy
		individual polygamy
	male homosexuality	effeminate behaviour
		virile behaviour
		concealed in behaviour

tional character, but appears to have been interested above all in the types of society created by the diverse nations and in the degree of civility that each of them had managed to achieve by the proper use of reason.

In so far as the deviser of the *Icones* was interested in explaining causes by means of comparison, he seems to have wanted to connect differences in civility with differences in political regime, technical ability, literacy, ethnic and religious homogeneity or heterogeneity, and family ethics. His view of the civilising potential of religion is strikingly secular. Christianity, Islam, and paganism are all found at different levels in the Asian hierarchy of civility. Each of the religions seems to adjust to the levels of civility rather than to be an autonomous civilizing force. Christianity is no guarantee of civil behaviour, as the Portuguese in Goa demonstrate. A high level of civility in China goes hand in hand with paganism. It is human activity rather than nature that seems to be important in explaining the hierarchy of civility. The influence of higher spiritual forces is discounted. God and the gods are only mentioned to show what ways of serving them people had devised and how civilised they were in that respect.

The *Icones* urge the reader not so much to look for causal explanations as to evaluate the Asian way of life in terms of the standards of European civility implicitly introduced by their deviser. This did not mean that Europeans in Asia would automatically come out on top. Portuguese Goa in fact ends up on the second rung in the hierarchy of Asian civility, above all as a result of the serious disruption of family ties among the Portuguese themselves. In the *Icones* this is connected to some extent with the Portuguese having 'gone native', but their acceptance of large-scale slavery—a phenomenon to be found in Portugal too, unlike north-western Europe—is another of its causes. Partly thanks to a judicious selection of texts, the Chinese score highest in the *Icones* with respect to both their 'policie' and the 'government of their houses', while no negative influence is attributed to their paganism. Large, peaceful, well-ordered states with many cities prospering based on the development of trade and industry, technical skill, respect for scholarship, and close family bonds represented the European ideal of civility. Ballagate and Malabar were seriously deficient in these respects. Conventional European prejudices against women and homosexuals are projected mainly onto these Asian southerners. Perhaps their dark skins made them objects of the white colour prejudice that was also directed against the black Mozambiquans.

All the same, the *Icones* do not seem to represent the barbarism of southern India as immutable and innate. Several passages—the praise of the clever use of the coconut palm, the report that the Canarim in Goa had abandoned some of their irrational heathen practices—betray an

urge to find glimmers of light in the barbarian darkness. Through their own efforts and by following the good European example, if the Europeans in Asia were capable of providing one, the Asians in the tropics could lead more civilised lives. As for the Portuguese, they would have to recognise the nefarious consequences of slavery and miscegenation. The evaluation of the four Asian societies applies a standard, but in each case there is some special pleading. The selection of facts is influenced to some extent by an emotional attitude toward the subject. A closed ethnocentrism dominated by fear and aversion to the unknown alternates in the *Icones* with an open ethnocentrism impelled by attraction and fascination. Definitions of self and other are rooted in mixed feelings.[151]

The discourse on the Asian hierarchy of civility that emerges from the comparison prompted by the engravings in the *Icones* comes closest to the argument of Alessandro Valignano, the visitor of the Jesuit missions during Linschoten's stay in Goa, in the *Summarium Indicum*. Valignano constructed a similar hierarchy of civility in that work, although with far less descriptive detail and with other intentions.[152] He was equally favourable to China (and Japan), and equally disparaging with regard to southern India and Mozambique. He also had his reservations about the Portuguese in Goa. He demonstrated a similar mixture of open and closed ethnocentrism. In his case, a minimal openness was prescribed, because he had to believe—by profession—that all Asians could be converted and prepared for salvation. His discourse, however, was intended to justify the mission strategy that he had adopted: a transfer of the centre of activity from India to China and Japan. The discourse of the *Icones* is less clearly influenced by practical concerns, although it might be argued that it was not entirely detached from the Dutch decision to make the Far East, not India, the centre of their trading activity. It estimates not the opportunities for missionary activities, but those for the largely autonomous perfection of civility in the different parts of Asia.

The Dominance of the Images in the Dialogue between Image and Text

The comparative and evaluative discourse on Asian morals was prompted by the plates, whose relation to the text was by no means transparent. The loose connection between the two components can already be seen in the way in which the text of the *Itinerario* refers to the plates. They are all mentioned, but hardly anything is said about them. It is left up to the reader to make something of them.[153] This forces the reader and viewer to make a continual comparison of these two components.

The answer to most of the questions raised by the plates can be found in the text, but there are illustrations—such as the engravings of boats and of the ambassador of the king of Ballagate—on which hardly a word is to be found either in the Latin comments accompanying the plates or in the *Itinerario* itself. There are elements that are probably significant in the visual narrative but whose precise significance is not clarified at all by the text, such as the Mozambiquan bow. In the case of other visual elements that may appear enigmatic at first sight, such as the male couples, the text does provide a clue, but it is unclear whether it applies to all three cases. Once the reader and viewer is struck by these riddles, the plates assume an active role in instructing him how to handle the text. They reveal the existence of lacunae in the text and prompt him to search for other images and texts to solve the remaining problems. The discrepancies between image and text may have been deliberately introduced to train him in the methodical collection of data, in disciplined curiosity.

Furthermore, it is the images that trigger the explanatory and evaluative comparison of Asian morals. Such a comparison is not explicitly made in the *Itinerario* itself, nor in the extensive Latin texts that accompany the plates in the *Icones.* Nor are the texts in the *Icones* tightly organised to distinguish the different aspects of morals and practices in a uniform way and to treat them in the same order. Instead, they confront the reader directly with the subject. They consist mainly of informative comments strung together in a relatively haphazard way, and only occasionally do they contain more discursive or narrative passages. It is the deployment of visual resources that invites the reader to systematic categorisation and comparison. They lead to the insight that the main theme of the series of plates is the systematic comparison and evaluation of the morals and practices, rather than the representation of Asian dress, means of transport, and fruits, plants, and trees.

The plates also indicate generally what does and does not belong to the comparative argument that they have triggered, and they suggest a way to structure it. All kinds of items that were important in the *Itinerario* proper—such as the information on trade—have been left out of the engravings. The plates focus the mind of the reader, distracted as it is by the proliferation of observations in the text, on a single theme: the morals and practices of the 'Indians and Portuguese living there'. The subjects that they propose—'policie' and the 'government of their houses' in their numerous aspects—structure the argument. The combination of the subseries, the pairs, and the clusters reveals a method for arranging and interpreting the information provided. The rhetoric of contrast and hierarchy provides a way of presenting the findings after they have been arranged and interpreted. The plates also ensure that religious polemic is practically avoided, an avoidance that is in line with Linschoten's text. Although they constitute an edifying series, they deal not with Christian

virtues and vices but with levels of civility and the corresponding morals and practices. The rhetoric of contrast and hierarchy within the images already programmes a moral judgement and an exhortation, but it does so in terms of the language of civility.

However, the texts of the *Icones* perform an active role as well. They specify the general notions and judgements that inform the series of plates. They also bring the engravings to life, partly because they do not shun rhetorical exaggeration, scabrous anecdotes, and asides. Without the lively texts the incitement of the stiff and artificial images to methodical reading could easily be wiped out by boredom. The varied, often crude descriptive details allow the plates to introduce the viewer and reader to the joys of method. The series of plates is not a work of art in the conventional sense of the term, but a skilfully devised instrument for handling the text of the *Itinerario* through categorisation and well-structured discourse. Once the method has been learned, it can be applied in other cases too.

In edifying prints of the sixteenth century, the word was generally expected to prevail over the image. Biblical texts, proverbs, sayings, or poetic texts accompanying an image were the key to a proper understanding of it.[154] To some extent this is true of the *Icones* as well. Without any descriptive titles and accompanying text, the plates would not even properly perform the elementary purpose of conveying the names and geographic location of the peoples of Asia they depicted. According to the interpretation offered above, however, the role of the plates was not confined to repeating information contained in the text in another form or supporting the credibility of the author. Rather, they encourage the reader to shape that text into a new kind of argument. The conventional relation between image and text seems to have been reversed, at least to some extent. This reversal seems to be based on the premise that observable reality consists of an overwhelming plethora of phenomena, whose coherence and meaning can only be discovered by systematic observation and classification.[155] The series teaches the viewer the importance of systematic and reasoned observation.

The comparative argument on Asian societies that has been constructed with the aid of the visual instrument is a transposition of the texts of the *Itinerario* proper into a different mode. It is an illustration of the process by which empirical accounts of journeys and eye-witness accounts of foreign customs were converted into 'anthropological' considerations.[156] The argument created shows some affinity with the more theoretical disquisitions on the diversity of human customs and practices written by various authors in the late sixteenth century. But it is no more than a preliminary outline, or exercise, for a disquisition of that kind.

The transposition in this case proceeded by means of the mutual interdependence of word and image. Without the input of the written description, the plates offer an empty framework and remain an example of uninspired illustration. Without the application of the instrument of the series of plates, the text remains a fairly shapeless presentation of observations and data. The series invites the reader to use his intelligence and to demand more than a simple representation of reality in word and image, no matter how true to life this pictorial or verbal representation may be. The same attitude to mimetic representations of reality can also be found in Karel van Mander. He held representations after nature to be useful, but they had to be elevated to a higher plane through the inventions of the spirit or imagination.[157] Seen in this light, the series of plates is a valuable supplement to the text of the *Itinerario* and contributes to a more reflective attitude toward empiricism.

Did Karel van Mander Devise the *Icones?*

Who devised this deftly composed visual instrument? Linschoten himself is not a likely candidate. Although clearly interested in the comparative analysis of morals and familiar with the idea of arranging societies in a hierarchy of civility,[158] he was probably not experienced enough in dealing with visual resources to design a series of plates as carefully constructed as the *Icones*. The inventor must have been someone with a demonstrable interest in the comparative study of the morals and practices of non-European peoples and a certain theoretical cast of mind, a skilful artist with a humanist education, preferably to be found among the circle of Cornelis Claesz and demonstrably in contact with Linschoten at the time when the *Itinerario* was being prepared for publication.

A candidate who comes close to satisfying these criteria is the Dutch Vasari, Karel van Mander. Born in the Southern Netherlands, this gentleman poet, painter, and art theoretician was a leading figure among the artists in Haarlem, where he lived from 1583 onwards. It is likely that he was in contact with Linschoten during the period in which the *Itinerario* was being prepared. In 1595/96 van Mander painted a memorial plaque for the jawbone of a whale that Linschoten had brought back from his voyages to the north and presented to his native city of Haarlem. The artist was also familiar with the poets from Hoorn who contributed the eulogies to the *Itinerario*. He collaborated, presumably around 1594, with Joannes van Doetecum junior, who engraved the ten border vignettes designed by van Mander for a map of the Middle East illustrating the Acts of the Apostles and Paul's journey. Cornelis Claesz published his poem *Dat hooghe Liedt Salomo* in 1598.[159]

Van Mander was certainly capable of coming up with the idea for a series of plates like the *Icones*. In his writings and in his practice as a painter he had concerned himself with instructive devices such as allegories, and he was clearly intrigued by the diversity of customs. In his work as an artist he dealt with this theme in the monumental engraving *Confusio Babylonica* executed around 1600 by Zacharias Dolendo. The scene includes Europeans, Asians, Africans, and American Indians, each with a different kind of script. This was an explanation of cultural diversity within the parameters of the religious tradition. In his literary work he compared customs and mores in various parts of the non-European world from a profane point of view. In his treatise *Den Grondt der edel vry schilder-const*, on which he worked in 1596/97, he mentioned the American Indians' lack of familiarity with an alphabet and paid attention to Mexican pictographic script and the Inca quipu. On the authority of Benzoni he records the praises of the 'West-Indians' for wine, iron, and glass, which were unknown to them until their introduction by the Spaniards. He also noted that the significance attached to the colours white and black by the Javanese was the opposite of the connotations that they held for Europeans. In the *Uutlegghingh op den Metamorphosis*, he cites Montaigne to put a criticism of excessive differences between rich and poor in Europe in the mouth of a Florida Indian. All of these scattered passages deal with subjects that also feature in the *Icones*: the significance of (skin) colour, literacy, social inequality, and differences in technological level. The formulations also make use of contrasts and hierarchies.

Moreover, Van Mander demonstrated a concern with the moral and political issues raised by the 'newly discovered lands', especially America. He translated Benzoni's account of America, a large-scale undertaking that he had probably completed before he started on *Den Grondt*. Benzoni attracted interest in Protestant circles as a critic of the Spanish atrocities in America. The *Icones* contained a similar criticism of Portuguese imperialism in Asia. Such 'black legends' of Iberian colonialism were also, in their more enlightened form, critiques of the widespread religious fanaticism, ruthless power politics, and unfettered desire for wealth that were not confined to Spain and Portugal. This critical attitude towards one's own culture could lead to an idealisation of foreign societies, as is the case with China in the *Icones*.[160]

The network to which van Mander belonged in the 1590s, the nature of his interest in the non-European world, and his views on the edifying character of art, suggest the possibility that he might have contributed to the series of plates in the *Itinerario*. On that hypothesis, the question remains of what his contribution might have been. The mediocre quality of the illustrations makes it unlikely that van Mander made the designs for the engravers, but he might have been responsible for the idea behind the series and indicated which visual resources were appropriate to it. Possibly it was enough to give experienced engravers like the van Doetecums precise instructions and to supervise the execution of the work. The fact that both designer and engravers lived in the same town would have facilitated a procedure of this kind.

Did van Mander carry out work of this advisory kind? He was known for suggesting designs, and the hypothesis outlined above finds support in the probability that it was van Mander who made recommendations on the decoration of a prestigious object in 1604, the very year of the publication of the *Icones*.[161] In that year the Amsterdam city council purchased a harpsichord for the city from Antwerp for the price of two hundred guilders, including transport. Pieter Isaacz was commissioned to paint the lid of the instrument for three hundred guilders. Karel van Mander apparently suggested the subject of the painting, for which he received a rose-noble (sixteen guilders and fourteen stuivers).

The instrument has not been traced, but the painted lid was recently discovered. The left-hand part of the decoration consists of an allegory of the city of Amsterdam receiving a ship and a pearl necklace, symbols of wealth and navigation. The foreground of the central and right-hand area comprises a strip of land with various scenes. In the background are three ships, possibly from the fleet that sailed to Asia in 1602, and a map of the whole world showing all the continents in a highly unusual projection. The Latin text on a tablet that is propped against an obelisk in the foreground contains the message of the painting: *Did you think that I would perish after being excluded from the Spanish West? In vain, for God's care has first opened for me the way to Africa and the Indies and to where exotic China extends, and the region of the world which not even the ancients knew [the West Indies and America]. Continue to favour us, God, and grant that they [the heathen] may know Christ.* Among the representations of the heathen on the right are three elements borrowed from the plates of the *Itinerario*. To the left of the obelisk stands the mosque, and on the extreme right the Hindu temple with its idol from plate 26. The king of Cochin and his Nayars are descending a hill behind it. The interpretation of the *Icones* offered above explains why precisely these scenes were chosen. They are from the Malabar cluster—that part of Asia that is presented in the *Icones* as the most degenerate and the one where there is the greatest need for the Word of God. If it was van Mander who provided the concept for the *Icones*, it becomes easier to understand why he selected these precise elements to illustrate the Dutch missionary task.[162]

Irrespective of who devised the series, the question draws attention once again to the central role of the instructions given by the print culture to the parties involved in the creation of the *Itinerario*. Linschoten himself emphasises this in the very first sentence of his book. His addiction to travel had been aroused by reading books. When his thirst for travel had been sated, he was impelled to record his experiences in a book.[163] He does not reveal how he became a draughtsman, but what he portrayed owes something at least to printed city views and possibly to costume books as well. Upon his return from Asia, there was an interest in his information and services on the part of traders in the provinces of Holland and Zealand who were engaged in setting up the sea route to Asia. Among them were those who urged him to publish what he knew. This led to the involvement of the publisher Cornelis Claesz in the project.

The constellation within which Claesz operated was more or less as follows. One of his activities was that of supplying the rapidly expanding world of Dutch maritime commerce with useful printed matter. During the period of preparation of the *Itinerario,* he published translations of foreign works that were considered important at the end of the sixteenth century by those Europeans who, for whatever reason, wanted to form a picture of America and Spanish colonialism, of sub-Saharan Africa, and of China. Most of these works were illustrated. From 1590 on the de Bry family demonstrated how these illustrated texts could be transformed into prestigious editions for the elites of Europe. These were publications that fired publishers and artists to emulation. There was no recent book on Portuguese Asia in the series of geographical works that enjoyed European favour at that time. Claesz saw Linschoten's text and images as an opportunity to do for Portuguese Asia what the de Bry family had done for America and black Africa. It would have to be a fairly expensive edition for his Dutch clients, as well as being accessible for a European public in translation. It is not far-fetched to assume that he was eager to find someone with the stature of a Karel van Mander to mastermind the pictorial side of the project in accordance with the rules of art.

A figure like van Mander may have had his interest in a comparison of non-European morals and practices stimulated by the rapid succession of Claesz's publications of older material on American cannibals and of more recent material on relatively civilised natives of the Congo and the highly civilised Chinese. De Bry's 1594 publication of Benzoni, a vivid diatribe against the Spanish atrocities in America, would probably have led such a reader to wonder how the Portuguese behaved in Asia.[164] As an artist and a patriot of the Netherlands, van Mander may have felt the challenge to create a series of plates that could rival those of the Frankfurt masters and at the same time become the first illustration of the black legend of Portuguese colonialism in Asia. The *Icones* are probably the joint product of a curious traveller, an energetic publisher who grasped how the traveller's material matched current practical and theoretical interests, and an artist who shared these theoretical interests and criticisms of Iberian imperialism and wanted to encourage others to form an opinion on these matters. The result was a pictorial narrative that—in the words of the title page of the *Itinerario*—would be 'very profitable and pleasant to all such as are welwillers, or desirous to heare and read of strange thinges'.

Notes

1. Jan Huygen van Linschoten, *Itinerario: Voyage ofte schipvaert naer Oost ofte Portugaels Indien, 1579–1592* (The Hague, 1955–1957), 1:xxxv. References to the *Itinerario* in the following notes are to this Dutch edition, edited by H. Terpstra, unless otherwise indicated. English translations are taken from the text of the London edition of 1598. For practical reasons the references in these citations are to the Hakluyt Society edition (*The Voyage of Jan Huyghen van Linschoten to the East,* ed. Arthur Coke Burnell and P. A. Tiele [London, 1885]), hereafter cited as '*Itinerario,* H.S. ed.' The English translation can also be consulted in the Roxburghe Club edition, which includes the *Itinerario* as well as the *Icones:* Ernst van den Boogaart, ed., *Jan Huygen van Linschoten and the Moral Map of Asia* (London, 1999).

2. Henry Beveridge, *A Comprehensive History of India* (1862; New Delhi, 1974), 279. The English also had other sources at their disposal. See G. V. Scammell, 'England, Portugal and the Estado da India, c. 1500–1635', in *Actas, II Seminário Internacional de História Portuguesa* (Lisbon, 1985), 443–58.

3. Donald F. Lach and Edwin J. Van Kley, *Asia in the Making of Europe,* vol. 3, bk. 1 (Chicago, 1993), 42–53, 73–78, 88–91, 93–95.

4. Ibid., 3:1:394, 515–20.

5. *Itinerario,* H.S. ed., 1:1. Apart from misspelling the name of the author the heading to chapter 1 of the 1598 English edition is a correct translation of the title of the 1596–98 Dutch edition. A new title page was designed for the English edition.

6. Donald F. Lach, *Asia in the Making of Europe,* vol. 2, bk. 1 (Chicago, 1970), 94.

7. Michael Giesecke makes a plausible case for this as characteristic of print culture. Michael Giesecke, *Der Buchdruck in der frühen Neuzeit: Eine historische Fallstudie über die Durchsetzung neuer Informations- und Kommunikationstechnologien* (Frankfurt, 1991), 499–501, 520–27, 599–602, 630. Giesecke summarises some of the main theses of his monumental study in his 'Von den skriptographischen zu den typographischen Informationsverarbeitungsprogrammen', in *Wissensliteratur im Mittelalter und in der frühen Neuzeit: Bedingungen, Typen, Publikum, Sprache,* ed. Horst Brunner and Norbert Richard Wolff (Wiesbaden, 1993), 328–46.

8. The Atlas van Stolk in Rotterdam has the only known exemplar of the title page of the set. The decoration for the title is taken from plate 29 of the *Exercitatio alphabetica* by Clemens Perret (1569), designed by Hans Vredeman de Vries and probably engraved by Jan and Lucas van Doetecum. Claesz owned the copperplates of Perret's work. He offered the *Exercitatio alphabetica* for sale in 1609 for the price of eighteen stuivers. Bert van Selm, *Een 'menighte treffelijcke boecken': De Nederlandse boekhandelscatalogi uit het begin van de zeventiende eeuw* (Utrecht, 1987), 220. Regarding Perret, see A. R. A. Croiset van Uchelen, 'De raadselachtige schrijfmeester Clemens Perret en zijn twee materie boeken', in *De Arte et Libris: Festschrift Erasmus, 1934–1984,* ed. A. Horodisch (Amsterdam, 1984), 43–60. The Herzog August Bibliothek in Wolfenbüttel, the Universiteitsbibliotheek in Amsterdam, and the Amsterdams Scheepvaart Museum own sets of the *Icones* without the title page. The set in Wolfenbüttel comprises the thirty plates. The set in Amsterdam lacks the plate with the two Chinese couples. Several prints are missing from the set in the Scheepvaart Museum.

9. Paludanus had already referred to the plates as the 'Habitus Indorum Orientalium' in his letter to Ortelius of 20 December 1598. James D. Tracy, ed., *True Ocean Found: Paludanus's Letters on Dutch Voyages to the Kara Sea, 1595–1596* (Minneapolis, 1980), 48, 58.

10. The known biographical information on Linschoten is summarised in Terpstra's introduction to his edition of the *Itinerario* (see n. 1). This was the factual basis for Charles McKew Parr, *Jan van Linschoten: The Dutch Marco Polo* (New York, 1964). A few additional data can be found in my 'Jan Huygen van Linschoten: Modern Curiosity and Its Beneficiaries', in *Jan Huygen van Linschoten and the Moral Map of Asia,* 1–21.

11. Fernand Braudel, *Civilisation matérielle, Économie et Capitalisme, XVe–XVIIIe siècle* (Paris, 1979), 3:178.

12. Little is known about Linschoten's early years. He was born in Haarlem, then one of the most important cities in the province of Holland, in late 1562 or early 1563. In the 1570s his parents moved to the port town of Enkhuizen, where his father worked as an innkeeper and notary. That is where Jan grew up. Enkhuizen was the first town in this part of Holland to join the revolt of William of Orange and to establish Calvinism as its official religion. The Linschoten family may have moved to Enkhuizen out of sympathy with the revolt, but this is not necessarily the case. Jan and his father both remained attached to Haarlem.

13. *Itinerario,* 1:5.

14. For several examples, see my 'Jan Huygen van Linschoten: Modern Curiosity and Its Beneficiaries', 3. See also John G. Everaert, 'Soldaten, diamantairs en jezuieten: Zuid- en Noord-Nederlanders in Portugees-Indië', in *Souffrir pour parvenir: De wereld van Jan Huygen van Linschoten,* ed. Roelof van Gelder, Jan Parmentier, and Vibeke Roeper (Haarlem, 1998), 80–94.

15. Justin Stagl, 'Die Apodemik oder "Reisekunst" als Methodik der Sozialforschung vom Humanismus bis zur Aufklärung', in *Statistik und Staats-*

beschreibung in der Neuzeit, vornehmlich im 16.–18. Jahrhundert, ed. Mohammed Rassem and Justin Stagl (Paderborn, 1980), 131–205, and Justin Stagl, *A History of Curiosity: The Theory of Travel 1550–1800* (Chur, 1995), 1–94.

16. The identity of the Venetian is unknown. The Englishmen were the merchants John Newberry and Ralph Fitch, the jeweller William Leedes, and the painter James Storey who had been despatched via the land route to the East by the London Levant Company. Michael Edwardes, *Ralph Fitch: Elizabethan in the Indies* (London, 1972).

17. J. W. IJzerman, ed., *Dirck Gerritsz Pomp alias Dirck Gerritsz China: De eerste Nederlander die China en Japan bezocht (1544–1604)* (The Hague, 1915).

18. *Itinerario,* 1:24, 87.

19. Linschoten was in Goa at the same time as several formidable critics of the Estado da Índia, such as Diogo do Couto and Francisco Rodrigues Silveira. See George Winius, *The Black Legend of Portuguese India: Diogo do Couto, His Contemporaries and the Soldado Pratico* (New Delhi, 1985). Nothing is known of his having any contact with them. For information about Ceylon, Pegu, and the Saint Thomas Christians that reached Linschoten via his work for the archbishop, see *Itinerario,* 1:63, 65, 75. This is probably also how he came to see the Japanese legates.

20. Roelof van Gelder, 'Paradijsvogels in Enkhuizen', in Gelder, Parmentier, and Roeper, *Souffrir pour parvenir,* 43.

21. Arie Pos, in the introduction to his Portuguese translation of the *Itinerario:* Jan Huygen van Linschoten, *Itinerário: Viagem ou Navegação as Índias Orientais ou Portuguesas* (Lisbon, 1997), 32.

22. See the introduction in Jas Elsner and Joan-Pau Rubiés, eds., *Voyages and Visions: Towards a Cultural History of Travel* (London, 1999), esp. 39–40. See also Stagl, *History of Curiosity,* 47–49. Linschoten considered taking the land route and thus returning via the Holy Land, as can be seen from the letter to his parents of 1584 published in IJzerman, *Dirck Gerritsz Pomp,* 8–13.

23. *Itinerario,* 3:40–50.

24. Kees Zandvliet, ed., *Maurits, Prins van Oranje,* exh. cat., Rijksmuseum (Amsterdam, 2000), 55.

25. *Itinerario,* 1:xci.

26. IJzerman, *Dirck Gerritsz Pomp,* 8–13.

27. *Itinerario,* 1:1.

28. *Itinerario,* 1:xci.

29. See Jan Huygen van Linschoten, *Itinerario,* vol. 3, ed. C. P. Burger and F. W. T. Hunger (The Hague, 1934), 249–68.

30. C. Koeman, *Lucas Janszoon Waghenaer: Sa vie et son 'Spieghel der Zeevaerdt'* (Lausanne, 1964).

31. See biography of Claesz in Selm, *Een 'menighte treffelijcke boecken',* 176–79. For a survey of his publications up to 1600, see Paul Valkema Blouw, *Typographia Batava 1541–1600* (Nieuwkoop, 1998).

32. J. G. van Dillen, ed., *Bronnen tot de geschiedenis van het bedrijfsleven en het gildewezen van Amsterdam* (The Hague, 1929), 1:680–81. The contract of 1594 is known only from a citation in a notarial act of 1610.

33. Marijke Spies, 'Betaald Werk? Poëzie als ambacht in de zeventiende eeuw', *Holland* 23 (1991): 214–17. C. P. Burger, 'De Historie ofte Beschrijvinghe van het Groote Rijck van China', *Het Boek* 19 (1930): 17–32.

34. Little is known about Hoogerbeets apart from what Velius reports on him in his chronicle of Hoorn. See *Nieuw Nederlands Biografisch Woordenboek,* vol. 9, cols. 1176–80. More of his poetry is mentioned in Chris L. Heesakkers, 'Petrus Forestus in gedichten en brieven', in *Petrus Forestus Medicus,* ed. H. A. Bosma-Jelgersma (Amsterdam, 1996), 126.

35. See the brief biography of Velius in R. E. O. Ekkart, ed., *Wilt Hooren 't Woort,* exh. cat., Rijksmuseum Meermanno-Westreenianum/Museum van het Boek (The Hague, 1979), 35–37.

36. Stagl, *History of Curiosity,* 65–66. For the relation between medical science and cosmography in the sixteenth century, see Wolfgang Neuber, *Fremde Welt im europäischen Horizont: Zur Topik der deutschen Amerika-Reiseberichte der Frühen Neuzeit* (Berlin, 1991), 60–61.

37. *Itinerario,* 1:lxxxv.

38. Linschoten's translation was published in 1598 by Jacob Lennaertsz Meyn in Enkhuizen and not by Cornelis Claesz. There seems reason to suppose that something went wrong in the relation between Claesz and Linschoten. Spies, 'Betaald werk?', 215.

39. The identity of the translator of the Latin edition published in 1599 in the Netherlands is not known. Could it have been Hoogerbeets?

40. Two exemplars of the first edition of the *Itinerario* are known with a parchment binding, stamped in both cases with a view of Amsterdam from the River IJ surrounded by Renaissance ornament. H. de la Fontaine Verwey considered that these bindings were added on the instructions of Claesz as the publisher. See 'Amsterdamse uitgeversbanden van Cornelis Claesz en Laurens Jacobsz', in H. de la Fontaine Verwey, *Uit de wereld van het boek,* vol. 2 (Amsterdam, 1976), 37–40. Bert van Selm refined the hypothesis by suggesting that Claesz had a few books bound in order to be able to show them to customers in his shop, but that he did not as publisher order the binding of the entire print run or a substantial part of it. In that case, it would be better to refer to these exemplars as book dealer's bindings. Selm, *Een 'menichte treffelijcke boecken',* 220–21, 302 n. 180. The same view is found in Jan Storm van Leeuwen, 'Some Observations on Dutch Publisher's Bindings up to 1800', in *Bookbindings and Other Bibliophily: Essays in Honour of Anthony Hobson,* ed. Dennis E. Rhodes (Verona, 1994), 290–91.

41. Five of the six topographical prints have dedications. In some cases the dedicatee supported Linschoten in the making of the *Itinerario:* the coastal profile of Saint Helena from the north, east, and west is dedicated to François Maelson; the coastal profile of Ascension, to Bernardus Paludanus; the coastal profile of Saint Helena from the south, to Philippus Eduardus and Octavianus Fugger and Marcus Matthaeus Welser, the merchants in whose employ Linschoten made the return journey; and the bird's-eye view of Angra, to Christophorus de Moura, the governor of Terceira who had received him so well. The most remarkable dedication is that of the bird's-eye view of Goa, to

Albert of Austria as viceroy of Portugal. A dedication could, but did not necessarily, lead to a financial gift from the body to which the book was dedicated. Linschoten received three hundred guilders from the States of Holland and West-Friesland. P. J. Verkruijsse, 'Holland "gededigeerd": Boekopdrachten in Holland in de 17ᵉ eeuw', *Holland* 23 (1991): 238. The dedications to the Fuggers and Welser and to de Moura will have been intended by Linschoten as a friendly gesture toward his patrons. In the introduction to the first edition of the *Itinerario* by the Linschoten Vereniging (1910), Robidé van der Aa supposed that Linschoten made this map for Albert in Goa on the archbishop's instructions. In 1596 Albert accepted the governorship of the Southern Netherlands.

42. In the 1598 English edition Linschoten's foreword was replaced with a foreword by the English publisher or translator.

43. *Itinerario,* 1:81, 137; 2:83, 94. Linschoten also used the expression *nae 't ooch afgebeelt* ('drawn from observation') in the coastal profile of the North Cape, included in his *Voyagie ofte Schipvaert van by Noorden om langs Noorwegen . . . tot voorby de revier Oby* (Franeker, 1601), an account of his voyages to the north.

44. *Itinerario,* 2:83. The issue facing Linschoten went back to the beginnings of typographic culture. Giesecke, *Der Buchdruck,* 342–61. Linschoten's experience shows that his socialisation in the typographic culture was partial. That was probably true of all those who were educated by the book, both before and after him.

45. Compare Michael Giesecke's comments on the place of typology in realistic descriptions and illustrations within the typographic information system. Giesecke, *Der Buchdruck,* 599–600.

46. Hessel Miedema, *Kunst, kunstenaar en kunstwerk bij Karel van Mander: Een analyse van zijn levensbeschrijvingen* (Alphen aan de Rijn, 1981), 21, 37–38, 122–27, 232. Claudia Swan, 'Ad Vivum, naer het leven, From the Life: Defining a Mode of Representation', *Word & Image* 11 (1995): 353–72. David Landau and Peter Parshall, *The Renaissance Print, 1470–1550* (New Haven, 1994), 237–59. Peter Parshall, 'Imago contrafacta: Images and Facts in the Northern Renaissance', *Art History* 16 (1993): 554–79. On the rise of North Netherlandish 'naturalism' see also Ger Luijten et al., ed., *Dawn of the Golden Age: North Netherlandish Art, 1580–1620,* exh. cat., Rijksmuseum (Amsterdam, 1993), especially the essays by J. Bruyn, 'A Turning-Point in the History of Dutch Art', and Nadine Orenstein et al. 'Print Publishers in the Netherlands 1580–1620'.

47. The term is borrowed from Svetlana Alpers. See her contribution 'The Mapping Impulse in Dutch Art', in *Art and Cartography: Six Historical Essays,* ed. David Woodward (Chicago, 1986), 51–96, and her *The Art of Describing: Dutch Art in the Seventeenth Century* (Chicago, 1983). For a survey of the heated controversy in the Netherlands surrounding this book, see Heidi de Mare, 'De verbeelding onder vuur: Het realisme-debat der Nederlandse kunsthistorici', *Theoretische Geschiedenis* 24 (1997): 113–37. Michael Giesecke discusses the codification of the realistic image and text in terms of his theory of the typographic information and communication system; Giesecke, *Der Buchdruck.*

48. Karen S. Pearson, 'The Multimedia Approach to Landscape in German Renaissance Geography Books', in *The Early Illustrated Book: Essays in Honor of Lessing J. Rosenwald,* ed. Sandra Hindman (Washington, D.C., 1982), 117–35. Wilfried Krings, 'Text und Bild als Informationsträger bei gedruckten Stadtdarstellungen der Frühen Neuzeit', in *Poesis und Pictura: Studien zum Verhältnis von Text und Bild in Handschriften und alten Drucken,* ed. Stephan Füssel and Joachim Knape (Baden-Baden, 1989), 295–335. Boudewijn Bakker, 'Maps, Books and Prints: The Topographical Tradition in the Northern Netherlands', in *The Dutch Cityscape in the Seventeenth Century and Its Sources,* ed. C. van Lakerveld, exh. cat., Amsterdams Historisch Museum / Art Gallery of Ontario (Amsterdam, 1977), 66–75.

49. Richard L. Kagan, 'Philip II and the Art of the Cityscape', in *Art and History: Images and Their Meaning,* ed. Robert I. Rotberg and Theodore K. Rabb (Cambridge, 1986), 115–36. Jürgen Schulz, 'Maps as Metaphors: Mural Map Cycles of the Italian Renaissance', in Woodward, *Art and Cartography,* 97–122. See also David Buisseret, ed., *Monarchs, Ministers, and Maps: The Emergence of Cartography as a Tool of Government in Early Modern Europe* (Chicago, 1992).

50. *Itinerario,* 2:48.

51. Given the lack of evidence, it is not possible to say to what extent Linschoten may have been capable of designing versions of the larger scenes himself. The illustrations in his *Reizen naar het Noorden* of 1601 were also engraved by Joannes and Baptista van Doetecum. They are mainly coastal profiles, a few bird's-eye maps, a 'realistic depiction' of the roadstead of Kilduyn with a settlement, and images of a fish smokehouse and a reindeer sleigh. Insets in the general map show three Samoyeds, Samoyed idols, and another sleigh. Linschoten also made sketches 'after life' on this journey, but only in the simpler genre, so these illustrations do not provide any supplementary information about his skill as a draughtsman.

52. Joannes van Doetecum (1530?–1605) was the father of the two other engravers of the plates in the *Itinerario,* Baptista van Doetecum (1551?–1611) and Joannes van Doetecum Jr. (1570?–1630). Joannes Sr. was born in Deventer and trained as a glazier, but he began working as a copper engraver and map painter early on. Between about 1559 and 1578 he and his brother Lucas engraved and etched in Antwerp for publishers like Hieronymus Cock and Gerard de Jode. There they produced ornamental and architectural prints after designs by Hans Vredeman de Vries and Cornelis Floris, landscapes after Pieter Breughel the Elder and Hans Bol, and above all many geographical charts. Joannes and his sons returned to Deventer in 1578, when it sided with William of Orange, and worked in their native city until its conquest by the Spaniards in 1587, after which they lived in Haarlem until the late 1590s. The collaboration with Cornelis Claesz certainly dates from 1589. The Doetecums were involved in the production of the most important Dutch cartographic works of the second half of the sixteenth century: in Antwerp the world atlases of Ortelius (1570) and Gerard de Jode (1578), in Deventer the *Spieghel der Zeevaert* (1584) of Lucas Jansz Waghenaer, and in Haarlem the same author's

Thresoor der Zeevaert (1592). Joannes Sr. and Waghenaer were also involved in the production of a famous series of naturalistic landscapes, a different type of landscape than is seen in the engravings of the *Itinerario*. Günter Schilder, *Monumenta Cartografica Neerlandica* (Alphen aan de Rijn, 1986), 1:1–37. H. J. Nalis, 'Joannes van Doetecum (overleden 1605)', in *Overijsselse Biografieën* (Meppel, 1990) 1:53–56; also his 'Baptista van Doetecum (overleden 1611), kaartmaker en graveur', in *Overijsselse Biografieën* (Meppel, 1993) 3:21–25, and *The Van Doetecum Family*, in the series *The New Holstein: Dutch and Flemish Etchings, Engravings and Woodcuts 1450–1700* (Rotterdam, 1998). T. A. Riggs, *Hieronymus Cock, Printmaker and Publisher* (New York, 1977), 36, 140–49, 312–13, 318–19, 364–66, 381–82. Joannes engraved twenty-four plates for the *Itinerario*, Baptista eleven. There was no specialisation by theme. Joannes Jr. was responsible for the map of the island of Mozambique and the Plancius world map.

53. Linschoten's style of illustration in the prints depicting ethnic types corresponds closely to that of the costume books. These appeared in print starting in 1562 in Venice and Paris, and from 1577 in the Netherlands. Before and after those dates, however, costume books circulated in the form of collections of drawings or paintings on paper. Heinrich Doege, 'Die Trachtenbücher des 16. Jahrhunderts', in *Beiträge zur Bücherkunde und Philologie: August Wilmanns zum 25. märz 1903 gewidmet* (Leipzig, 1903), 429–44. Lach, *Asia in the Making of Europe,* vol. 2, bk. 1, 90–92. Daniel Defert, 'Collections et nations au XVIe siècle', in *L'Amérique de Théodore de Bry: Une collection de voyages protestante du XVIe siècle,* ed. Michèle Duchet (Paris, 1987), 47–67. The printed collections contain very few Asian types. The same is true of the manuscript collections from the sixteenth century in the Lipperheidische Kostümbibliothek, part of the Kunstbibliothek der Staatlichen Museen in Berlin and probably the largest collection of this kind of material in Europe. The Codex Casanatense 1889 also follows the conventions of the costume books.

54. Linschoten seems to have missed opportunities too. Shortly after his arrival he had the opportunity to see Japanese in Goa. They formed part of the delegation formed by the Jesuit Alessandro Valignano to urge Philip II and the pope in Europe to lend more support to the mission in Asia. Linschoten mentions their arrival and also their return in 1586–87, but he did not sketch them—at least, there are no illustrations of Japanese in the *Icones,* although the *Itinerario* does have a chapter on Japan.

55. A comparison with the text rules out the possibility that any of the prints was devised in its entirety on the basis of information from the *Itinerario*. The corpus of illustrations made by Europeans in Asia in the sixteenth century is still in need of exhaustive description. The best impression is provided by Lach, *Asia in the Making of Europe,* vol. 2, bk. 1, 80–90.

56. There are two editions of the Codex Casanatense: Luís de Matos, ed., *Imagens do Oriente no século XVI* (Lisbon, 1985), primarily to be consulted for the commentary and excerpts from Portuguese sources; and *Oltremare: Codice Casanatense 1889: Con il Libro dell'Oriente di Duarte Barbosa* (Rome, 1984), which has better reproductions. In 1586 Sassetti appreciatively mentioned a contact with an Indian painter of plants in Cochin. Lach, *Asia in the Making of*

Europe, vol. 2, bk. 1, 66. Linschoten could have had a contact of this kind in Goa. The English painter John Storey, who was released from imprisonment by the Portuguese through the mediation of Linschoten and who remained in Goa, could also have helped him to make a visual record of his stay in Asia. The text of the *Itinerario* reveals nothing about this. In what follows—mainly in the notes—all kinds of similarities and differences in the choice of themes and in the illustrative techniques of the *Icones et Habitus Indorum* and the Codex Casanatense are indicated. This is intended to make clear that there are more similarities than one might at first suppose and to support the hypothesis that there could have been a Luso-Asian model for Linschoten's series.

57. C. R. Boxer, ed., *South China in the Sixteenth Century* (London: 1953), 139, 165, 261, 283. Philipp Ludwig II, count of Hanau, visited Paludanus's cabinet of curiosities in November 1592, shortly after Linschoten's return. Afterward he saw the collection of another, unnamed citizen of Enkhuizen, which included a 'Painting from China'. The depictions of Chinese in the *Itinerario* could have been made in Enkhuizen on the basis of such a painting. Gelder, 'Paradijsvogels in Enkhuizen', 43.

58. In English the contemporary term 'husbandry' more explicitly refers to the economic aspects of the 'government of their houses'.

59. For the sixteenth-century preoccupation with dress in relation to national identity in Europe see Harald Hendrix and Ton Hoenselaars, eds., *Vreemd Volk: Beeldvorming over buitenlanders in de vroegmoderne tijd* (Amsterdam, 1998), especially the contribution by Hoenselaars, 'Kleren maken de man: Mode en identiteit in het vroegmoderne Engeland'.

60. See Karel van Mander, *The Lives of the Illustrious Netherlandish and German Painters,* ed. Hessel Miedema (Doornspijk, 1994), 1:282. The multiple meanings of clothing are still important for anthropologists. See Anton Blok, 'Epiloog: Naar een historisch-antropologisch onderzoek van sexualiteit', in *Soete Minne en Helsche Boosheit: Seksuele voorstellingen in Nederland, 1300–1850,* ed. Gert Hekma and Herman Roodenburg (Nijmegen, 1988), 256. In the depiction of dress realism came second to making it function in accordance with the accepted code. A number of items, such as the dress of the mandarin and his wife, the Indian *dhoti* (a large, draped loincloth), the *choli* (a bodice), and the long cloaks of the men in India, do display some similarity to what was worn in the sixteenth century. Charles Fabri, *Indian Dress* (1960; New Delhi, 1977), 6, 70, 80. Zhou Xun and Gao Chumming, *Le costume chinois* (Paris, 1985), 153, 244–45. Texts from Portuguese sources that provide some information on Asian dress are collected by Luís de Matos in his commentary on the Codex Casanatense. See Matos, *Imagens do Oriente*. Roelof van Gelder drew my attention to the fact that Paludanus's cabinet of curiosities also included a considerable quantity of exotic clothing. It is conceivable that Paludanus's cabinet was consulted for the making of the prints. Details such as the hairstyle of the *chauderim* man, the elongated earlobes of the people of Malabar, and the cross branded onto the faces of the Abyssinian Christians are probably all derived from actual observations. The Chinese commoners (pl. 2, left), on the other hand, appear to be wearing imaginary costumes. This suggests that

the aim was less to document variations in dress of different nations accurately than to record what dress revealed about the manners of those who wore it. The maker of the series may have believed that this gave him some leeway. In some instances he did know qualities of a social group that certainly must have been reflected in their dress, but he did not know precisely what dress they wore. In such a case, he allowed himself to fit the figures out with a type of dress appropriate to their known qualities.

61. George Huppert, 'The Idea of Civilization in the Sixteenth Century', in *Renaissance Studies in Honor of Hans Baron,* ed. A. Molho and J. Tedeschi, 759–69 (Florence, 1970). C. Vivanti, 'Alle origini dell'idea di civiltà: Le scoperte geografiche e gli scritti di Henri de la Popelinière', *Rivista Storica Italiana* 84 (1962): 225–49.

62. Both in the Codex Casanatense and in Linschoten's series a selection has been made from the peoples with whom the Portuguese came into contact. The range of the Codex is wider than that of the *Icones.* From eastern Africa it presented not only 'Kaffirs from the Cape' but also Abyssinians and Black Nubians (remarkably, however, no Mozambiquans); from the peoples around the Red Sea and the Persian Gulf, eight groups besides the Arabs; and from the Indian subcontinent and islands the Cambaians, the *canarim* from near Goa, the Moors, Hindus, and Saint Thomas Christians from the Malabar coast, as well as people from Sindh, Rajputs, and Pathans in the north, Jews from Malabar, Cingalese, Calos from the Maldives, Badagas from the southernmost tip of India, and people from Orissa and Bengal. Southeast Asia is poorly represented in both series: only the people of Pegu and the Malays, but no Thai, Cambodians, or Vietnamese. Both series contain Chinese but no Japanese.

63. The representation of the peoples of the newly dicovered territories by a man and a woman, sometimes accompanied by a child, goes back to Hans Burgkmair in the *Merfahrt* of Balthasar Sprenger from 1508. Franz Hümmerich, *Quellen und Untersuchungen zur Fahrt der ersten Deutschen nach dem portugiesischen Indien 1505–1506* (Munich, 1918). Beate Borowka-Clausberg, *Balthasar Sprenger und der frühneuzeitliche Reisebericht* (Munich, 1999), 30–44. One of the first Dutch examples is a sheet printed by Jan van Doesborch in Antwerp ca. 1520. See the facsimile edition by M. E. Kronenberg, *De Novo Mondo* (The Hague, 1927).

64. 'China' is the most precise of the geographical terms used here. It refers to the Ming Empire, with which the Portuguese were in contact through Macao. 'Ballagate' usually refers to the territory under the authority of the 'king' of Bijapur to the east of Goa, but it can also refer to a much larger area, perhaps best described as east of the Ghats and north of the kingdom of Narsinga. 'Goa' is the city of Goa and its environs that were under Portuguese rule. In the past Goa had been a part of 'Ballagate', and—as we shall see— 'Goa' and 'Ballagate' tend to shift in both the text and the illustrations. 'Malabar' is here a coastal strip that begins somewhere south of Goa and includes at any rate the Moorish domain of Cananor and the Hindu domain of Cochin. Malabar stands here for a culture area—to use an anachronism—in

the southwestern coastal region of India.

65. *Itinerario,* 2:29.

66. In the text of the *Itinerario* Linschoten describes the Jews in Cochin as one of the ethnic-religious groups of Malabar. They are not illustrated in the *Icones.* They are illustrated in the Codex Casanatense.

67. The territorial position of the Arabs is ambiguous. They represent Arabia but also a very poor ethnic group in Goa. The suggestion regarding the significance of the bare feet of the woman is based on this information, taken from Linschoten's text. The territorial position of the Abyssinians and Mozambiquans and the inhabitants of Ballagate is ambiguous in the same way, as will be further explained below.

68. This also applies to the Codex Casanatense, where a Portuguese nobleman on horseback with servants and a Portuguese noblewoman in an open litter are illustrated on separate pages. Another page shows a meeting between a Portuguese on foot and two unmarried Indian Christians. In a few other cases, for example those of the Pathans and the Cingalese, the men and women who represent a people are spread over two pages as well. The reason for this is not known.

69. The three Portuguese couples represent three conditions: unmarried, married, and widowed. The explanation for this is to be found in the distinction that the Portuguese in Goa made between *soldados* (unmarried) and *casados* (married), and in the difference between the treatment of widows in Goa and in Ballagate. The Portuguese widower, whose clothing is not very different from that of the *casado,* is added as a counterpart to the widow but does not by himself seem to signify anything in particular.

70. The Codex Casanatense does not contain any male couples as representatives of a people, ethnic group, or social stratum. The only male couple consists of two yogis, each from a different ascetic denomination.

71. As far as the dominant contemporary representation is concerned, the term 'homosexuality' is an anachronism for the sixteenth century, at least according to current insights of Dutch historians. D. J. Noordam, 'Homoseksuelen en sodomieten in Nederland: Verbranden of tolereren?', in *Stigmatisering en strafrecht: De juridische positie van minderheden in historisch perspectief,* ed. J. W. ter Avest and H. Roozenbeek (Leiden, 1990), 87–93. Idem, *Riskante relaties: Vijf eeuwen homoseksualiteit in Nederland, 1233–1733,* (Hilversum, 1995), esp. chap. 3. Theo van der Meer, *Sodoms zaad in Nederland: Het ontstaan van homoseksualiteit in de vroegmoderne tijd* (Nijmegen, 1995), esp. 41–58, 74–75. Pieter Spierenburg, 'Homoseksualiteit in preïndustrieel Nederland: Twintig jaar onderzoek', *Tijdschrift voor Geschiedenis* 109 (1996): 485–493. See too Jonathan Goldberg, ed., *Queering the Renaissance* (Durham, 1994). For a tradition in the visual arts in Italy, see Andreas Sternweiler, *Die Lust der Götter: Homosexualität in der italienischen Kunst von Donatello zu Caravaggio* (Berlin, 1993), esp. 249–51. For the Netherlands, see J. Schenk, 'Homosexualiteit in de Nederlandse beeldende kunst voor 1800', *Spieghel Historiael* 17 (1982): 576–83.

72. The first wave of persecution of sodomites in Europe extended from the end of the fifteenth century to the beginning of the seventeenth through

the south European Inquisitions. E. William Monter, *Frontiers of Heresy: The Spanish Inquisition from the Basque Lands to Sicily* (Cambridge, 1990). Stephen Haliczer, *Inquisition and Society in the Kingdom of Valencia, 1478–1834* (Berkeley, 1990). For a view of sodomy in Portugal, see Ronaldo Vainfas, *Trópico dos pecados: Moral, sexualidade e Inquisição no Brasil* (Rio de Janeiro, 1989), 144–162. Luiz Mott, 'Justitia et misericordia: A Inquisição portuguesa e a repressão ao nefando pecado de sodomia', in *Inquisição: Ensaios sobre mentalidade, heresias e arte* (São Paulo, 1992), 703–38. I have not been able to determine whether sodomites were condemned by the Inquisition during Linschoten's stay in Goa.

73. *Itinerario,* 1:74–75, which also connects sodomy with the Pegu penis bells, which Linschoten had given to Paludanus. Cf. Anthony Reid, *Southeast Asia in the Age of Commerce, 1450–1680* (New Haven, 1988), 1:148–49, and B. N. Teensma, 'Literaire, filologische en moralistische bespiegelingen over de Siamese penisbel', *Bijdragen tot de Taal-, Land- en Volkenkunde* 147 (1991): 128–39.

74. Another indication that the man is a sodomite may be provided by the position of the plate in the series as a whole. Plate 24 forms a pair with plate 25, on which the sodomite from Pegu is depicted. In each of these plates we see a pair of men on the left and a male-female couple on the right. This suggests a correspondence between the couples on the two plates. A contrast is chiastically introduced between the male couples on the two plates: the virile as opposed to the effeminate sodomite (the man from Pegu), and the armed Moluccan warrior as opposed to the unarmed banana grower. A drawing by Jan Saenredam (1565–1607) provides some support for the interpretation advanced here. It shows a male inhabitant of Sodom who presents himself with his lance in a rather similar way. Arthur M. Hind and Arthur E. Popham, eds., *Catalogue of Drawings by Dutch and Flemish Artists Preserved in the Department of Prints and Drawings in the British Museum* (London, 1915–32), 5:177, no. 2. Saenredam was a member of the circle of Haarlem artists for whom the Doetecums worked. Accusations of sodomy were a theme of both Catholic and Protestant propaganda at this period. See Schenk, *Homosexualiteit in de Nederlandse beeldende kunst,* 580–81.

75. The aphrodisiac properties of betel are mentioned in *Itinerario,* 1:157 and 2:106. Figures with leaves in their hands are found in plates 1 (Javanese woman), 11 (Portuguese woman on the right), 14 (small female servant on the right), 15 (merchant from Ballagate), 16 (the bride and the Brahman), 17 (one of the women on the right), 18 (one of the servants on the left), 24 (the Polya man), and 30 (the woman in the foreground). The leaves in plates 11 and 30 are betel leaves without a shadow of doubt. The assumption that the other leaves are also those of the betel is based on Linschoten's account of the widespread and continuous use of these leaves by both men and women in India. *Itinerario,* 2:104.

76. Here too the position of the plates within the series as a whole may provide confirmation. Plates 15 and 19 form a pair. The dominant contrast is here between the two plates instead of between the left and right halves of

each plate, as was the case with plates 24 and 25. There is probably a suggestion of a chiastic correspondence between the two merchants, without a woman, and the *lascaryn* and *balhadeira,* who constitute a male-female couple but who are unmarried because of their professions. The *balhadeira* had the reputation of being a prostitute. Her opposite partner, the merchant with the betel leaves, may thus not have been as chaste as he looks.

77. In sodomy trials in the Netherlands in the seventeenth century, a distinction was made between active and passive roles, which were associated with masculinity and femininity. Noordam, *Riskante Relaties,* 56. This and the interpretation of the pairs of males in the *Icones* advanced here indicate that sodomy may be dealt with in penal law purely as an unnatural act, but that it was also taken to be connected with a specific 'orientation' and specific forms of public behaviour.

78. Flowers but not children or betel leaves are found in the Codex Casanatense as markers for couples. As in the *Icones,* flowers may be attributes of either men or women, but the vast majority of them are attributed to women. Why the Abyssinian, the man from Sindh, the Javanese, and the Pegu man in the codex have flowers as attributes is an open question. Another attribute that occurs in the codex, but not in the *Icones,* is a bowl with fruit; it is only found in a few cases, and is exclusively connected to women.

79. The woman is almost always to the left of the man in the Codex Casanatense too. The exceptions there are, for as yet unexplained reasons, the Rumes, Peguans, Sumatrans, and Javanese.

80. One might expect that once a marking had been introduced, it would be used in every relevant case, and that deviant marking or the absence of a mark would thus be significant. The lack of empirical data need not stand in the way of marking, because the process takes place on the basis of the north-centre-south grid. It depends instead on how faithfully the designer wants to cling to what reality has to offer for representations from life. Why several couples are not marked with a flower, betel leaf, or functional equivalent is unclear, especially since some could use an attribute. The Christian Abyssinians, the Saint Thomas Christians, and the Christian Mozambiquans are not just poor, they are also deprived of attributes. Perhaps this was done to underline their deviance from European Christianity.

81. Couples with children are found in early-sixteenth-century representations of Asians. For references see note 63. To the best of my knowledge, children are not depicted in the early costume books. In the Codex Casanatense they are found only in two bathing scenes, not among the couples.

82. The fact that the Mozambiquan couple is Muslim can be seen from the combination of plates 21 and 22 and the brief caption.

83. Jan Bremmer and Herman Roodenburg, eds., *A Cultural History of Gesture from Antiquity to the Present Day* (Cambridge, 1991), is useful for further research.

84. Where visible, the breasts of other women are firm and not pendulous. Perhaps the hanging breasts of the black African women are a marker of wildness, as Bernadette Bucher assumed to be the case for the American 'sauvage

aux seins pendants' in the illustrations to the Grands Voyages of de Bry. Bernadette Bucher, *La sauvage aux seins pendants* (Paris, 1977), 46–47. This distinguishes them physically from European and Asian women. Giving suck over the shoulder also marks them as culturally different. This is probably connected with the position of Mozambiquans as slaves in Goa, as shown in plate 5. The representation from the *Itinerario* is continued in the illustrations to *Beschrijvinge ende historisch verhael van het Gout Koninckrijk van Gunea* by Pieter de Marees, published by Cornelis Claesz in 1602. On this see Jennifer Morgan, '"Some Could Suckle over Their Shoulder": Male Travelers, Female Bodies, and the Gendering of Racial Ideology, 1500–1770', *William and Mary Quarterly,* 54 (1997): 181–88.

85. That the presence or absence of weapons in this series is used to distinguish two types of elites is mainly an extrapolation from the pairings of China/Goa and Ballagate/Cochin, where this distinction—as we shall presently see—is a criterion. The underlying idea is that, generally speaking, the ruling elite consists of warriors, knights, or nobles. Similarly, in the Codex Casanatense the only woman portrayed with a weapon is the Patana from north India, where womenfolk were expected to join in the fighting. The only unarmed men among the couples in the Codex are the merchant from Cambaia, the man from the Maldives, and the yogis. In the case of the merchant from Cambaia, this may be because, as a Jain, he was expected not to kill humans or animals. (This may also have influenced Linschoten in his decision not to portray the Cambaian with a weapon.) The yogis had also renounced the use of weapons in their asceticism. The man from the Maldives in the Codex stands for the minimum of civilisation; there is no longer a proper social hierarchy, and there are thus no armed or unarmed elites. As in the *Icones*, one function of the plates with more than one figure in the Codex may have been the elaboration of the theme of social stratification.

86. In the case of the man from Pegu, the absence of a weapon may be connected more with the main purpose—the representation of an effeminate sodomite—than with the intention of depicting an unarmed elite. The absence of weapons among the Christian Abyssinians and one of the Mozambiquan couples may be connected with their slave status in Goa.

87. The meaning of *mandil* here is enigmatic.

88. *Faraz* is the term applied to one of the lowest castes in Goa. See Sebastião Rodolfo Dalgado, *Glossário Luso-Asiatico*, 2 vols. (Coimbra, 1919–21).

89. In fact, the *negros* will have been *escravos* as well.

90. The Codex Casanatense also contains several procession scenes, but their composition is more varied than in the *Icones*. The king of Cambaia who is depicted in the Codex must represent something completely different from Linschoten's king of Cochin. To judge from the number of illustrations, the Codex is centred on Cambaia rather than on Goa.

91. Remarkably, there is no display of firearms among the Portuguese, except in the plate depicting the fust from Goa/Malabar. This supports the suggestion made above that the type of weapon is not a marker in the hierarchy of civilisation.

92. This marker is also found in the plate of the ambassador from Ballagate and in those of the Arabs and Mozambiquans, where it is more closely connected with their position as the proletarians of Goa.

93. The seated figure on the right in the boat does not have a beard or moustache, unlike the other male Chinese, and is thus probably a woman. We can recognise in the pair of servants the Chinese commoners from the series of ethnic couples. It is striking that the woman paddles and thus propels the boat, while the man serves at table, but it is not clear whether any importance should be attached to this.

94. The text of the *Itinerario* makes no mention of any delegation from Ballagate in Linschoten's time. This plate may have been entirely concocted from elements derived from the other plates.

95. Jean Deloche, *Transport and Communications in India prior to Steam Locomotion,* vol. 2, Water Transport (Oxford, 1993), 187–93.

96. L. Audemard, *Les jonques chinoises,* 6 vols. (Rotterdam, 1957–66). This work offers hardly any points of contact by which to judge the accuracy of the illustration of the junk in plate 4.

97. This supposition is based on other deviations from regular left/right patterns. See below.

98. The Portuguese carrack is missing from the series. The mention of reed sails and a wooden anchor in the case of the junk should perhaps be taken as a reference to European superiority in shipbuilding. The choice of the boat as a gauge of civility may be motivated by the fact that the moderns incontrovertibly surpassed the ancients in navigating the oceans. This topos of Portuguese humanistic literature could be found in authors like Camões, with whose work both Linschoten and Cornelis Taemsz were well acquainted. R. Hooykaas, *Humanism and the Voyages of Discovery in 16th Century Portuguese Science and Letters* (Amsterdam, 1979), 152–53. See also the comments on the European assessment of African and Asian vessels in Michael Adas, *Machines as the Measure of Men. Science, Technology, and Ideologies of Western Dominance* (Ithaca, N.Y.: 1989), 37, 47–49.

99. There is no such series in the Codex Casanatense.

100. Anthropocentric definitions of the natural world are as old as the scriptographic information and communication system. Giesecke, *Der Buchdruck,* 574. A new form of representation appropriate to the typographic information and communication system is being used here for an old idea.

101. *Itinerario,* 2:106.

102. Dalgado, *Glosário Luso-Asiatico,* 2:461, translates such cases with 'superstructure', 'elevation'. These are probably the pleasure houses *(speelhuys)* to which Linschoten referred; see the following note.

103. *Itinerario,* H.S. ed., 1:178, notes, 'They commonly have their Gardens and Orchards at the backe side of their houses [in town] full of all kinde of Indian fruites: as also the whole Iland through, they have many pleasant Gardens and farmes, with houses to play in, and trees of Indian fruites, whether they goe to sport themselves, and wherein the Indian women take great delight'. The house with a verandah on the first floor looks too big for a 'house to play in'.

104. *Itinerario,* 2:101.

105. For an interpretation of the water-carrying buffalo tethered to the *arbore triste,* see the following section.

106. The practice of decorating the borders of maps with personifications of nations, profiles of cities, and suchlike appears to have come into fashion in the Netherlands toward the end of the sixteenth century. Schilder, *Monumenta Cartografica Neerlandica,* 3:123. Plancius's world map of 1592 (Colegio de Corpus Christi, Valencia) is decorated with representations of plants and animals from the newly discovered regions of the world. His 1594 world map and the one published by Vrients go further in the same direction. These last two maps occur alternatively in the earliest impressions of the *Itinerario.* They are certainly not purely decorative additions.

107. See *Itinerario,* vols. 1 and 2, chaps. 27–44.

108. *Itinerario,* vol. 1, chaps. 4–26, esp. pp. 79–81, 86–87, 94–108.

109. The binding of the feet of married women is contrasted with the burning alive of widows in Ballagate. It is thus an argument for the superiority of the Chinese. The text on China, an extract from Gonzalez de Mendoza, is here being read selectively. The text mentions that after the death of a high-ranking mandarin, many of his servants and wives were killed to escort him to the afterworld. *Itinerario,* 1:100.

110. The Codex Casanatense does not have any direct pendants to these scenes, but it does have similar ones. The page with the *xaroffo* and his public comes close to Linschoten's depiction of the market in Goa. There are two representations of women bathing, but in a totally different context. On the other hand, the Codex contains appreciably more scenes of labour in the countryside. See note 122.

111. For a recent study of this topic with exhaustive references to the literature, see Elizabeth A. Honig, 'Country Folk and City Business: A Print Series by Jan van de Velde', *Art Bulletin* 78 (1996): 511–26, and her book *Painting and the Market in Early Modern Antwerp* (New Haven, 1998).

112. *Itinerario,* H.S. ed., 1:183: The drinking water for the city of Goa was drawn from a well a quarter of a mile outside the city, 'which the slaves fetch in pots and sel it in the towne'.

113. The woman with a headscarf (behind the crier) and the man with the naked torso (to the left of the slave girl) cannot be identified from the text.

114. *Itinerario,* H.S. ed., 1:185.

115. Cäcilie Quetsch mentions a woodcut of a Turkish slave market by Erhard Schön dated ca. 1532. Cäcilie Quetsch, *Entdeckung der Welt in der deutschen Graphik der beginnenden Neuzeit,* (Erlangen-Nuremberg, 1983), p. 123, pl. 205.

116. In their edition of the *Itinerario* the de Bry brothers added legenda to the plate of the market in Goa. They describe the female figure with the jar as a slave prostitute. Friedemann Berger, ed., *De Bry: India Orientalis* (Leipzig, 1979), vol. 1, pl. 51.

117. *Itinerario,* 1:139.

118. *Itinerario,* H.S. ed., 1:185.

119. *Itinerario,* 2:10–11: 'for although men were of iron or steele, the un- chaste life of a woman, with her unsatiable lustes were able to grinde him to powder, and swéep him away like dust; which costeth many a mans life'. On the fraternities of the Misericordia, see Isabel dos Guimarães Sá, *Quando o rico se faz pobre: Misericórdias, caridade e poder no império português, 1500–1800* (Lisbon, 1997), chap. 5 (on Goa).

120. At the end of the sixteenth century slavery was a matter on which a local court or government in Zealand or Holland had to make occasional pronouncements because pirates tried to sell black slaves that they had seized. In 1596 the States of Zealand decided to prohibit the sale of what were assumed to be baptised black slaves. W. R. Menkman, *De Geschiedenis van de West-Indische Compagnie* (Amsterdam, 1947), 27–28.

121. Several features in the architectural of the village are also hard to identify on the basis of the text. A small shop or workshop seems to be standing next to the hut on the left. The open building in the background on the far left resembles the *bayleo* (pleasure house) in plate 28.

122. The Codex Casanatense contains illustrations of *canarim* rice growers, launderers (*mainatos,* also mentioned by Linschoten), and smiths. The codex makes hardly any visual distinction between the city and the countryside. The floral decoration in most of the other scenes suggests a rural rather than an urban setting. The exception is the scene showing the *xaroffo* in Cambaia, the equivalent in the codex to the market in Goa in the *Icones.* The scene of ploughing and sowing in the codex is also situated in Cambaia, making this the only place in the codex where a distinction is genuinely made between the countryside and the city.

123. *Itinerario,* 2:4, 25–28, 51.

124. *Itinerario,* H.S. ed., 1:226–27.

125. *Itinerario,* 2:26, 51. Compare Linschoten's observations on the poverty with what Gita Dharampal-Frick reports on the economic observations in early German-language texts on the Indian subcontinent: *Indien im Spiegel deutscher Quellen der Frühen Neuzeit (1500–1700): Studien zur einer interkulturellen Konstellation* (Tübingen, 1994), 162–73.

126. Norbert Elias, *Über den Prozess der Zivilisation: Soziogenetische und psychogenetische Untersuchungen,* vol. 1, (1939; Bern/Munich, 1969). The Codex Casanatense also has two illustrations of women bathing, but their composition is completely different from that in the *Icones.* One scene is situated in Muscat, the other in Cambaia. The significance of these scenes is unknown. The passages from Portuguese chroniclers cited by Luís de Matos only emphasise the fact that men and women frequently bathed. Apparently this was a stock theme in series of prints on the peoples of Asia.

127. Ilja M. Veldman, *Leerrijke reeksen van Maarten van Heemskerck* (Haarlem, 1986); idem, *De Wereld tussen goed en kwaad: Late prenten van Coornhert* (The Hague, 1990).

128. In the Codex Casanatense, the men and women from Patana are illustrated on separate folios. All the same, this resource underlines the fact that they belong to the same world, i.e., they both fight on horseback. The wives of Cambaian merchants appear together with their husbands, but they are also

illustrated on a separate folio fetching water and bathing. A folio with women bathing on their own represents Muscat. Their menfolk are not illustrated at all. The interpretation of these scenes is open. The Portuguese in Goa are only illustrated on three folios of the codex. The first shows a meeting between a Portuguese man in full dress, on foot, with a servant, and two decorously dressed, unmarried Indian Christian women with their servants. One of these 'Indian' Christians may be an Abyssinian. The other two illustrations show a Portuguese man on horseback and a Portuguese woman in an open litter that is very similar to the corresponding plate in the *Icones*. There is no reason to suppose that these illustrations play on the opposition between public virtues and private vices.

129. The Codex Casanatense contains an illustration of a fight between two Arab pirate ships. There is no parallel with the print from the *Icones*.

130. This passage seems to be an echo of Ovid, *Metamorphoses,* 1:139–50.

131. This adult practice is represented in the print of the market of Goa, probably as a pendant to the baby that sucks at the wetnurse's breast. Both scenes exemplify the 'going native' of the Portuguese.

132. Linschoten's criticisms are in accord with those of Diogo do Couto and Francisco Rodrigues Silveira. See Winius, *Black Legend of Portuguese India.* Compare also the discussions in *Indian Economic and Social History Review* 23 (1986): 330–31 and in *South Asia* n.s. 10 (1987): 91–93. And see Silveira's *Reformação da milícia e governo do estado da Índia Oriental,* ed. B. N. Teensma (Lisbon, 1996).

133. Linschoten's account influenced European views on the art of India. Partha Mitter, *Much Maligned Monsters: History of European Reactions to Indian Art* (Oxford, 1977), 21–22.

134. *Itinerario,* 2:24.

135. *Itinerario,* H.S. ed., 1:224. This passage is not included in the excerpt that accompanies plate 16 of the *Icones*. The de Bry brothers connected this plate with the correct passage in their edition of Linschoten. Their interpretation is followed here. Berger, *De Bry,* vol. 1, pl. 24.

136. The Codex Casanatense pays considerably more attention to Hinduism than the *Icones,* and does so in a more confrontational way. It includes a very elaborate scene of a Hindu wedding. It does not have a suttee, but it does include a scene of a widow being buried alive. It does not represent a Hindu temple or a mosque, but it does contain a scene of the ritual suicide beneath the juggernaut and no fewer than three forms of the ritual suicide of a Brahman.

137. The free status of the Arab sailors is mentioned in the *Itinerario,* 2:29. Linschoten also mentions the sale of children into slavery (2:35) and the disruptive consequences of slavery for family life (1:159). It would have been fitting if the plates had alluded to Islamic polygamy. This does seem to be the case. Islamic customs are characterised rather poorly throughout the series.

138. Linschoten's characterisation of the Mozambiquans seems more negative than was usual in Portuguese sources on eastern Africans of his day. See W. G. L. Randles, *L'image du Sud-est Africain dans la littérature européenne au XVIe*

siècle (Lisbon, 1959), esp. chaps. 7–9.

139. The Nayars are a classic puzzle of Western sociology of the family. Randall Collins, *Weberian Sociological Theory* (Cambridge, 1986), 297–321.

140. For Linschoten's place in European reports of Elephanta, see Mitter, *Much Maligned Monsters,* 36–39.

141. *Itinerario,* H.S. ed., 2:84

142. Compare William B. Ashworth Jr., 'Emblematic Natural History of the Renaissance', in *Cultures of Natural History,* ed. N. Jardine, J. A. Secord, and E. C. Spary (Cambridge, 1996), 17–37. F. David Hoeniger, 'How Plants and Animals Were Studied in the Mid-Sixteenth Century', in *Science and the Arts in the Renaissance,* ed. John W. Shirley and F. David Hoeniger (Washington, 1985), 130–48.

143. See the arguments in chapter 5 of Bodin's *Methodus ad facilem historiarum cognitionem* (1566) and in book 5 of his *Six Livres de la République* (1576 and 1586). His theory became famous through various literary works, including *Les Colonies* by Guilaume du Bartas, part of his unfinished *Seconde Sepmaine.* Waldemar Zacharasiewicz, *Die Klimatheorie in der englischen Literatur und Literaturkritik von der Mitte des 16. bis zum frühen 18. Jahrhundert* (Vienna, 1977), 76–82, 149–82. Bartas was also known in the Netherlands. A. Beekman, *Influence de Du Bartas sur la littérature néerlandaise* (Poitiers, 1912). Cornelis Taemsz was inspired by him in the composition of his ode for the *Reys-Gheschrift.* Spies, 'Betaald Werk?', 216. Frank Lestringant, 'Du Bartas entre Du Plessis-Mornay et Jean Bodin: À propos des "Colonies", in his *L'expérience huguenote au nouveau monde (XVIe siècle)* (Geneva, 1996), 317–28. See too Lestringant on Bodin in his *Écrire le monde à la Renaissance: Quinze études sur Rabelais, Postel, Bodin et la littérature géographique* (Caen, 1993), 255–92.

144. For contemporary English views on the tropics see Karen Ordahl Kupperman, 'Fear of Hot Climates in the Anglo-American Colonial Experience', *William and Mary Quarterly* 41 (1984): 213–40.

145. It is conceivable that Linschoten gave instructions for the colouring of the plates to bring out differences in skin pigmentation, but this does not seem to have been the case. In the coloured prints in the first impressions in Rotterdam and Johannesburg the black Africans are usually coloured an appropriate dark grey, but it is doubtful whether the minimal differences in tint among the figures should be regarded as an attempt to indicate differences in skin pigmentation 'after life' in any systematic way.

146. Such a differentiation between black and white populations in Asia is not typically Dutch or north European. The same distinction can be found in the writings of the great organiser of the Jesuit mission, the Italian Alessandro Valignano, who was in Goa at the same time as Linschoten. Lach, *Asia in the Making of Europe,* vol. 1, bk. 1, 258–59. Dauril Alden, *The Making of an Enterprise: The Society of Jesus in Portugal, Its Empire, and Beyond, 1540–1750* (Stanford, Calif., 1996), 56.

147. Skin pigmentation does play a role in the classification of peoples in the Codex Casanatense, as can be seen from the consistent application of differences.

148. See the scheme in an English translation of Pierre Charron, another propagator of Bodin's theory of climate, reproduced in Lach, *Asia in the Making of Europe,* vol. 2, bk. 2, pl. 17.

149. For similar conceptual schemes from the contemporary apodemic literature, see Antoni Maczak, *De ontdekking van het Reizen: Europa in de vroegmoderne tijd* (Utrecht, 1998), 215. Stagl, *History of Curiosity,* 61.

150. On early modern views of national characters, see Louis van Delft, *Littérature et anthropologie: Nature humaine et caractère à l'âge classique* (Paris, 1993), chap. 4.

151. A few recent studies of this inexhaustible subject are Herfried Münkler, ed., *Die Herausforderung durch das Fremde* (Berlin, 1998), and idem, *Furcht und Faszination: Facetten der Fremdheit* (Berlin, 1997).

152. The place accorded the Asians in the hierarchy of civility in the *Icones* is heavily influenced by the work of Gonzalez de Mendoza (1585). Linschoten only became familiar with this work after his return, but he could have come across a similar classification in Jesuit circles during his stay in Goa. For the views of Alessandro Valignano, see Josef Franz Schütte S.J., *Valignanos Missionsgrundsätze für Japan* (Rome, 1951), 1:169–77, and the versions of his *Summarium Indicum* in Josef Wicki S.J., ed., *Documenta Indica,* vol. 13 (1583–1585) (Rome, 1975), 5–13, 144–49, 196–207.

153. For a closer relation between word and image in the literature of the technical professions see Giesecke, *Der Buchdruck,* 628 ff.

154. H.-J. Raupp, ed., *Wort und Bild: Buchkunst und Druckgraphik in den Niederlanden im 16. und 17. Jahrhundert* (Cologne, 1981), 15–17.

155. This view of the visible world differs from what is usually regarded as the premise of Dutch 'realist' art: the artist and the viewer believed that the true significance of the only apparently easily accessible and comprehensible world was situated in an underlying, invisible world, a state of affairs to which the deceptive realism of the 'counterfeits from life' referred. See, for example, Justus Müller Hofstede, '"Wort und Bild": Fragen zu Signifikanz und Realität in der holländischen Malerei des XVII. Jahrhunderts', in *Wort und Bild in der niederländischen Kunst und Literatur des 16. und 17. Jahrhunderts,* ed. Herman Vekeman and Justus Müller Hofstede (Erftstadt, 1984), xii–xix. Wayne Franits, *Looking at Seventeenth-Century Dutch Art: Realism Reconsidered* (Cambridge, 1998). A relation between word and image in travel accounts different from the one advanced here for the *Icones* is discussed by Wolfgang Neuber in his 'Imago und Pictura: Zur Topik des Sinn-Bilds im Spannungsfeld von Ars Memorativa und Emblematik (am Paradigma des "Indianers")', in *Text und Bild, Bild und Text: DFG-Symposion 1988,* ed. Wolfgang Harms (Stuttgart, 1988), 245–61. Carsten-Peter Warncke, *Sprechende Bilder, sichtbare Worte: Das*

Bildverständnis in der frühen Neuzeit (Wiesbaden, 1987). This last work came to my attention too late to be used in this study. However, it is an essential addition to the literature on the subject.

156. Joan-Pau Rubiés, 'New Worlds and Renaissance Ethnology', *History and Anthropology* 6 (1993): 157–97, and idem, 'Instructions for Travellers: Teaching the Eye to See', *History and Anthropology* 9 (1996): 139–90.

157. Miedema, *Kunst, kunstenaar en kunstwerk,* 122–27

158. The *Historia natural y moral de las Indias* by José de Acosta, which Linschoten translated, contained a 'programme for comparative ethnology', according to Anthony Pagden, *The Fall of Natural Man: The American Indian and the Origins of Comparative Ethnology* (Cambridge, 1982), 146–97.

159. Cornelis Taemsz wrote a eulogy on van Mander's translation of the *Georgics* (1597). Peter Hoogerbeets wrote verse in praise of van Mander's painting *The Adoration of the Three Kings.* Van Mander drew a portrait of Hoogerbeets, engraved by Jan Saenredam. Marjolein Leesberg, 'Karel van Mander as a Painter', *Simiolus* 22 (1993–94): 5–58, esp. 6–7. See too the commentary on van Mander's biography by Hessel Miedema in Mander, *The Lives of the Illustrious Netherlandish and German Painters,* vol. 2 (Doornspijk, 1995). For the collaboration between van Mander and Joannes van Doetecum, see Nalis, *Van Doetecum Family,* no. 926.

160. Reindert Jacobsen, *Carel van Mander (1548–1606): Dichter en prozaschrijver* (1906; Utrecht, 1972), 83, 211. Benjamin Schmidt, '"O Fortunate Land!": Karel van Mander, a West Indian Landscape, and the Dutch Discovery of America', *Nieuwe West-Indische Gids* 69 (1995): 5–44. See Hessel Miedema's commentary on van Mander in Mander, *Den grondt der edel vrij schilder-const,* 2 vols. (Utrecht, 1972), 1:273–274; 2:613 n. 35, 633, 635. For the *Confusio Babylonica* see *America: Bride of the Son,* exh. cat., Koninklijk Museum voor Schone Kunsten (Antwerp, 1992), 320–21.

161. Hessel Miedema, 'Het stadsklavecimbel van Amsterdam', *Bulletin van het Rijksmuseum* 48 (2000): 259–79, esp. 260–61.

162. Zandvliet, *Maurits, Prins van Oranje,* 367–71.

163. This cycle of the processing and collecting of information is described by Giesecke in 'Von den skriptographischen zu den typografischen Informationsverarbeitungsprogrammen'.

164. The Huguenot La Popelinière compared the Portuguese colonisation of Asia favourably with that of the Spaniards in America in *Les Trois Mondes* (1582) to counter the anticolonialist sentiment in Protestant circles. Frank Lestringant, *Le Huguenot et le sauvage* (Paris, 1990), 258–59. The *Icones* draw the attention of Protestants and others to the problematic aspects of Portuguese mercantile imperialism.

Bibliography

Adas, Michael. *Machines as the Measure of Men: Science, Technology, and Ideologies of Western Dominance*. Ithaca, N.Y.: Cornell University Press, 1989.

Alden, Dauril. *The Making of an Enterprise: The Society of Jesus in Portugal, Its Empire, and Beyond, 1540–1750*. Stanford, Calif.: Stanford University Press, 1996.

Alpers, Svetlana. *The Art of Describing: Dutch Art in the Seventeenth Century*. Chicago: University of Chicago Press, 1983.

———. 'The Mapping Impulse in Dutch Art'. In *Art and Cartography: Six Historical Essays*, ed. David Woodward, 51–96. Chicago: University of Chicago Press, 1987.

America: Bride of the Son. Exh. cat., Koninklijk Museum voor Schone Kunsten. Antwerp, 1992.

Ashworth Jr., William B. 'Emblematic Natural History of the Renaissance'. In *Cultures of Natural History*, ed. N. Jardine, J. A. Secord, and E. C. Spary, 17–37. Cambridge: Cambridge University Press, 1996.

Audemard, Louis. *Les jonques chinoises*. 10 vols. Rotterdam: Museum voor Land- en Volkenkunde, 1957–66.

Bakker, Boudewijn. 'Maps, Books and Prints: The Topographical Tradition in the Northern Netherlands'. In *The Dutch Cityscape in the Seventeenth Century and Its Sources*, ed. C. van Lakerveld, 66–75. Exh. cat., Amsterdams Historisch Museum/Art Gallery of Ontario. Amsterdam: Landshoff, 1977.

Beekman, A. *Influence de Du Bartas sur la littérature néerlandaise*. Poitiers: Masson, 1912.

Berger, Friedemann, ed. *De Bry: India Orientalis*. Leipzig: Gustav Kiegenheuer Verlag, 1979.

Beveridge, Henry. *A Comprehensive History of India*. 1862; New Dehli: Associated Publishers House, 1974.

Blok, Anton. 'Epiloog: Naar een historisch-antropologisch onderzoek van seksualiteit'. In *Soete minne en helsche boosheit: Seksuele voorstellingen in Nederland, 1300–1850*, ed. Gert Hekma and Herman Roodenburg, 255–61. Nijmegen: SUN, 1988.

Blouw, Paul Valkema. *Typographica Batava, 1541–1600*. Nieuwkoop: De Graaf, 1998.

Boogaart, Ernst van den, ed. *Jan Huygen van Linschoten and the Moral Map of Asia*. London: Roxburghe Club, 1999.

Borowka-Clausberg, Beate. *Balthasar Sprenger und der frühneuzeitliche Reisebericht*. Munich: Iudicium, 1999.

Boxer, Charles R., ed. *South China in the Sixteenth Century, Being the Narratives of Galeote Pereira, Fr. Gaspar da Cruz, O.P., Fr. Martín de Rada, O.E.S.A.* London: Hakluyt Society, 1953.

Braudel, Fernand. *Civilisation matérielle, Économie et Capitalisme: XVe–XVIIIe siècle*. 3 vols. Paris: A. Colin, 1979.

Bremmer, Jan, and Herman Roodenburg, eds. *A Cultural History of Gesture from Antiquity to the Present Day*. Cambridge: Polity Press, 1991.

Bruyn, J. 'A Turning-Point in the History of Dutch Art'. In *Dawn of the Golden Age: Northern Netherlandish Art, 1580–1620*, ed. G. Luijten et al., 112–21. Amsterdam: Rijksmuseum; Zwolle: Waanders, 1993.

Bucher, Bernadette. *La sauvage aux seins pendants*. Paris: Hermann, 1977.

Buisseret, David, ed. *Monarchs, Ministers, and Maps: The Emergence of Cartography as a Tool of Government in Early Modern Europe*. Chicago: University of Chicago Press, 1992.

Burger, C. P. 'De Historie ofte Beschrijvinghe van het Groote Rijck van China'. *Het Boek* 19 (1930): 17–32.

Collins, Randall. *Weberian Sociological Theory*. Cambridge: Cambridge University Press, 1986.

Croiset van Uchelen, A. R. A. 'De raadselachtige schrijfmeester Clemens Perret en zijn twee materie boeken'. In *De Arte et Libris: Festschrift Erasmus, 1934–1984*, ed. A. Horodisch, 43–60. Amsterdam: Erasmus Antiquariaat en Boekhandel, 1984.

Dalgado, Sebastião Rodolfo. *Glossário Luso-Asiatico*. 2 vols. Coimbra: Imprensa da Universidade, 1919–21.

Defert, Daniel. 'Collections et nations au XVIe siècle'. In *L'Amérique de Théodore de Bry: Une collection de voyages protestante du XVIe siècle: Quatre études d'iconographie*, ed. Michèle Duchet, 47–67. Paris: Editions du Centre Nationale de la Recherche Scientifique, 1987.

Delft, Louis van. *Littérature et anthropologie: Nature humaine et caractère à l'âge classique*. Paris: Presses Universitaires de France, 1993.

Deloche, Jean. *Transport and Communications in India prior to Steam Locomotion*. Vol. 2, *Water Transport*. Oxford: Oxford University Press, 1993.

Dharampal-Frick, Gita. *Indien im Spiegel deutscher Quellen der Frühen Neuzeit (1500–1700): Studien zur einer interkulturellen Konstellation*. Tübingen: Niemeyer, 1994.

Dillen, J. G. van, ed. *Bronnen tot de geschiedenis van het bedrijfsleven en het gildewezen van Amsterdam*. Vol. 1. The Hague: M. Nijhoff, 1929.

Doege, Heinrich. 'Die Trachtenbücher des 16. Jahrhunderts'. In *Beiträge zur Bücherkunde und Philologie: August Wilmanns zum 25. märz 1903 gewidmet*, 429–44. Leipzig: O. Harrassowitz, 1903.

Edwardes, Michael. *Ralph Fitch: Elizabethan in the Indies*. London: Faber, 1972.

Ekkart, Rudolf E. O., ed. *Wilt Hooren 't Woort.* Exh. cat. The Hague: Rijksmuseum Meermanno-Westreenianum, 1979.

Elias, Norbert. *Über den Prozess der Zivilisation: Soziogenetische und psychogenetische Untersuchungen.* Vol. 1, *Wandlungen des Verhaltens in den weltlichen Oberschichten des Abendlandes.* 1939; reprint, Bern/Munich: Franck, 1969.

Elsner, Jas, and Joan-Pau Rubiés, eds. *Voyages and Visions: Towards a Cultural History of Travel.* London, 1999.

Everaert, John G. 'Soldaten, diamantairs en jezuieten: Zuid- en Noord-Nederlanders in Portugees-Indië'. In *Souffrir pour Parvenir: De wereld van Jan Huygen van Linschoten,* ed. Roelof van Gelder, Jan Parmentier, and Vibeke Roeper, 80–94. Haarlem: Arcadia, 1998.

Fabri, Charles. *Indian Dress: A Brief History.* 1960; reprint, New Delhi: Orient Longman, 1977.

Fontaine Verwey, Herman de la. 'Amsterdamse uitgeversbanden van Cornelis Claesz en Laurens Jacobsz'. In *Uit de wereld van het boek,* vol. 2, 33–48. Amsterdam: Israëls, 1976.

Franits, Wayne. *Looking at Seventeenth-Century Dutch Art: Realism Reconsidered.* Cambridge: Cambridge University Press, 1998.

Gelder, Roelof van. 'Paradijsvogels in Enkhuizen'. In *Souffrir pour parvenir: De wereld van Jan Huygen van Linschoten,* ed. Roelof van Gelder, Jan Parmentier, and Vibeke Roeper, 30–50. Haarlem: Arcadia, 1998.

Giesecke, Michael. *Der Buchdruck in der frühen Neuzeit: Eine historische Fallstudie über die Durchsetzung neuer Informations- und Kommunikationstechnologien.* 3d ed. Frankfurt: Suhrkamp, 1998.

———. 'Von den skriptographischen zu den typografischen Informationsverarbeitungsprogrammen'. In *Wissensliteratur im Mittelalter und in der frühen Neuzeit: Bedingungen, Typen, Publikum, Sprache,* ed. Horst Brunner and Norbert Richard Wolf, 328–46. Wiesbaden: Ludwig Reichert, 1993.

Goldberg, Jonathan, ed. *Queering the Renaissance.* Durham: Duke University Press, 1994.

Haliczer, Stephen. *Inquisition and Society in the Kingdom of Valencia, 1478–1834.* Berkeley: University of California Press, 1990.

Heesakkers, Chris L. 'Petrus Forestus in gedichten en brieven'. In *Petrus Forestus Medicus,* ed. H. A. Bosma-Jelgersma, 119–241. Amsterdam: Duivendrecht, 1996.

Hekma, Gert, and Herman Roodenburg, eds. *Soete minne en helsche boosheit: Seksuele voorstellingen in Nederland, 1300–1850.* Nijmegen: SUN, 1988.

Hind, Arthur M., and Arthur E. Popham. *Catalogue of Drawings by Dutch and Flemish Artists Preserved in the Department of Prints and Drawings in the British Museum.* 5 vols. London: Trustees of the British Museum, 1915–32.

Hoeniger, F. David. 'How Plants and Animals Were Studied in the Mid-Sixteenth Century'. In *Science and the Arts in the Renaissance,* ed. John W. Shirley and F. D. Hoeniger, 130–48. Washington, D.C.: Folger Shakespeare Library; London: Associated University Presses, 1985.

Hoenselaars, Ton. 'Kleren maken de man: Mode en identiteit in het vroegmoderne Engeland'. In *Vreemd Volk: Beeldvorming over buitenlanders in de vroegmoderne tijd,* ed. Harald Hendrix and Ton Hoenselaars, 93–120. Am-

sterdam: Amsterdam University Press, 1998.

Honig, Elizabeth A. 'Country Folk and City Business: A Print Series by Jan van de Velde'. *Art Bulletin* 78 (1996): 511–26.

———. *Painting and the Market in Early Modern Antwerp.* New Haven: Yale University Press, 1998.

Hooykaas, R. *Humanism and the Voyages of Discovery in 16th Century Portuguese Science and Letters.* Amsterdam: Noord-Hollandsche Uitgevers Maatschappij, 1979. Mededelingen der Koninklijke Nederlandse Akademie van Wetenschappen, Afd. Letterkunde: Nieuwe Reeks, v. 42, no. 4.

Hümmerich, Franz. *Quellen und Untersuchungen zur Fahrt der ersten Deutschen nach dem portugiesischen Indien 1505–1506.* Munich: Verlag der Königlich Bayerischen Akademie der Wissenschaften, 1918. Abhandlungen der Bayerischen Akademie der Wissenschaften, Hist. Klasse, vol. 30.

Huppert, George. 'The Idea of Civilization in the Sixteenth Century'. In *Renaissance Studies in Honor of Hans Baron,* ed. A. Molho and J. Tedeschi, 759–69. Dekalb: Northern Illinois University Press, 1970.

IJzerman, J. W., ed. *Dirck Gerritsz Pomp alias Dirck Gerritsz China: De eerste Nederlander die China en Japan bezocht (1544–1604).* The Hague: M. Nijhoff, 1915.

Jacobsen, Reindert. *Carel van Mander (1548–1606): Dichter en prozaschrijver.* 1906; reprint, Utrecht: HES, 1972.

Kagan, Richard L. 'Philip II and the Art of the Cityscape'. In *Art and History: Images and Their Meaning,* ed. Robert I. Rotberg and Theodore K. Rabb, 115–36. Cambridge: Cambridge University Press, 1986.

Koeman, Cornelis. *Lucas Janszoon Waghenaer: Sa vie et son 'Spieghel der Zeevaerdt'.* Lausanne: Sequoia, 1964.

Krings, Wilfried. 'Text und Bild als Informationsträger bei gedruckten Stadtdarstellungen der frühen Neuzeit'. In *Poesis und Pictura: Studien zum Verhältnis von Text und Bild in Handschriften und alten Drucken: Festschrift für Dieter Wuttke zum 60. Geburtstag,* ed. S. Füssel and J. Knape, 295–335. Baden-Baden: Körner, 1989.

Kronenberg, M. E., ed. *De novo mondo: Antwerp Jan van Doesborch.* Facsimile of a broadsheet printed ca. 1520. The Hague: Nijhoff, 1927.

Kupperman, Karin Ordahl. 'Fear of Hot Climates in the Anglo-American Colonial Experience'. *William and Mary Quarterly* 41 (1984): 213–40.

Lach, Donald F. *Asia in the Making of Europe.* Vols. 1 and 2. Chicago: University of Chicago Press, 1965, 1970.

Lach, Donald F., and Edwin J. Van Kley. *Asia in the Making of Europe.* Vol. 3. Chicago: University of Chicago Press, 1993.

Landau, David, and Peter Parshall. *The Renaissance Print, 1470–1550.* New Haven: Yale University Press, 1994.

Leesberg, Marjolein. 'Karel van Mander as a Painter'. *Simiolus* 22 (1993–94): 5–58.

Leesberg, Marjolein, Hugen Leeflang, and Christiaan Schuckman, eds. 'Karel van Mander'. In *The New Holstein: Dutch and Flemish Etchings, Engravings and Woodcuts 1550–1700.* Rotterdam: Sound & Vision Publishers, 1999.

Leeuwen, Jan Storm van. 'Some Observations on Dutch Publisher's Bindings up to 1800'. In *Bookbindings and Other Bibliophily: Essays in Honour of Anthony Hobson,* ed. Dennis E. Rhodes, 287–319. Verona: Valdonega, 1994.

Lestringant, Frank. 'Du Bartas entre Du Plessis-Mornay et Jean Bodin: À propos des "colonies"'. In *L'expérience huguenote au nouveau monde (XVIe siècle),* 317–28. Geneva: Droz, 1996.

——. 'Europe et théorie des climats dans la seconde moitié du XVIe siècle'. In *Écrire le monde à la renaissance: Quinze études sur Rabelais, Postel, Bodin et la littérature géographique,* 255–76. Caen: Paradigme, 1993.

——. *Le Huguenot et le sauvage.* Paris: Aux amateurs de livres, 1990.

Linschoten, Jan Huygen van. *Itinerario.* Vol. 3. Ed. C. P. Burger and F. W. T. Hunger. The Hague: Nijhoff, 1934. Werken van de Linschoten Vereniging 39.

——. *Itinerario: Viagem ou Navegação as Índias Orientais ou Portuguesas.* Trans. and introduced by Arie Pos. Lisbon: Commissão Nacional para as Comemorações dos Descobrimentos Portugueses, 1997.

——. *Itinerario: Voyage ofte schipvaert naer Oost ofte Portugaels Indien, 1579–1592.* 3 vols. Reprint of 1910–39 edition. Rev. and ed. H. Terpstra. The Hague: Nijhoff, 1955–57. Werken Linschoten-Vereeniging 57, 58, 60.

——. *The Voyage of Jan Huygen van Linschoten to the East.* 2 vols. Reprint of 1598 edition. Ed. Arthur Coke Burnell and Pieter Anton Tiele. London: Hakluyt Society, 1885. Hakluyt Society, first series vols. 70 and 71.

——. *Voyagie ofte Schipvaert van by Noorden om langs Noorwegen . . . tot voorby de revier Oby.* Franeker: Gerard Ketel, 1601.

Luijten, Ger, Ariane van Suchtelen, Reinier Baarsen, Wouter Kloek, and Marijn Schapelhouman, eds. *Dawn of the Golden Age: Northern Netherlandish Art, 1580–1620.* Exh. cat. Amsterdam: Rijksmuseum; Zwolle: Waanders, 1993.

Maczak, Antoni. *De ontdekking van het reizen: Europa in de vroeg-moderne tijd.* Utrecht: Het Spectrum, 1998.

Mander, Karel van. *Den grondt der edel vrij schilder-const: Uitgegeven door Hessel Miedema.* 2 vols. Utrecht: Haentjens Dekker & Gumbert, 1972.

——. *The Lives of the Illustrious Netherlandish and German Painters.* 6 vols. Ed. Hessel Miedema. Doornspijk: DAVACO, 1994–99.

Mare, Heidi de. 'De verbeelding onder vuur: Het realisme-debat der Nederlandse kunsthistorici'. *Theoretische Geschiedenis* 24 (1997): 113–37.

Matos, Luís de, ed. *Imagens do Oriente no século XVI: Reprodução do codice português da Bibliotheca Casanatense.* Lisbon: Impr. Nacional-Casa da Moeda, 1985.

Meer, Theo van der. *Sodoms zaad in Nederland: Het ontstaan van homoseksualiteit in de vroegmoderne tijd.* Nijmegen: SUN, 1995.

Menkman, W. R. *De geschiedenis van de West-Indische Compagnie.* Amsterdam: P. N. van Kampen, 1947.

Miedema, Hessel. *Kunst, kunstenaar en kunstwerk bij Karel van Mander: Een analyse van zijn levensbeschrijvingen.* Alphen aan den Rijn: Canaletto, 1981.

——. 'Het stadsklavecimbel van Amsterdam'. *Bulletin van het Rijksmuseum* 48 (2000): 259–79. Amsterdam.

Mitter, Partha. *Much Maligned Monsters: History of European Reactions to Indian Art.* Oxford: Clarendon Press, 1977.

Monter, E. William. *Frontiers of Heresy: The Spanish Inquisition from the Basque Lands to Sicily.* Cambridge: Cambridge University Press, 1990.

Morgan, Jennifer L. ' "Some Could Suckle over Their Shoulder": Male Travelers, Female Bodies, and the Gendering of Racial Ideology, 1500–1770'. *William and Mary Quarterly* 54 (1997): 167–92.

Mott, Luiz. 'Justitia et misericordia: A Inquisição portuguesa e a repressão ao nefando pecado de sodomia'. In *Inquisição: Ensaios sobre mentalidade, heresias e arte,* ed. Anita Novinsky and Maria Luiza Tucci Carneiro, 703–38. Rio de Janeiro: Expressão e Cultura; São Paulo: Edusp, 1992.

Münkler, Herfried, ed. *Furcht und Faszination: Facetten der Fremdheit.* Berlin: Akademie Verlag, 1997.

——. *Die Herausfordrung durch das Fremde.* Berlin: Akademie Verlag, 1998.

Nalis, Henk J. 'Baptista van Doetecum (overleden 1611), kaartmaker en graveur'. In *Overijsselse biografieën: Levensbeschrijvingen van bekende en onbekende Overijsselaars,* vol. 3, 21–25. Meppel: Boom, 1993.

——. 'Joannes van Doetecum (overleden 1605)'. In *Overijsselse biografieën: Levensbeschrijvingen van bekende en onbekende Overijsselaars,* vol. 1, 53–56. Meppel: Boom, 1990.

——. *The Van Doetecum family.* 4 vols. Rotterdam: Sound and Vision Interactive, 1998. The New Hollstein: Dutch and Flemish Etchings, Engravings and Woodcuts, 1450–1700.

Neuber, Wolfgang. *Fremde Welt im europäischen Horizont: Zur Topik der deutschen Amerika-Reiseberichte der Frühen Neuzeit.* Berlin: Erich Schmidt, 1991.

——. 'Imago und Pictura: Zur Topik des Sinn-Bilds im Spannungsfeld von Ars Memorativa und Emblematik (am Paradigma des "Indianers")'. In *Text und Bild, Bild und Text: DFG-Symposion 1988,* ed. Wolfgang Harms, 245–61. Stuttgart: J. B. Metzler, 1990.

Noordam, D. J. 'Homoseksuelen en sodomieten in Nederland: Verbranden of tolereren?'. In *Stigmatisering en strafrecht: De juridische positie van minderheden in historisch perspectief,* ed. J. W. ter Avest and H. Roozenbeek, 87–93. Leiden: Stichting Leidschrift, 1990.

——. *Riskante relaties: Vijf eeuwen homoseksualiteit in Nederland, 1233–1733.* Hilversum: Verloren, 1995.

Oltremare: Codice Casanatense 1889: Con il Libro dell'Oriente di Duarte Barbosa. Milan: Ricci, 1984.

Orenstein, Nadine, Huigen Leeflang, Ger Luijten, and Christiaan Schuckman. 'Print Publishers in the Netherlands 1580–1620'. In *Dawn of the Golden Age: Northern Netherlandish Art, 1580–1620,* ed. G. Luijten et al., 167–200. Amsterdam: Rijksmuseum; Zwolle: Waanders, 1993.

Pagden, Anthony. *The Fall of Natural Man: The American Indian and the Origins of Comparative Ethnology.* Cambridge: Cambridge University Press, 1982.

Parr, Charles McKew. *Jan van Linschoten: The Dutch Marco Polo.* New York: Crowell, 1964.

Parshall, Peter. 'Imago contrafacta: Images and Facts in the Northern Renaissance'. *Art History* 16 (1993): 554–79.

Pearson, Karen S. 'The Multimedia Approach to Landscape in German Renaissance Geography Books'. In *The Early Illustrated Book: Essays in Honor of Lessing J. Rosenwald,* ed. S. Hindman, 117–35. Washington, D.C.: Library of Congress, 1982.

Pisters, Ine, ed. *America: Bruid van de zon: 500 jaar Latijns-Amerika en de Lage Landen.* Antwerp: Koninklijk Museum voor Schone Kunsten, 1991.

Quetsch, Cäcilie. *Entdeckung der Welt in der deutschen Graphik der beginnenden Neuzeit.* Diss., Friedrich-Alexander-Universität, Erlangen-Nuremberg, 1983.

Randles, W. G. L. *L'image du Sud-est Africain dans la littérature européenne au XVIe siècle.* Lisbon: Centro de Estudos Historicos Ultramarinos, 1959.

Raupp, H.-J., ed. *Wort und Bild: Buchkunst und Druckgraphik in den Niederlanden im 16. und 17. Jahrhundert.* Cologne: Belgisches Haus, 1981.

Reid, Anthony. *Southeast Asia in the Age of Commerce, 1450–1680.* Vol. 1. New Haven: Yale University Press, 1988.

Riggs, Timothy A. *Hieronymus Cock, Printmaker and Publisher.* New York: Garland, 1977.

Rubiés, Joan-Pau. 'Instructions for Travellers: Teaching the Eye to See'. *History and Anthropology* 9 (1996): 139–90.

———. 'New Worlds and Renaissance Ethnology'. *History and Anthropology* 6 (1993): 157–97.

Sá, Isabel dos Guimarães. *Quando o rico se faz pobre: Misericórdias, caridade e poder no império português, 1500–1800.* Lisbon: Comissão Nacional para as Comemorações dos Descobrimentos Portugueses, 1997.

Scammell, G. V. 'England, Portugal, and the Estado da India, c. 1500–1635'. In *Actas, II Seminário Internacional de História Portuguesa,* 443–85. Lisbon: Instituto de Investigação Cientifica Tropical, 1985.

Schenk, J. 'Homoseksualiteit in de Nederlandse beeldende kunst voor 1800'. *Spieghel Historiael* 17 (1982): 576–83.

Schilder, Günter. *Monumenta Cartographica Neerlandica.* 6 vols. Alphen aan den Rijn: Canaletto, 1986–96.

Schmidt, Benjamin. ' "O Fortunate Land!": Karel van Mander, a West Indian Landscape, and the Dutch Discovery of America'. *Nieuwe West-Indische Gids* 69 (1995): 5–44.

Schulz, Jürgen. 'Maps as Metaphors: Mural Map Cycles of the Italian Renaissance'. In *Art and Cartography: Six Historical Essays,* ed. D. Woodward, 97–122. Chicago: University of Chicago Press, 1987.

Schütte S.J., Josef Franz. *Valignanos Missionsgrundsätze für Japan.* Vol. 1. Rome: Edizioni di storia e letteratura, 1951.

Selm, Bert van. *Een 'menighte treffelijcke boecken': Nederlandse boekhandelscatalogi in het begin van de zeventiende eeuw.* Utrecht: HES, 1987.

Silveira, Francisco Rodrigues. *Reformação da milícia e governo do estado da Índia Oriental.* Ed. B. N. Teensma. Lisbon: Fundação Oriente, 1996.

Spierenburg, Pieter. 'Homoseksualiteit in preïndustrieel Nederland: Twintig jaar onderzoek'. *Tijdschrift voor Geschiedenis* 109 (1996): 485–93.

Spies, Marijke. 'Betaald werk? Poëzie als ambacht in de zeventiende eeuw'. *Holland* 23 (1991): 210–24.

Stagl, Justin. 'Die Apodemik oder "Reisekunst" als Methodik der Sozialforschung vom Humanismus bis zur Aufklärung'. In *Statistik und Staatsbeschreibung in der Neuzeit, vornehmlich im 16.–18. Jahrhundert,* ed. Mohammed Rassem and Justin Stagl, 131–205. Paderborn: Schöningh, 1980.

———. *A History of Curiosity: The Theory of Travel 1550–1800.* Chur, Switzerland: Harwood, 1995.

Sternweiler, Andreas. *Die Lust der Götter: Homosexualität in der italienischen Kunst von Donatello zu Caravaggio.* Berlin: Verlag Rosa Winkel, 1993.

Swan, Claudia. 'Ad Vivum, naer het leven, From the Life: Defining a Mode of Representation'. *Word & Image* 11 (1995): 353–72.

Teensma, Benjamin N. 'Literaire, filologische en moralistische bespiegelingen over de Siamese penisbel'. *Bijdragen tot de Taal-, Land- en Volkenkunde* 147 (1991): 128–39.

Tracy, James D., ed. *True Ocean Found: Paludanus's Letters on Dutch Voyages to the Kara Sea, 1595–1596.* Minneapolis: University of Minnesota Press, 1980.

Vainfas, Ronaldo. *Trópico dos pecados: Moral, sexualidade e Inquisição no Brasil.* Rio de Janeiro: Editora Campus, 1989.

Vekeman, Herman, and Justus Müller Hofstede, eds. *Wort und Bild in der niederländischen Kunst und Literatur des 16. Und 17. Jahrhunderts.* Erftstadt: Lukassen, 1984.

Veldman, Ilja M. *Leerrijke reeksen van Maarten van Heemskerck.* Exh. cat., Frans Halsmuseum, Haarlem. The Hague: Staatsuitgeverij; Haarlem: Frans Halsmuseum, 1986.

———. *De wereld tussen goed en kwaad: Late prenten van Coornhert.* The Hague: SDU, 1990.

Verkruijsse, P. J. 'Holland "gededigeerd": Boekopdrachten in Holland in de 17ᵉ eeuw'. *Holland* 23 (1991): 225–42.

Vivanti, C. 'Alle origini dell'idea di civiltá: Le scoperte geografiche e gli scritti di Henri de la Popelinière'. *Rivista Storica Italiana* 84 (1962): 225–49.

Warncke, Carsten-Peter. *Sprechende Bilder, sichtbare Worte: Das Bildverständnis in der frühen Neuzeit.* Wiesbaden: Harrassowitz, 1987. Wolfenbüttler Forschungen, vol. 33.

Wicki, Josef, ed. *Documenta Indica,* vol. 13, 1583–85. Rome: Institutum Historicum Societatis Iesu, 1975.

Winius, George D. *The Black Legend of Portuguese India: Diogo do Couto, His Contemporaries, and the Soldado Prático: A Contribution to the Study of Political Corruption in the Empires of Early Modern Europe.* New Delhi: Concept, 1985.

Zacharasiewicz, Waldemar. *Die Klimatheorie in der englischen Literatur und Literaturkritik von der Mitte des 16. bis zum frühen 18. Jahrhundert.* Vienna: Braumüller, 1977.

Zandvliet, Kees, ed. *Maurits, Prins van Oranje.* Exh. cat. Amsterdam: Rijksmuseum, 2000.

Zhou Xun and Gao Chumming. *Le costume chinois.* Fribourg: Office du Livre; Paris: Vilo, 1985.

The Plates

Images of the dress and customs of the Indians and of the Portuguese who live in India, of the
sanctuaries, houses, trees, fruits, herbs, spices. Furthermore their religious practises, polity, and family life.
Description of trade, how and where it is carried out. Various noteworthy events, summarised
in a brief account and compiled by Jan Huygen van Linschoten.
Amsterdam, by Cornelis Claesz, 1604

The title page is reproduced from the copy in the Atlas van Stolk, Rotterdam. Plate 2 is reproduced from that in the Herzog August Bibliothek, Wolfenbüttel. The other plates are reproduced from the set in the Universiteitsbibliotheek, Amsterdam. The captions are translations of the short texts in Dutch that appear, together with the Latin poems by Petrus Hoogerbeets, on the plates themselves, and of longer descriptive passages drawn from the Latin text of the *Icones*. The Latin texts were first translated into Dutch by C. L. Heesakkers. His Dutch version was translated into English by Peter Mason.

ICONES,

HABITVS GESTVSQVE
INDORVM AC LVSITANORVM PER
INDIAM VIVENTIVM, TEMPLORVM, AEDI-
VM, ARBORVM FRVCTVVM, HERBARVM,
AROMATVM,

MORES ITEM GEN-
tium circa facrificia, Politiam ac rem familiarem, Enarratio Mercaturæ quomodo & ubi ea exerceatur. Memorabilia gefta varia breui defcrip-
tione comprehenfa, & à Ioanne Hugone Linfchotano congefta.

Amftelredami apud Cornelium Nicolai.　1604.

Inhabitants of Malacca, who outstrip all other Indians in language, fine manners, and amorosity.
An islander from Java, an obstinate and stubborn people.

Malacca is inhabited by Portuguese and natives. The Portuguese have a fortress there like the one in Hormuz. It has a bishop, but he is subordinate to the archbishop of Goa. It flourishes thanks to an enormous body of merchants. The air is unhealthy, which is why there are few Portuguese settlements. But when desire for wealth is the driving force, fear of evil, even evil itself, is no deterrent. Thus despite a certain deterioration in their health, through their incessant activity of buying and selling, a very large number of merchants from every part of the East have made Malacca immensely splendid. The situation of the place is exceptionally suitable and comfortable for trade. In the past resources were small and it was the home of seven or eight fishermen, a small hamlet, but in a relatively short period its population has grown, it has acquired the form of a city, and its inhabitants have striven for specific qualities and created a language different from that of the other peoples. That language, called Malay, grew in prestige and influence with the city itself and is spoken by almost all Indians, like French among us, and without the assistance of that language a person is hardly of any account. The people themselves are educated, friendly, and civilised, and are more affable than any other people of the East. The women have just as large an innate interest for music and rhetoric as the men and a confidence of achieving more in those fields than other peoples. They all equally value the combination of music and song. So has nature endowed them with the beauty of talent.

The natives of the island of East Java have a stubborn and harsh character. They are yellow in colour like the Malaccans, not unlike the peoples of Brazil, but they have robust and sturdy hips, chubby faces, broad and prominent cheekbones, large eyebrows, small eyes, and a thin beard, and their hair is not thick either, though it is black. In general they trade with the Malaccans and in exchange for spices they receive linen that has been prepared in all kinds of ways. It would be easy to begin trading with them, for they have no fear of the Portuguese, who do not sail to Java, while the Javanese themselves regularly visit Malacca.

PLATE I

Malayos *Yauvas*

Ioann: à Doet: fec:

Malachę incolę sermone et moribus quam reliqui Indi
cultioribus et magis comes.

Inwoonders van Mallacka welcke alle andere Indianen in
taele courtosije ēn amoreusheÿt te boven gaen.

Insulanus e Iava gens durę cervicis.

Een eÿlander awt Iava welcks volck is hart:
neckich ēn opstinaet.

24 en 25

Malacca à Lusitanis & indigenis habitatur. Arx ibi Lusitanis est, ut Ormutij. Episcopum
habet, sed Goënsis Archiepiscopi suffraganeum & celeberrima negotiatorum frequentia floret. Aere laborat malesano, ideo paucorum illic Lusitanorum sedes. Verum cupiditate divitiarum impellēte, neque timor mali alicujus, imo nec ipsum malum deterret; ita Malaccæ summus ex omnibus Orientis partibus numerus mercatorum, assiduo studio emptionum ac venditionum, non obstante certo valetudinis detrimento, ingentem splendorem addidit. Et est loci situs aptissimus ac ad negotiationem commodissimus. Parvæ ante erant opes; habitaculum septem aut octo Piscatorum, exiguus tum Vicus, sed nō ita pridem, aucti incolæ, erecta civitatis forma, & ambivere singulares notas, composito sermone à cæteris gentibus diverso. Is sermo Malayo dictus, cum ipsa urbe honorem ac incrementum suscepit, inde omnibus fere Indis in ore est, ut nobis Gallicus ; & sine hujus linguæ præsidio, vix quis in aliquo

numero sit. Ipse populus cultus, comis & ad civilitatem compositus, omnes Orictis nationes affabilitate superat. Mulieribus juxta ac viris Musicæ ac Rhetorices natiuum studium, & quædam præstandi ante cæteras gentes fiducia. Rhytmi ac Cantiones omnibus promiscuè cordi sunt; ita natura illos amænitate ingenij imbuit.

Iavæ Orientis Insulæ habent indigenas pertinacis ac crudelis animi, colore fusco, qui & Malaccensium, Brasiliæ populis non absimiles, sed robustis & validis lateribus, facie plena, genis extantibus & latis, palpebris magnis, oculis minutis, rara barba, neque crine denso, sed nigro. Negotiantur fere cum Malaccæ incolis, & in vicem Aromatum Linteamina diverfimode laborata accipiunt. Facile cum ijs incunda esset mercaturæ ratio, nam ibi nullus metus à Lusitanis, qui Iavam non proficiscuntur, cum & ipsi Iavenses Malaccam sere frequentent.

Dress of the people of China, a kingdom overflowing with all beauty and sumptuousness.

The Kingdom of China contains much that is well worthy of mention. This is especially true of the people's friendliness and excellence in all the arts and social graces. This print illustrates the clothing and robes of the Chinese. Very often the clothes of the highest-ranking are made of silk and distinguished by their colours. The commoners use cotton clothing to cover their bodies. They cannot manufacture woollen or velvet fabrics even though the material is abundantly available. That is why they are surprised at these products among the Portuguese. The women dress in exquisite clothing, in long broad robes, with many gold ornaments decorating their hair and other parts of their body. Their hands are covered, they seldom go out of doors, and they usually live in seclusion. Slender, small feet are regarded by them as particularly attractive. To that end they are swaddled and bound from early childhood to prevent them from growing at all. The women thus often stumble and walk with difficulty, their feet being misshapen and unsuitable because of the binding. That elegance is primarily required by their menfolk. Because of their tendency to jealousy and their suspicion of female wantonness, provoked by their own lust and pleasure, they declared this to be attractive, so there results a greater need for women to stay at home, because their walking is hindered, as if it were prohibited. Persons of distinction are borne on chairs and litters, which are covered with curtains of silk embroidered with silver thread and have small grids through which the occupants see everything without being seen themselves.

The natives themselves have a by no means inelegant figure. They are generally fat and corpulent, with a round and broad face and small eyes, thick eyelids and prominent eyebrows, a flat nose, and a thin beard with seven or eight hairs above and below the mouth; but on their chin they have very black hairs, which they do not shave but tend, clean, and nourish with great care.

Those who live near Macao and Canton, toward the coast, are dark, like the Moors in Barbary and some of the Spaniards. Those in the central region, however, closely resemble the Germans and Dutch in colour. China also has blacks with a thick beard and staring eyes. They are not really Chinese, though, but are descended from the Tartars, who engaged in intensive trade with the Chinese in the past. They let their left nails grow long but trim the right nails. This is required by their traditional religion. The character of the people can easily be seen in their very salutary ability to rule in peace and wartime, their excellent morals, and their exceptional proficiency in all kinds of handiwork. As this is all related in the accounts of numerous historians, and there is no ground to suspect falsehood, there is hardly any reason to doubt that such a level of civility exists among those whom we call barbarians.

PLATE 2

H. Linschoten

Ioa: a Doe: fe:

Habitus e China regno pretiosę elegantię et rerum omnium affluentissimum

Cleedinge van die wt China een Coninckryck overvloedich van alle schoonheyt ēn costelickheyt

32 en 33

IN Regno Chinēsi multa sunt memoratu dignissima, praecipua autem incolarum Comitas est & in omni arte ac amaenitate excellens ingenium. Hæc tabula monstrat habitum ac vestimenta Chinensium. Et plurimum sunt ex bysso coloribus diviso apud illos, qui dignitate præstant. Cæteri ex plebe Vestibus gossypinis utuntur ad tegumenta Corporis. Pannum ex Lana; aut etiam holosericum conficere non norunt, etsi abunde sit materia, ideo hic apparatus in Lusitanis admirationi illis est. Mulieres incedunt egregio vestitu, latis ac longis togis, crinibus cæterisque corporis partibus multo auro squallentibus. Manus tectas habent, raro in publicum prodeunt, clausæ plurimum. Inprimis ornamentum illis est pes gracilis, ac minutus; ideo jam à teneris unguiculis ita stringunt ac comprimunt pedem, ut omne maius incrementum prohibeant. Sic difficili gressu mulieres passim claudicant, informi & inepto ob adhibita vincula pede. Ea nimirum elegantia à Maritis primum orta est. Nam ipsi Zelotypiæ adfectu & Luxuriæ ac Libidinis stimulis in suspicionem fœmineæ levitatis adducti, hoc ornamenti loco posuerunt, ut ita mulieribus impedito & velut interdicto gressu, major mansionis necessitas sit. Qui nobiliores sunt Cathedris & sedilibus gestantur: Ex velamentis ex bysso argenti filo inducto tectæ sunt, admissis fenestris Cancellatis, quarum beneficio se-

dens omnia conspicit, à nemine ipse visus.

Ipsi incolæ corporis forma haud illaudata, pingues ferè & distenti sunt; rotunda lataque facie, oculis minutis, palpebris grandibus, supercilio provecto, naso plano, barbâ rarâ, septem aut octo crinibus supra ac infra os extantibus; à mento autem nigerrimi crines, quos nec radunt, sed magna cura tractant, purgant & nutriunt.

Qui circa Machau & Canton habitât, ad maris Littus fusci sunt, ut in Barbaria Mauri, & partim Hispani: Qui autem Mediterranea habitant, colore Germanis, aut Belgis haud absimiles sunt; habet China & nigros quosdam, densâ barbâ, ac oculis patentibus. Verum Chinenses ij proprie non sunt, sed à Tartaris Orti, quibus olim magnum cum Chinensibus commercium fuit. Vngues lævæ lōgiores nutriunt, dextræ abscissos; ita dictabat illis Religio antiqua. Cæterum populi ingenium ex saluberrimis ibi regnandi in pace & bello artibus, ex imsijs moribus & in omni artificio insigni præstātia facile cognosci potest; quæ tamen multorum Historicorum celebrata testimonijs, ademtâ omni suspicione mendacij, vix adhuc dubitandi causas tollût, Si inter eos, quos Barbaros appellamus, tanta humanitas exiltat.

How the mandarins of China, who are the principal authorities of government,
are carried and delight in cruising on the rivers.

Among the Chinese there is no one who claims an area of authority as a private ruler, no count, no baron, no duke. The king does grant land to some people, but it is not inherited. Upon the death of the recipient it reverts to the king, who can retain it but usually leaves it to the children, at least if they are suitable, with a renewal of the oath of allegiance. In every provincial capital there is a statue of the king, covered with a veil of cloth woven with gold, which is venerated by the king's servants; the Loitias and the mandarins pay it the highest respects too, as if the king were present. The king's servants, dignitaries who hold honorary positions, are selected not from the wealthier and higher aristocracy but from the most highly educated, and are experienced in all the sciences. They are appointed to the most prestigious positions and enjoy the greatest respect from the people. They live in luxury and cheerfulness. They are gods on earth. These notables are called Loitias and mandarins. Because of their status they are carried in chairs and litters, covered with a veil of silk and cloth woven with gold. They are prone to pleasure and luxury and are self-indulgent, which is a quality of all Chinese. None of these dignitaries is a governor in his own region; no one occupies honorary offices in his place of birth. The king decided this to prevent the magistrate in legal cases from being corrupted by kin or family ties.

Every place in China is filled with books and historical works. They are fond of the laws and political science, and in this respect they are like the ancient Greeks and Romans. They affably greet guests and passersby; in general they touch their breast with their left hand clasped in their right hand in humble veneration, as a sign that their heart is filled with love. The mandarins, however, close both hands and fold their arms, which form, as it were, a circle. Standing thus with their heads bowed, and moving their whole bodies, they make friendly competition to grant each other honourable precedence.

No one in China goes about armed or has a weapon at home without the king's permission, which he grants to the soldiers and to their children who also have military dignity.

The Chinese are idolaters, without adulteration by the Mohammedan sect. They worship the devil so that he will do them no harm, make sacrifices to the sun and moon as man and wife, and believe in the immortality of the soul and in rewards for good and evil after death.

There are many universities throughout this kingdom where the laws of the kingdom and the principles of philosophy are taught. So for students in the sciences the road to prestigious reward—honorary positions and administrative functions—lies open.

PLATE 3

Lectuli, et ratio, quibus Chinę proceres primarij (Mandorinos vocant) gestantur, cymbęq̃, quibus ad oblectationem per fluvios vehuntur.

Maniere als haer die Mandoryns van China welcke het princepael gover: nement hebben laten draegen en op die revieren vermeyen vaeren.

32 en 33

APud Chinenses nullus est, qui privato Dominatù aliquod Imperium usurpet, non Cõmes, non Baro, non Dux.Rex tamen quibusdam feudum aliquod indulget,quod hereditariũ non est, sed post mortem beneficiati ad Regem transit,qui illud retinere potest,liberis tamen fere relinquit,si modo idonei sunt, renovato fidelitatis Iuramèto.Imago regis in Metropolitana Vrbe cujusq̃; Provinciæ, velo ex attalico panno tecta, à Regijs ministris colitur; nam & Loitiæ & Mandorini summo illam honore venerantur; ut præsente Rege.Ministri autè Regis, qui dignitates ac honores gerunt, nõ ex opulentioribus aut nobilioribus eligũtur, sed ex doctissimis,ac in omni scientia peritissimis. Hi ad illustria munera vocãtur,& in maxima veneratione apud populum sunt; Vivunt lautè ac hilariter. Dij in terris. Hos optimates,Loitias ac Mandorinos vocant, qui honoris causa in sellis ac cathedris gestantur, velo ex serico & Attalico panno tecti. Proclives sunt in de-litias & Luxum,indulgentes genio;quod & omnibus Chinensibus commune est. Ex his proceribus nemo patriæ præficitur,nemo in natali terra honores gerit,Ita Regi visum ne respectus aut adfinitatis; aut cogna-tionis,Iudicem in audiendis causis pervertat,Plena in China omnia libris & Historicis sunt. Leges ac poli-ticam disciplinam amant, veteribus Romanis & Gręcis, haud absimiles. Comiter salutant hospites & ob-vios,vulgò,sinistra manu clausa,quam dextra tegit,pectus tangunt submissa veneratione, amore toto corde conceptum demonstrantes. At Mandorini utranque manum claudunt,flexis ad modum circuli brachijs.Ita stantes capite submisso, totaque corporis commotione magno comitatis certamine pugnant de transitu, quem alter alteri honoris causa gestit concedere.

In China nemo armatus incedit,aut telum domi habet, nisi Regis permissu, qui id militibus indulget, etiam Liberis eorum, quos etiam militaris dignitas sequitur.

Idololatræ sunt Chinenses,sine Mahometicæ sectæ admixtione,Diabolum colũt ne noceat.Soli & Lunæ, velut conjugibus sacrificant. Immortalitatem animarum tenent, & pretium boni malique operis post mortem.

Multæ passim in hoc Regno Academiæ extant, in quibus Leges Regni & Philosophiæ dogmata tradũ-tur,Ita studiosis disciplinarum,postea honestissimo præmio ad honores ac Magistratus iter est.

Vessels of China and Java, with reed sails and wooden anchors.

The Kingdom of China is watered here and there by numerous rivers. They make the most plenteous land fertile and provide the inhabitants with a good opportunity for trade. Almost all the villages and settlements are beside a river, to the great convenience of the residents, who fill the whole area in a wondrous way with countless ships and barges. To give an example: there are more ships or barks in the harbour and river of Canton than in the whole of Spain. However, they also use reed sails and wooden anchors, as this illustration shows. They pay attention to the de-tails with great skill so that absolutely nothing is overlooked. As they do everything with striking skilfullness, they also invented waggons with sails. They are shaped like ships with wheels, and with a favourable wind they can travel on open land as fast as Liburnian vessels on water. The art of printing was also in use among the Chinese before all times, as were the cannon and gunpowder, to our great surprise. What we claim to be specific to our world and a new showpiece of our age was already passé among them, and its origin goes back beyond human memory.

PLATE 4

Naves e China et Iava velis ex arundine
contextis et anchoris ligneis.

Schepen van China ēn Iava met rietten
ſeÿlen ēn houten anckers

32 en 33

Chinenſe Regnum multis paſſim irrigatur fluminibus: Illa & fœcunditatem, lætiſſimæ terræ, & incolis facilem mercandi facultatem permittunt. Adjacent omnia fere oppida ac vici, alicui fluvio, ſingulari commodo incolarum, qui navibus ac ſcaphis ſine numero omnia implent, ad miraculum. Et ut exemplum accipias. In portu & fluvio civitatis Cantō duntaxat, plures ſunt Naves ſive Barcæ, quam in univerſa Hiſpania. Vtuntur autem & velis ex arundine contextis & anchoris ligneis, ut præſens figura docet, magno ad ſingula ingenio attenti, ne quid ratibus deſit. Vt ſane inſigni omnia artificio agunt, ita & invenere currūs, velis ſuccinctos, navium forma, quibus rotæ ſunt & favente vento in patentibus campis faciles curſus, ut Liburnicis in pelago. Etiam Typographia ante omne tempus Chinenſibus in uſu fuit, bombardæ quoque & pulvis tormentarius, magno noſtro ſtupore. Ponimus enim velut ſingulare Orbis noſtri & ſæculi decus novum, quod jam apud illos obſoletum erat, & quoad originem extra omnium hominum memoriam.

A clear record of the market of Goa, with its shops, wares, and daily traders.

Do you see what a large area lies open on the market of Goa, spacious, with many houses, dazzling, rich in goods? How one hastens to sell merchandise glittering with precious gems and gold, another to sell his slaves from afar? Here you can see the produce of the Ganges and the Indus, and the largest islands in the Eastern sea. P. HOOGERBEETS

The city of Goa, capital of the whole of the East Indies, which enjoys the honour of being the residence of the archbishop and the viceroy of India, is very famous among the cities of the whole world that owe their prosperity to trade. An immense quantity of goods are displayed in a vast array as if on stage, and the unparalleled wealth of Arabia, Armenia, Persia, Cambaia, Bengal, Pegu, Siam, Malacca, Java, China, etc. is sold there according to a fixed and universal agreement. The laws of Portugal apply to the residents. The heathen, Moors, and Turks have religious freedom, but on the instructions of the archbishop they refrain from a shameful manner of marriage and burial. He ensures that nothing is done contrary to the law of nature. However, much goes on in secret religious services.

In the city of Goa there is a daily meeting of all kinds of people, a sort of exchange, as it is called. It is also open to the nobility. All the merchandise of India is traded there for money, but only in the morning, from seven to nine o'clock. Then it is very crowded on the market. After noon the heat of the sun prevents all trading.

The excellent site of this meeting is popularly called Leylon, that is, the place of announcement. For it is there that the heralds, who are appointed for this function by the city council, announce all kinds of merchandise. As they are making their announcements they go about decorated with precious gems, gold and silver jewellery, rings, and pearls, followed by a large crowd of men and women of various origins, destined to work as slaves and servants. Anyone can buy freely as he chooses. Thus through cruel fate humans are separated one from the other like cattle. Arabian horses are on sale here as well, and all kinds of medicinal herbs and perfumes, gently aromatic salves, unusually fashioned clothes from Phrygia, and other wondrous products from the Indian world, from Cambaia, Sunda, Bengal, China, etc., all as a result of the indescribable activity of buyers and sellers at fixed times, because their minds are remarkably attuned to the desire for profit.

The property of the dead is also sold on this spot in accordance with a common custom, including the goods of the viceroy, with the good intention of preventing the widow and orphans from being exposed to the injustice and malice of the creditors. This auction is held often because of the high mortality rate among the Portuguese. For many die prematurely because of the unhealthy air and the excesses of a dissolute life.

Portuguese married men and those who keep a family derive considerable profit from their slaves, because they are maintained at little cost. They each have ten, twenty, or even thirty servants who help their masters with their labour and with the money they earn for carrying and selling water (there is a great shortage of fresh water in the city) and make a profit for them. The female servants are very skilled at making confitures from Indian fruits and at needlework, which they bring to the market to sell. Their decorous appearance and blooming beauty beguile not only the well-intentioned buyer but also the generous lover. They also sell their bodies for profit, and these girls are sought not so much for their merchandise as for intercourse. This is, as it were, a regular profession. The payment is kept for the master, and the profit amassed by these slave girls serves to keep the family. There is also a large number of money changers in these markets. They adjust the rate of the Spanish and Indian currency at fixed times and make a considerable profit on the transaction. There are also those who earn a considerable sum from palms, for they are the most important product of this country that is sold for a profit. Planted fields are also rented out, like our estates, so that a single tree can earn a carolus guilder a day. One field comprises three to four hundred trees. The streets are organised separately by trade. In some streets you see gold everywhere, others display a great abundance of textiles, silk, cotton, fine linen, half silk, precious stones, and pearls. The Indian idolaters are especially cunning in buying and selling. There are also many middlemen among them who are most fluent in speech and adapt their eloquence to both parties. There is an infinite number of barbers in the city, who are prepared to do anything and take on the meanest work for a low wage. Many of the heathen are very well acquainted with medicine. They help not only the Indians but also the Christians, the archbishop, and the viceroy with more dedication than the Europeans.

The activity of the money changers in the city of Goa is absolutely essential, for without them no one dares to accept a coin for fear that it be counterfeit. They are exceptionally acute in recognition, very good at calculating, clear proof of their lively intelligence.

The Indians have the following tradition of pagan superstition. No one may alter his craft, and once a trade is in their family it stays. That is why the son of a carpenter is a carpenter, etc. They also marry with people from the same profession. It is their only way of identifying a family, so that if you ask from whom they are descended, they reply: from the family of goldsmiths, carpenters, fishers, etc.

Who can adequately describe the other riches and products in this city? It is as if it has been chosen as the seat of such great majesty because it surpasses the other areas that produce gold and gems in its incomparable wealth. Let antiquity no longer stand in awe of Corinth or Alexandria as the leading cities of the maritime powers, because it is bound to admit that it has been outstripped by the greatness of the wealth and the sublimity of the empire and brilliance of this city.

PLATE 5

O Leilao que se Faz cada dia pola menhã na Rua direita na Cidade de Goa Feito Polo natural por Ioan de Linschoten framengo.

Xaraffo
Wisselaer

Porteiro
Wtroeper

Pingues
Arbeiders

Ama
Voester

Sande Peert yder.

Goënsi se quanta foro viden area pandat
Plana frequens tectis splendida dives opum?

Vt mercem hic properet gemmis auroque nitentem
Ille abducta procul vendere mancipia?

Congesta huc videas Ganes quæ portat
Insulæ et Eoo maxime in Occano.

Urbs Goa, Metropolis totius Indiæ Orientalis, Archiepiscopi & Proregis Indiæ domicilio decorata, inter vniversi Orbis vrbes, mercaturæ subsidio florentes, clarissima est, ibi tantæ opes, velut ad spectaculum, amplissimo tractu exponuntur, & certo ac universali cōventiculo venduntur Arabiæ, Armeniæ, Persiæ, Cambaiæ, Bengalæ, Pegu, Sian, Malaccæ, Iavæ, Chinæ, &c. incomparabiles divitiæ. Incolæ Lusitaniæ legibus reguntur. Ethnicis, Mauris, Turcis, libera relligio est; à turpi tamen sepeliendi ac nubendi ritu abstinent, Archiepiscopi jussu. Is ne quid inhumanum contra naturæ Legem contingat providet, secretis tamen adhuc multa religionibus exercentur.

Quotidiana in vrbe Goa cōventio est omnium mortalium, & quasi quædam Bursæ ut vocant species, sed etiam nobilibus ad eam aditus est. Ibi omnia Indiæ mercimonia pretio distrahūtur; tantum antemeridiano tempore. A hora septima ad nonam, tum foro sua celebritas est, post meridiem solis calor omne cōmetcium prohibet.

Hujus conventionis potissimus Locus, vulgo Leylon nuncupatur, id est, Præconium. Ibi enim Præcones ad id munus à magistratu electi, omne genus mercium publicāt, qui hoc præconij tempore Gemmis auteis

argenteisque monilibus, annulis & margaritis cincti incedūnt, subsequēte insuper magna virorum ac mulierum caterua, ex omni gente ad servitutem & mancipium. Cuique ex his libera pro arbitrio emptio est, ita homines dira sorte ut pecora distrahuntur. Vænales etiam hic equi ex Arabia prostant, herbarum ad usus medecinæ ac Aromatum omnia genera, vnguenta suaviter olentia, Phrygiæ vestes singulari artificij, multaque alia Orbis Indici miracula, ex Cambaja, Sunda, Bengala, China, &c. indicibili vendentiū ementiúque statis temporibus industria, ad lucri cupiditatem mirifice incitatis mentibus.

Facultates etiam defunctorum hoc in loco venduntur communi post interitum more, quem etiam Proregis bona subirent; bono fine ne viduæ ac Orphani injuriæ ac mali gnati creditorum subijciantur. Sæpe hæc auctio bonorum habetur, ob mortes Lusitanorum crebriores. Nam aeris intemperie, & vitæ non compositæ excesibus multi cadunt ante diem.

Lusitani mariti, & qui familiam alunt ex mancipijs multum lucri consequuntur, parvis quippe aluntur sumptibus, & sunt singulis decem viginti ac triginta famuli, qui labore, & aquæ (est enim in urbe aquæ dulcioris potus magna inopia) portandæ ac vendendæ pretio heros adjuvant & quæstu adficiunt. Cæterum fa-

mulæ ex Indicis fructi tioni deserunt, ibi tur beralem amatorem at caufa, quam concubi hisce mācipijs corrad Illi Hispanicæ & Indi cuntur. Sunt & qui lucrum est, & locantu cipit, & sunt trecentæ sunt plateæ; sunt in qu sum, subsericum, Gen niosissimi sunt Indi I tranque partem accor

PLATE 5

A. Misericordia

Sande. Peert yder.

Joannes à Doetechum fecit.

'huc videas Ganes quę portat et Indus lç ét Eoo. maxime in Occano. Hoogerb.

Fori Goensis tabernarum mercium et mercatorum illud frequentantium aperta explicatio. per N.Linschoten

Claere opdoeninge vande merckt van Goa met haer winckelen waren en ·daegelickse Cooplwÿden. door I. H. V. Linschoten

44 en 45

t magna virorum ac mutmulę ex Indicis fructibus Hypotrimmata scitè conficiunt, ac laborata ex filo affabre, eaque ad forum vendia pro arbitrio emptio est, tioni deferunt, ibi tum eę regie compræ, & forma hilariore non tantum lubentem emptorem, sed etiam liostant, herbarum ad usus beralem amatorem aucupantur, Corpore enim quæstum faciunt, & expetuntur hę puellæ, non tam merciũ singularis artificij, mul-causa, quam concubitus; est hoc quasi proprium munus. Precium heris servatur, & sufficit lucrum quod ex li vendentiũ ementiũque hisce mācipijs corraditur, ad alendam familiam. Argetariorum quoque in hisce nundinis magna est copia.

Illi Hispanicæ & Indicæ pecuniæ valorem stato tempore captant, ex eaque reinsignem quæstum nancis1 more, quem etiam Pro-cuntur. Sunt & qui exceditibus Palmarum victitant, satis liberaliter, nam præcipuum illud hujus terræ rum subiciantur. Sæpe lucrum est, & locantur agri côsiti, ut apud nos villæ, ita aliquis ex una arbore singulis diebus carolinum acmperie, & vitę non com-cipit, & sunt trecentæ aliquadringentæ arbores in uno fundo. Cæterum officinis singulatim distributæ

sunt plateæ; sunt in quibus Aurum passim squallere videas, sunt quæ linteamina, sericum, Byssum, Carbar, parvis quippe aluntur sum, subsericum, Gemmas ac Margaritas, &c. longo apparatu ostentant, in his vendendis emendisque inget enim in urbe aquæ dul-niosissimi sunt Indi Idolclatræ. Inter hos etiam multi proxenetæ sunt, quibus egregia sermonis ars, & in u-1 adficiunt, Cæterum fa-tranque partem accommodata facundia. Infinitus autem est in urbe tonsorum numerus, ij ad omne offi-

cium parati, etiam minuto præmio vilia munera subeunt. Ex Ethnicis multi Medecinæ peritissimi, nõ tantum Indis sed etiam Christianis, Archiepiscopo ac Viceregi serviunt, majore fidelitate quam Europæi.

Argentariorum autem in urbe Goa necessarium summopere munus est, sine his enim nemo aliquod genus pecuniæ audet accipere, falsitatis suspicione & sunt in cognoscenda pecunia acutissimi, in rationibus subducendis certissimi, magno argumento parati ingenij.

Ethnicæ superstitionis Indis mos hic est. Nemo artificium suum mutare potest, & quod semel in familia fuit id persistit. Ideo parés faber & filium habet fabrum, sic deinceps. Matrimonia quoque ejusdem artificij homines inter se contrahunt, neque est aliud generis argumentum; ut si quæras qua sit stirpe ortus, respondeat ex genere Aurificum, fabrorum, Piscatorum, &c.

Divitiarum ac opum in hac urbe reliqua, quis pro dignitate enarret. Electa est hæc velut sedes tantæ majestatis, quæ auriferis ac gemmiferis Regionibus incomparabili quæstu præsit, Vt jam antiquitas Corinthũ aut Alexandriam velut ad maris Imperia urbes præcipuas jactare desistat, magnitudine opum, majestate Imperij & splendore urbis hujus certissima confessione devicta.

Indian huts, country houses and villages near Goa.

This illustration shows the country estates and houses of the Canarim. They live more or less on the outskirts of Goa, especially in the district that they call Bardes, which extends toward the northern part of the city and is known for its production of Indian palms. The viceroy, the archbishop, and the other clerics derive their incomes and food from these estates by renting them annually to the Canarim natives. They live in simple houses built near the coast and beside lakes and river banks, because the palms grow on sandy soil and near the coast but are not found further inland. The palms yield an enormous profit for the farmer and the master. That is why many inhabitants of Goa make a living from fields planted with palms, which are regarded as the richest source of income of the estates, with an inexhaustible profit. The palms are the special preserve of the Canarim, who make a living from this rustic and simple way of life as the lowest of mortals. They are sober in their eating and drinking. Banana leaves serve a variety of functions: table, serviette, plate. They drink from a cruse, holding it in the air and pouring the beer into their mouth without touching the vessel with their lips. They smear their houses with cow dung, a well-tried remedy against flies. They are clean, and both men and women wash their body with their left hand after answering the call of nature; they eat with the right hand. Nowadays they are mostly Christians and are acquainted with the higher arts.

PLATE 6

Indorum casæ, villæ, et vici
circa Goam.

Indische hutte Lanthuysen ēn dorpen
ontrent Goa.

44 en 45

HÆc imago Canarinorum villas & casas repræsentat. Hi fere circa Goam habitant, præcipue in terra quam Bardes vocant, ad Septentrionalem partem urbis porrecta, multo proventu palmarum Indicarum nobili. Ex hisce agris Vice-rex, Archiepiscopus, cæterique Ecclesiastici proventus suos ac alimenta habent, annua locatione in Canarinos indigenas, Hi circa Littus & Lacus ac ripas extructis humilibus casis habitant. Nam palma crescit in locis arenosis & Littoribus; interior terra has arbores non fert, & est mirificus ex ijs fructus Agricolæ ac Domino. Ideo multi incolæ urbis Goæ ex agris palmiferis, tanquam ex abundantissimo villarum reditu vivunt, inexhausta utilitate. Estque illa velut peculiaris cura Canarinorum, qui infimi mortalium, hoc vivendi rustico simplicique genere vitam sustentant. Comedunt ac bibunt parcè: folia Fici pro mensa, Mappa, Catino, omnigena utilitate serviunt. Poculum habent ex ære, ex eo cerevisiam desuper ori infundunt, neque labris admovent: Casas simo vaccarum inungunt, efficaci adversus pulices remedio. Mundi sunt & crebris lavationibus corpus post universos naturæ actus viri juxta ac fœminæ abluunt, quod læva quidem manu faciunt: nam dextra cibum capiunt. Christiani nunc ferè sunt & melioribus imbuti disciplinis.

Comportment and dress of the Portuguese citizens and soldiers in East India as they appear in the streets.

The Portuguese in the city of Goa can be divided into two categories. One comprises the married men and heads of households, the other the unmarried men, called soldiers or mercenaries in popular usage. That is a very highly esteemed title among them, though not so much because they serve under the military banner or are bound by oath to the standards, because that form of recruiting soldiers is not practised anywhere in India. When Portuguese sent from Spain arrive in India, they are free to go where they please, and there is no compulsion at all to stay in a particular place. However, they are registered on a list and this is sent to India every year. It includes the first and second names of the departing men and the level of their pay as determined by the king. They are all distinguished by their titles and rank. Some of them are called Fidalgo da caza del rey nosso Senhor, a very prestigious title, because they are nobility of the royal family. Others are called Mosos fidalgos, and they too are held in high esteem; they are sons of nobility or are elevated to that rank by the king. The Cavalheiros fidalgos, comparable to the golden knights, are also held in high esteem and delight in this title because of their prowess during an expedition. It is easy for the Portuguese to acquire this rank, because when there is a menace of war or when it is in full swing, this equestrian title is readily obtained from the commander or from a nobleman. It is so common that even cooks, camp followers, and water carriers, the lowest rank, are not turned down. In addition, there are others who are called Mosos da Camara, do Numero, and do Serviço. They are chamberlains of the king, members of the Number, and members of the Service, the first step toward honorary positions. This is a stepping-stone toward higher ranks, above all through rivalry dominated by the thirst for honour, for they consider these titles and empty names more important than the multiplication of their wealth.

The Escuderos fidalgos also have their own honour. The others on the list constitute the Homens honrados, the distinguished men. The designation of soldier is conferred on the lowest in rank, without the addition of a title. They are looked down upon and are recruited from the common people.

The benefit of this registration grows through protracted periods of service in war and peace, which are reported to the king in accordance with the title of the rank occupied and increased with yet higher positions of rank. For in Portugal remuneration is based on title. The list of the names of the Portuguese who leave for India is itself kept by an official appointed for that purpose by the king. Like all other civil servants, this position rotates every three years. Its occupant has three or four assistant clerks. He himself is called the scrivener general of the matricula.

A specific and authentic characteristic of the Portuguese is their love of splendour and their respectable dignity. The Portuguese commoners also compete with the monarch by being escorted by slaves and servants who protect them from the sun and the rain. Eight to ten soldiers live in one house. They eat together and have one or two servants to wash their linen and clothing. They eat cheap rice and are content to drink water. The eight to ten of them have only one silk robe, which they make available to the one who goes out. The others are content with a shirt and cotton trousers and spend the day indoors. For no one wears clothing indoors because of the heat. The greatest income of the soldiers is derived from the generosity of the women of the other Portuguese, and even of the Christians of India. For the women in this region, driven by an insatiable lasciviousness beyond all human needs, seek contact with foreigners, and are not deterred by any fear of the wrath of their husbands, which means certain death, or any sense of shame.

PLATE 7

H.linschoten

Ioann: a Doct: fec.

Gestus et habitus tam civium que militum Lusitanorum in
oriente agentium. cum publicum prodeunt.

Contenancijen en habyten der Portugeesers so burgers als
Soldaten in oost Indien als se op die straten comen.

46 en 7

IN Vrbe Gòa Lusitani in duo genera sunt distincti . Etenim unum mariti ac Patres familiarum constituunt, alterum cælibes;hos communi vocabulo Soldatos sine milites Stipendiarios appellant, & illud inter eos honestissimum nomen,non quod sub signis sint,aut ullo juramento ad vexilla constricti,nam in universa India is militum scribendorum modus non est in usu . Cæterum ubi in Indiâ Lusitani ex Hispania missi veniunt,liberū illis quo velint iter est, nullaque mansionis certe necessitate arctantur. Albo tamē ascripti sunt, & mittitur illud quotannis in Indiam;id eo modo conficitur, ut nomina ac agnomina proficiscentium cōtineat,& stipēdij à Rege statuti magnitudinē.Distincti autē sunt omnes titulis & prærogativa dignitatis,Ex his quidam Fidalgi da caza del Rey nossa Señor nuncupantur præstantissimo elogio , nam nobiles hi sunt regiæ domus; alios Mosos fidalgos vocant,& sunt sane & isti honorati,ac nobiliū filij, vel à Rege ad illud dignitatis genus provecti. Cauaileri fidalgi Equitum auratorū vice illustres quoque sunt, & gaudent hoc titulo ob natam in aliqua expeditione operâ.Hujus sane dignitatis apud Lusitanos parabilis modus est, instante enim bello,aut in ipso ardore belli,facile aliquis à Duce aut nobili quodam hāc equestrem prærogatiuam optinet, ita vulgariter; ut Coci,Lixæ; ac aquarij,vilissimi homines,haud repellantur,Sunt præter hos alij quos Mosos da Camara,do Numero & do Serviço appellant:Hi aut Cubicularij Regis, aut ex numero; aut ex ministerio habentur,primo ad honores gradu, nam ex hoc ad majora insignia conscendunt, ambitioso inprimis certamine,cum hos titulos & sumosa nomina,pluris quam augmentum multarum divitiarū æstiment, Escude-

ris fidalgis honor quoque suus est.Ceteri Homes otterados,id est,honorabiles viri;relicto humilibus Soldati nomine, sine alicujus tituli appendice,& sunt isti sane contemptiores; ac ex fæce populi.
Hujus autem in scriptiones fructus ex diuturnis in pace belloque officijs Regi exhibitis secundum dignitatis titulum crescit,ac majoribus honoribus paratur. Nam ex titulo in Lusitania præmiorum ratio constat. Album ipsum quo Lusitanorum in Indiam proficiscentium nomina notātur,apud destinatum huic muneri à Rege servatur , is ut cæteri omnes ministri, post tres annos mutatur; habet subsidiarios tres aut quatuor scribas. Ipse,scriba generalis matricolæ,indigitatur,
Peculiaris vero ac genuina Lusitanorum omnium magnificētia est, & quædam cōposita gravitas. Etiam ex plebe Lusitani, principem æmulantur,servis ac famulis comitātibus & umbellam adversus solis calorem ac pluviæ injuriam ferentibus.Ipsi Milites decem aut octo in una domo habitant, communi victu , ministro uno aut altero ad Linteamina ac vestimenta purganda. Vescuntur Oriza,tenui sumptu,aquæ potu contenti, Vnicum vestimentum ex serico octo isti decē mūc habent,id exeunti traditur ; Cæteri camisia & pannicularia bracca contenti, domi diem interim terunt: Ob calorem enim nemo vestibus domi utitur . Summum Lucrum militum est ex liberalitate conjugum cæterorum Lusitanorum ; aut etiam Indiæ Christianorum. Nam inexplebili libidine in hoc tractu mulieres, supra omnia humana congressum advenarum expetunt, ñ ullo metu ab irato marito,cum certa morte;aut alio pudore deterritæ.

How the Portuguese noblemen, governors, and councillors commonly ride through the streets.

The Portuguese, who hold the highest positions in the East Indies, maintain their families in a grand manner. They have ten or twenty slaves in well ordered services. They go about in dazzling clothing and accoutrements, and change their shirt every day for refreshment from the heat that is fierce in that region. They proceed calmly, never forgetting their good name, and there is no distinction between nobility and commoner: they all share the same arrogance, the same sense of self-importance, and the same conviction of their excellence. One of their servants carries an umbrella or parasol, another a raincoat, for protection against rain and sun; a third carries the sword so that it will not disturb their dignity. A servant brings a cushion of pure silk for his master before a meal and places it before him to kneel and perform the religious services.

They are very formal in their manner of greeting, with due observance of obligation aimed at the display of honour by both parties. Lack of courtesy on the part of someone who does not respond with the correct degree of respect is punished very severely. They summon their friends to punish the miscreant with death, and that crime, carried out with a good deal of ceremony, is very glorious. The streets are filled with equestrians, not just noblemen but also others, merchants and artisans, as long as they can afford a horse. They all have the same self-confidence. No one works with his hands. If they are craftsmen, they run their workshops with slaves and servants and spend their time idling on the street with a broad and proud gait. They visit their friends at home and enjoy life. During marriage ceremonies all the friends, neighbours, and relatives accompany the bride to church on horseback, to the accompaniment of loud trumpet and flute music. The ostentation is enormous, but the meal is sober. The guests are the best friends, who do not hinder the pleasure of the bride with the bridegroom for long. The friends also come on horseback when a child is baptised, striking in every respect as regards outer appearance, but sober in eating and consumption. All the same, they employ mercenaries with a measure of generosity, and the nobility have the greatest confidence in recruiting with gifts individuals who are devoted to them and prepared to engage in nocturnal expeditions and to avenge crimes. Most of the Portuguese have married native women. The children born of such a union are called half-bloods. They are yellow in complexion and through their ancestry and further propagation they come more and more to assume the colour of the people of Deccan.

PLATE 8

Hoc habitu, qui e Lusitanis Nobilitate aut dignitate clariores in India fere conspiciuntur per plateas obequitant.

Op dese maniere rijden gemeenlick over straeten die Portugeesche Edellieden Regierders en Raetsheeren.

46 en 47

LUsitani (quibus in Orientalis Indiæ partibus summa imperia sunt) magnificè familiã alũt. Decem ac viginti servos habent, compositis ministerijs. Nitidi in vestimentis ac cætero habitu, mutant singulis diebus camisias, ad mitigandos calores, qui in eo tractu vehementes sunt. Gressu incedunt tranquillo, magna cum existimationis ratione, neque aliquod inter nobilem aut ignobilem discrimen est. Par arrogantia, par æstimatio, simili præstantiæ opinione. Ex famulis unus umbellam fert, alter penulam, pluviæ aut solis causa, tertius ensem, ne & is gravitatis ordinem impediat. Ante prandium ex famulis quidam pulvinar ex holoserico fert, quod flectenti genua domino, ac intento Ecclesiasticis ministerijs substernat.

In salutationibus officiosissimi sunt, crebra veneratione in mutuum cultum intenti. Incivilitatem non resalutantis pari adoratione, extrema vindicta prosequuntur, còvocatis amicis ad unius miseri necem, & est illis tale facinus tanta gestum mole gloriosissimum Equites plateas obeunt, non tantũ nobiles, sed etiã cæteri, qui modo equum alere possunt mercatores

& artifices. Omnibus eadem est fiducia. Artificium aliquod nemo exercet, si qui sint artifices, ij officinam per servos ac famulos habent, ipsi ociosi plateas, spacioso & superbo gressu invadunt, amicorum habitacula visentes & genio indulgentes. In solemnitatibus Nuptiarũ, amici omnes, vicini ac cognati, equites sponsam ad templum deducunt, magno sonitu tubarum ac tibiarum Apparatus, ingens est, frugale tamen convivium, ad quod eximij amicorum invitati, Sponsæ cum Sponso voluptatem non diu remorantur. Etiam quando infans unda baptismi abluitur, amici equites conveniunt, in omnibus rebus exteriore magnificentia celebres, cæterum in victu ac sumptibus sobrij. Liberalitate tamen quadã stipendiarios in officio continét, & est illa nobilium maxima fiducia, parare muneribus quosdam, velut devotos, ac paratos in nocturnas expeditiones, & injuriæ vindictam. Plurimi Lusitanorũ cum indigenis mulieribus contraxere matrimonium, vocanturque liberi ex hujusmodi Connubio nati Mixti, qui colore flavo sunt, & ductu stirpis ac longiore generatione in formã & coloré Decaninorũ abscedũt.

How the wealthy Portuguese of high birth are carried.

This illustration shows the form of the palanquin or litter. The Portuguese use them when they do not feel like riding or walking, especially the most prominent ones, the ones whom the king has promoted to new dignities after years of service. The motivations for these promotions are provided by the witnesses of the viceroy and the captain general, by which the excellence and uprightness of the recipients—without exception important persons—are guaranteed. After receiving this rank they undertake the tedious and dangerous journey to Spain, pay a visit to the king, show that their loyalty and excellence are backed up by documents, and request a reward, including in the request mention of the function which they have already chosen as appropriate. All positions of rank in India are filled for a period of three years. The person who requests a position must fulfil it himself, unless special permission is granted to use the income from such a function for selling or for giving a daughter in marriage. In such a case a record is kept in the king's chancery and registered on a list pending ratification by the viceroy of India. Sometimes there are many candidates for one position and their names are registered on a roll. The order is adjusted when a position becomes vacant as a result of the decease or departure of the previous incumbent.

As in Portugal, the law is enforced throughout India from Goa by consuls and councillors. The sitting is presided over by the viceroy, but certain appeals are referred to the tribunal of Portugal. Who could describe the splendour of the viceroy in words? He rarely appears in public. On holidays, however, he goes to church accompanied by a very large retinue of noblemen and servants to extremely loud trumpet and flute music. He is entrusted with authority for three years. The kings of Portugal did not want a longer period in office. Is that a salutary or a detrimental policy? At any rate, a governor who expects a successor after such a short period is less concerned about the state. That is why many matters which concern the interests of the king or the well-being of the inhabitants are neglected, because the viceroy is only interested in his own profit.

PLATE 9

Hac forma Lusitanorum nobiliores et qui opulen⸱
tiores se gestari jubent⸺

Op dese maniere laeten haer die Portugeesen draegen
die van affcomtste en vermoegen zyn.

46 en 47

PRæsens figura Pallanquinorum, sive gestatoriarum sellarum formam demonstrat. Iis Lusitani utuntur, ablubescente equitatus aut ambulationis voluptate. Imprimis nobiliores. Hi sunt, quos Rex post longa ministeria ad novas dignitates evexit; Faciunt autem fidem testimonia Proregis & Capitanei generalis, quibus constat virtus ac probitas viri, sine exceptione magni. His instructi fastidiosum illud & periculosum iter in Hispaniam suscipiunt, Regem adeunt, fidem ac virtutem tantis documentis probatam ostendunt, præmium implorantes, designato etiã supplicatione munere, quod jam ante ut conveniens electum habebant, Trium annorum termino dignitates omnes Indiæ temperantur: Ipsus qui implorat administrare debet, nisi specialis favor suffragetur, ad venditionem aut compendium filiæ maritandæ, talis officij proventu. Nam tum hujus modi Literæ in Cancellaria, Regis notantur; & in album re-

feruntur, confirmatione Proregi Indiæ servata, Multi aliquando ad idem munus adspirant, & notantur in rotula nomina. Ordine tamè, facto loco, morte, aut absentia præcedetis, sequeti. Ius autem à Consulibus ac consiliarijs, ut in Lusitania, administratur ex Goa per totam Indiam. Ipse Prorex Iuri præest; sed appellationes quædam ad Lusitaniæ tribunal reijciuntur. Magnificentiam & pompam Vice-Regis quis fando explicet? raro prodit. Diebus autè festis ad templum maxima incedit frequentia nobilium ac famulorum, summo musices, tubarû tibiarumque; strepitu trium annorum dominatione insignis, Non placuit Regibus Lusitaniæ longior potestas. Salubri ne an damnoso concilio? Certe minor cura Reip: magistratui inest, qui successorem post tam breve tempus exspectat. Ideo multa quæ vel ad Regis utilitatè, vel ad Incolarum salutem pertinent negliguntur, occupato tantum Prorege in copendia privata⸱

Ships which the Portuguese and their enemies the Malabars use in war and for trade.

The worst enemies of the Portuguese are those who live in the Malabar region of India. They often go to sea in warships and attack the ships of the merchants like degenerate pirates. They are cunning and untrustworthy, but courageous and tough fighters. They go about naked except for their genitals. A fleet sails from Goa every year to curb their activities. A herald announces its departure to the sound of a tambourine at the beginning of the summer around September, and those who wish to serve the king in the war at sea come in crowds for the payment of the wage. The viceroy appoints a supreme commander, who has other subordinate commanders under him in charge of each of the warships or the vessels. A yacht often has a hundred men on board, a warship three hundred. They are paid in accordance with the list or matricula, depending on their titles. Noblemen receive more than common soldiers. The commanders still attract the best soldiers and bind them to themselves with new remunerations as a sort of bonus in addition to what the king pays. They provide the ships with plenty of provisions, eat their meals at the same table as the soldiers, and constantly take care to ensure that they are at ease. Otherwise they would not listen well and would be disobedient. The commanders derive a special reputation from the excellence and bravery of their soldiers.

This fleet protects the sea until April and follows on the heels of the Malabars, so that they do not engage in hostilities. Toward the end of April the fleet returns to Goa and the ships are brought on land, because it is winter in that region. After the conclusion of the expedition the soldiers are dismissed and return home as they choose.

The inhabitants of Malabar are very skilled in all the martial arts and are as adept as the Portuguese. Although they are surrounded by the bulwarks of the Portuguese, they break out in certain places, such as Chale, Calicut, Cunhale, Panane, etc. They also use sea vessels with oars or sails, which they are able to manoeuvre extremely skilfully. Those ships also travel easily and have many uses in the transport of merchandise. The inhabitants are black in complexion, but they have a shiny smooth skin and enhance the sheen with salves and oil. They let their hair grow and tie it in a knot on top, both men and women. Their earlobes are opened up and they consider that to be elegant. They hardly differ from Europeans in physique. The men are hairy. They are more lascivious than any other people, and young girls lose their virginity before they reach the age of ten, as if the recollection of chastity has been entirely effaced. The Malabars are divided into two castes, the Nayars, or noblemen and soldiers, and the Polyas, that is, the common people.

PLATE 10

Naves çeloces seu biremes, quibus Bello et transportandis mercibus utuntur Lusitani, et eorum hostes Malabares.

Fusten welcke die Portugeesen en haer vianden die Malabaren gebruycken ter oorloch, en om coopmanschap te voeren

46 en 47

INfestissimi Lusitanorum hostes sunt, qui Malabar Regionem Indiæ inhabitant. Hi crebro Liburnicis mari incumbunt, & piratica pravitate mercatorum navigia expugnant: Subdoli homines, & fidei non validæ, fortes tamen ac pugnaces, incedunt nudi & pudenda tantum tecti. Ad comprimendos horum motus, quotannis Classis ex Goa solvit, ideoque in Septembrem initio æstatis, ad sonum tympani præco profectionem indicit; ut ad stipendij solutionem accurrant, qui Regi ad marini prælij usum servire volunt. Ibi tum à Prorege Dux supremus constituitur, qui alios minores sub se Duces habet, singulis Liburnicis aut Celocibus præfectos, ita subinde Celox centum viros capit, Liburnica vero triginta. Hi juxta tenorem albi, sive Matriculæ, habitá titulorum ratione, stipendium consequuntur, aliud enim homo nobilis; aliud gregarius miles accipit. Etiamnum Duces vltra Stipendium à Rege debitum nouis præmijs, ac velut donativo præstantissimos milites sollicitant & ad se trahunt, naves omni apparatu ciborum largiter instruunt, cum militibus una in mensa cibum capiunt, semper intenti, ut illis bene sit; alioquin parum audiétes & obsequentes haberent; & posita est Ducibus specialis quædam gloria in præstantia ac virtute militum,

Classis hæc, usque ad Aprilem mare custodit, & Malabarenses insequitur, ne quid hostile tentent. Circá finem Aprilis Goam revertitur, & subducuntur rates; tunc enim in illo tractu hyems est, sic expeditione finita milites absoluti, ad sua pro arbitrio se referunt.

Incolæ Malabar in omni arte bellica peritissimi, Lusitanis vix cedunt, & quanquam propugnaculis Lusitanorum obsessi, ex locis tamen quibusdam furtim erumpunt, ut sunt Chale, Calcut, Cunbale, Panane, &c. Vtuntur etiam Liburnicis, quas remigio aut præsidio velorum, egregia scientia norunt regere. Etiam in vehendis mercibus harum navium facilis cursus est, & promiscuus usus; sunt hi incolæ colore nigro, cute tamen nitida ac plana, & affectant nitorem unguentis ac oleo. Comam nutriunt & in nodum supra verticem cogunt, viri juxta ac fœminæ. Auriculas habet patentes; daturque id elegantie. Corporis statura ac forma ab Europeis vix differunt. Viri pilosi sunt. Luxuriosi supra omnes mortales & puellis jam arte ætatem annorum decem erepta virginitas, velut extincta memoria castitatis. In duo genera divisi sunt Malabarenses; in Naïros sive nobiles vel milites; & in Polias, id est, plebeios.

Dress and costume of a Portuguese maiden in India. Dress and ornament of a Portuguese married woman.
Dress and costume of the Portuguese widows, which they abandon if they remarry and resume
the dress of a married woman. Dress and covering of women indoors, irrespective of their estate and age.

The wives of the half-bloods or Christian-Indian Portuguese are more or less confined to the walls of their house. They never appear in public except for certain legitimate purposes. They go about dressed in very expensive clothing, dazzlingly adorned with golden armbands and necklaces, pearls and precious gems. Their cloak is of checked damask or pure silk. A cloth of ordinary silk is regarded as inferior. Indoors they uncover their heads and do not wear a veil, and they wear a tunic called a *baiu* that reaches the navel and is so thinly woven that the naked body can be seen through it. From the navel down they are covered by a multi-coloured cloth wrapped two or three times around their body. This cloth is very skilfully woven and decorated with all kinds of figures and scenes, and it is proof of exceptional artistic skill. The rest of the body is uncovered. They walk barefoot on sandals, as the men also do. This is the indoor dress for young and old, rich and poor. They rarely go out and are entirely dedicated to domestic activities. The other work is done by servant girls. The women and servants do not eat bread, not because of a lack of grain but because traditionally they prefer rice. No one puts food into his mouth with a spoon; that would be unworthy and a clear sign of dishonour. Boiled rice, mixed with the fruit they call mango, is eaten with the fingers. They drink from a long-necked cruse from which the liquid emerges drop by drop so that it makes a noise, and they do not put the vessel to their lips. This is regarded as elegant. Those who have recently arrived from Portugal and try to drink from the cruses easily spill onto their breast because they are not versed in the art. This clumsiness provokes laughter from the women who are used to the cruse. Such

a person is called Reynol, a nickname among the Portuguese that is given to those who are not familiar with Indian customs.

Generally speaking, the women are very keen on domestic propriety. They strive for special elegance in their clothing and person and wash their body time after time with untiring enthusiasm to clean themselves after every call of nature. They avoid work and devote themselves with great dedication to aromatic herbs and the preparation of incense. They rub sandalwood oil into their head and forehead to attain the charm of a pleasant scent. They constantly chew betel and the herb areca, and their teeth and lips are therefore black and red, which alarms anyone who is not used to it. This custom originally came from the Indians and the heathen. They claim that these herbs are very good for the preservation of the teeth, according to a persistent tradition, so they go nowhere without chewing. If the husband is away, they sit behind their rush screen chewing their betel and watch the passersby without being seen themselves, or if someone catches the eye of the lady of the house, she raises the screen modestly as a display of special favour. This is the start of all the wantonness that they engage in with astonishing skill and with the connivance of the female servants. They are very hostile to chastity and therefore consider the betel and areca important to provoke lust. They also eat scented herbs of all kinds to provoke heat, as well as certain biscuits called cachunde, which are made of all kinds of aromatic herbs. They are very skilful in finding ways to be immodest by all kinds of tricks, while the unlucky husband vainly watches over the family honour, which is rarer than a black swan in these parts.

PLATE II

Hinfchoten

Io:à Do:
fec.

Donzella

Cazada.   Viuua.

| Virginis Lufitanę in India gestus et amictus.

Cleedinge en dracht van een Portugeefche Dochter ofte Maecht in Indien. | Matronarum et conjugatarum foras prodeuntium veftitus et ornatus.

Der Portugeefen gehoude Vrouwen, habyt en cyraet. | Viduarum Lufit. amictus quem iterum nuptę deponunt resumpto nuptiar habitu.

Cleedinge en dracht der Portugeefcher Weduwen welcke weder houwende aflegge, weder acu nemende der gehouder dracht. | Vestitus et comptus Mulierum cujus cunque ordinis et ætatis intra ædes.

'Der Vrouwen cleedinge en hulfel binnen fhuys van wat staet en ouderdom die zyn.   48 en 49 |

Lufitanorum, Mixtorum, fiue Chriftianorum Iudorum uxores, domo ac mūris fere feptę, nunquam in publicum prodeunt nifi certis juftifque de caufis. Veftitu prætiofiffimo incedunt, armillis, cathenis aureis, gemmis & margaritis fplendidè in ftructę. Veftis, Damafcena, fcurulata; aut Holoferica, indumentum ex ferico vile eft. Aperto capite & fine velo domi degunt, indui camifiam, quam Baiu vocant, ufque ad umbilicum, ita tenuirer laboratam, ut nudum corpus perluceat. Ab umbilico picto linteamine, eoque duplicato; aut triplicato teguntur. Id Linteamen fumma arte elaboratum, varijs figuris & imaginibus excultum, fingulare artificium oftendit. Cætera corporis fine tegumento, nudis pedibus foleis incedunt, ut etiam viri. Hic habitus domefticus eft, & cōmunis vetulis ac junioribus, diuitibus & pauperibus, raro enim exeūt, familiaribus intentæ rebus: Munera cætera famulæ fubeunt. Mulieres panē non comedunt, neq; etiã mancipia, non caritate frumenti, fed cōfuetudine ad Orizam procliues. Cochlearibus autē cibum ori nemo admovet, indignū hoc effet & certa nota infamiæ. Orizam decoctã, ac fructu, quē Mangas vocat, temperatam, manu contrectãt. Bombylijs utuntur ad potum, ita guttatim diftillante liquore ut fonitū edat, nec ori admouent; datur enim id elegantiæ. Qui ex Portugallia recentes adveniunt, ex his Bombylijs bibere conantes, pectus facile perfundunt, ignari artificij, Ea imperitia in rifum vertit fuetas huic poculo, Talis ergo Reynol

vocatur ludicro apud Lufitanos nomine, ac in rudes Indicorum rituum jactato.
Mundicies fæminis communiter gratiffima eft in ædibus, veftitu & corpore quæ fita fpecialis elegantiæ; crebris ita lauationibus corpus purgãt; poft actus univerfos naturæ inexhaufto lavandi ftudio. Laborem furgitant, deditæ fummopere odoriferis aromatibus & thurificationi; fandalo caput ac fronte ungunt, ad conciliandam boni odoris gratiam. Bettelam continuo manducant, & herbam Arrecam, ideo dentibus labrifque niger ac rubicundus color eft, terrore quodam non fuetis. Ab Indis Ethnicifq; mos hic primum fluxit, ad dentium infuper cuftodiã utiliffimas effe has herbas autumant, pertinaci confuetudine, ut fine hac rumination e nufquam fint. Viro abfente poft Stoream fedentes Bettelam identidem dentibus terunt, ac prætergredientes fpectant, ipfæ à nemine vifæ, vel fi aliquis ad Dominæ oculum tranfit, levãt ftoream modeftè, quafi in arham tenerioris adfectus. Principia hæc omnium Libidinum, quas mirifico ingenio, famularum opera, exercent. Caftitati inimiciffimæ, & ideo Bettellam, ac Arrecquam cre tenent incitandę Luxurię. Aromata quoq; diverfi generis comedunt. ad caloris incitamentum; etiã Liba quædam cachūde dicta, ex omni aromatum genere confecta; artificiofiffimæ per varias artes in inftrumenta incontinentię, necquicquam cuftodiente mifero marito familię pudicitiam, quæ in hifce partibus atro Cygno rarior eft.

Litters on which the Portuguese women and daughters are borne under cover.

The Portuguese women are borne on litters or couches, which they call palanquins, covered by a veil. The husbands decided on this to protect female modesty. They are very prone to jealousy and all men are prohibited from visiting women, even those with whom they are close friends; as the poet says: 'Only from my mistress must you stay far away' [Propertius, *Elegies* 2, 34, 14].

Access is somewhat easier for in-laws and relatives in the course of outings of the whole family, surrounded on all sides by a mass of servants, to gardens and country houses. Whenever anyone happens to knock at the door, the women immediately conceal themselves so that they are not seen by some kind of Actaeon. Only the husband remains behind to receive guests. Members of the household who have passed adolescence are forbidden to mix with the womenfolk too. The males are transferred to separate rooms in another part of the house, so that a brother no longer has any contact with his sister, because they live separately. After all, the criminal passion goes so far in many cases that brothers throw themselves into the arms of sisters, and nephews of aunts, paying no heed to human and divine laws. They do not know any other way of life, and the husband's alertness is in vain. That is why practically all the women choose a lover from among the soldiers to fulfil the husband's duties. And there are thousands of devices to encourage and create the opportunity for illicit intercourse. In that region there is a herb called dutroa that is effective. When it is sprinkled into food or drink, it causes drowsiness and befuddles the brain. They give it to their husbands, and when they are overmastered by a dishonourable sleep and are deprived of their senses, as it were, they make fun of them with their adultery. The result is poisonings, attempts on the lives of the husbands, toxic drinks which cause death after a certain time; it is deferred, but it never fails to come. Similarly the women are certain to be killed by their enraged husbands, because Portuguese law recognises a wife's adultery as legitimate grounds for manslaughter. This punishment is carried out every day because the crime is committed every day and is present everywhere. But the women themselves (who could believe it?) consider nothing better than in the name of Love—that is what they call lust—to undergo even the cruellest death and to offer their blood to the divine Venus, eternally loyal to their fire of love.

You therefore see nothing so often in those parts as the violent deaths of men and women. When the wrath is justified, the man demands the appropriate penalties for the crime, and punishment even on the grounds of suspicion alone is considered justified. Similarly, when passion sets the woman's heart aflame, it is permitted to kill the adulterer to safeguard the husband's love.

PLATE 12

Lectuli quibus Vxores et Filię Lusitanorum
contecte gestantur.

Coetskens daer de Portugeesche Vrouwen en Dochters
bedeckt in gedraegen worden.

48 en 49

IN sellis siue lecticis, quas Pallamquinos vocāt, Lusitanorum mulieres gestantur, velo tectæ. Ita maritis visum, ad custodiam muliebris pudicitiæ. Zelotypia enim maxime laborant, interclusa mulierum visitatione omnibus masculis, etiam amicitia arctè junctis: ut ait Poeta

        A domina tantum te modo tolle mea.

    Conjugatis tamen & Compatribus liberior accessio est, universali totius familiæ ambulatione ad hortos & villas, circumfusa mancipiorum undique turba. Si quis forte fores Pulset, continuo sese mulieres abdunt, ne temere ab aliquo Actæone conspiciantur. Ibi tum vir solus remanet, ad excipiendos hospites. Etiam ex familiaribus, qui ex ephebis excesserit, à consuetudine cum mulieribus repellitur, separatis mansionibus, & in aliam partem ædium trāslatis masculis; ita nec fratri ullū cū sorore cōmercium, discreta habitatione. Etenim multis exēplis eo pervenit scelerata Libido, ut fratres in sororum, cognati in amitarū amplexus ruerent, contēptis humanis divinisq; legibus. Nō aliter illis vita cōstat, frustra custodiēte marito. Inde oēs

fere matronæ amasium quendā ex militibus adsciscunt, qui viro succidaneā operam nauet. Et sunt mille artes ad incitamēta ac opportunitatē captandā furtiui cōcubitus. Est herba in hisce partibus, quā Durtoā vocāt, efficaci virtute ad sommū ac stolidū soporē, si potui aut cibo inspergatur. Hanc maritis prębēt, ijsq; turpi sommo victis, ac velut mēte captis adulterino coitu illudunt. Inde veneficia, paratæ in maritorū caput insidię, &noxia potio, morte in certū tempus, eventu nunquam irrito destinata ac prorogata. Et pariter fæminis ab irato marito certa mors, Lusitanorū jure causa cædis in adulterā muliere approbata. Atq; quotidiana hæc pæna est, ut & crimē quotidianum & vulgare. Verum ipsæ mulieres (quis credat?) Nihil pulchrius existimant, quam Amoris causa, ita luxum istum indigitant, mortem etiam atrocissimam subire, libato diuæ veneri, in æternam flammæ fidem sanguine.

    Itaque nihil in his partibus jam crebro intelligas; quā violentos maritorum fæminarūmq; interitus: ubi justa ira, pænas etiam justas nefandi operis exigit, & vel ex suspicione punitio recta æstimatur: inflammante identide animum muliebrē libidine, permissa & injuncta adultero ad securiores amores maritorū morte.

Manner in which the Portuguese women and daughters are borne, when it rains and at other times,
with their slaves and servants before, behind, and beside them.

This plate shows the covered litter and the servants who walk in front of it, behind it, and beside it. When the weather is rainy and cloudy, the wives of the Portuguese are carried, veiled and sitting on the palanquins, and pay visits to the churches and altars accompanied by a number of servants. It is virtually their only opportunity to leave the house and go outside, for their husbands try to curb their lasciviousness in every possible way by preventing them from going for a walk. And perhaps this jealousy serves to increase their desires, because the oppressive guarding of the women by the men stimulates their lust.

'He races past what lies in reach, but chases that which flies away' [Horace, *Satires* 1, 2 108].

This illustration also shows the wet nurse, or *ama*. She is a servant or Indian woman and follows the litter of the female head of the household carrying the child. The children of the Portuguese, the half-bloods, and the other Christians go about naked, dressed only in a short tunic called a *baiu*, until they are a bit bigger, when they usually wear trousers.

PLATE 13

Ratio qua coelo pluvio et alias Lufitanę gestantur
comutantibus ante retro et utriumq3 famulis

Maniere vandie Portugeesche vrouwen en dochters te draegen
alst regent en oock op ander tÿden met haer slaven
en dienaers voor achter en besÿden

48 en 49

Hæc tabula tectam Lecticam oftendit, famulos ante ambulones, incitantibus maritis.
fequentes & à latere incedentes. Cœlo enim pluvio ac nubiloso, Transvolat in medio pofita ac fugientia captat.
mulieres Lufitanorum Pallanquinis infidentes velatæ geftantur, & co- Etiam in figura hac oftenditur nutrix, quam Amam vocant. Illa aut
mitatæ familiarium turba templa ac altaria vifitant, unica fere exeundi famula eft aut Indica mulier, & lecticam matronæ fequitur, puerū ba-
& fpaciandi occafione: nam quovis modo ftudent mariti coercere mu- julans. Liberi vero Lufitanorum, mixtorum, cæterorumque Chriftia-
lierum intemperiem, refecata omni ambulatione: & eft fortaffe zeloty- norum, nudi incedunt, tunica tantum, quam Baiu vocant tecti, ufque
pia hæc ad acuendos appetitus, difficili cuftodia, mulierum libidinem, ad ætatem majorem, tunc confuetum veftimentum eft bracca.

A Portuguese woman accompanied by her husband and slaves visiting the churches at night.

At night the Portuguese families often visit the churches for a religious service. Then the women are a little freer to go outdoors on foot, because that is how they go to religious services, and they leave the show of litters and chairs behind. These nights are often keenly desired by the women, and they look forward to them for a long time. The female servants accompany them, and while the housewives are praying, they go out in search of lovers. At a given sign they go to a shop or tavern and immediately perform the sacred service of Venus there and deceive their master, who is occupied with the more important religious duties. They regard themselves as very fortunate if they can attract a whiter or Portuguese man, and with immodest exaggeration they praise the beauty and excellence of their lovers among one another, fired by a fervent and militant enthusiasm. That is why they squander the money of their master and reduce it by liberal gifts to these lovers. Their 'payment' of the Portuguese soldiers is very generous, more generous than what the king pays. The children borne by these female servants are the property of the master and he delights in the expansion of the number of his servants, except when the children are the result of a union with a Portuguese or free man. For then the father can redeem a son for a small fee within eight days of birth and give the child freedom. However, once the fixed eight or ten days are past, the child whose father is a free man becomes a slave and remains the property of the master of the servant. The master can sell him for any price or bring him up himself. This is the only procedure that is allowed here. Seldom or never does the mother in these parts allow the child to be taken away, not even in the worst poverty or slavery. Because it is the special pride of this group, if the woman carries the child of a white man. Therefore she watches closely over her child and will not relinquish it to the father at any price, unless it is stolen or kidnapped. So they regard the fertility of their womb as a compensation for all wealth.

There are monasteries and churches of most of the monastic orders (to mention this too) in Goa, just as in Lisbon, but there are no nunneries. For there is no way to get women to adopt chastity, and every endeavour in favour of this virtue is in vain. They will not be virgins at any price.

PLATE 14

Lusitana, templa noctu invisura, comitata
marito, et servis.

Een Portugeesche vrouwe verselschapt met hare man
en slaven des snachts die kercken besoeckende.

48 en 49

NOcturno tempore subinde ex religionis ritu familia Lusitanorum.Templa visitat , tum uxori liberior
exitus est,pedibus ; nam in supplicationibus ita incedūt , remota lecticarum cathedratumque magnificentia. Hæ noctes passim mulieribus optabiles sunt,& jam ante longa spe conceptæ. Etiam famulæ
comitantur,quæ occupata precibus domina,furtim Amasijs operam dant, & in officinam aut tabernā dato
signo se conjiciunt,ac ibi peractis cōtinuo Veneris sacris, Domino,majoribus religionis curis occupato,il-
ludunt.In amore Viri candidioris, sive Lusitani , magnam reponunt fælicitatem & lactantia inter æquales
lasciva,formam ac virtutem proci, ardentibus adversisque studijs prędicant. Inde peculium heri crebro in-
vertunt,ac imminuunt,largitione in hosce amatores procliui,Estque illud uberrimum Lusitanorum militum stipendium,Regia largitate copiosius. Liberi ex hisce ancillis nati Heri sunt,& gaudet is auctus servis,
nisi ex,Lusitano aut libero concepti sint, Nam tum intra octo dies à natiuitate pater filium paruo precio re-

dimere potest,vindicato in Libertatem infante. Verum octo decemue statis diebus elapsis, servus est etiarā
ex libero conceptus & Domini ancillæ manet . Is potest quovis precio vendere , aut sibi alere, neque fas est
aliter cum hoc agere. Raro aut nunquam mater in hisce partibus infantem tollit, etiam summa paupertate
aut servitute pressa:Nam ea peculiaris huic generi gloria est, imprimis si ex albi coloris viro gravida sit. Itaque studiose infantem custodit,patri nullo precio tradita,nisi furtim aut clam auferatur.Ita omnium fere
divitiarum æstimatione fœcunditatem uteri pensant.

Sunt autem in Goa(ut & hoc addamus)monasteria ac Templa ut Lisbonæ plurimorum monachorum;
virginum tamen claustra nūsquam . Nam mulieres nullo fervore tanguntur ad studium castitatis , & vani
hic omnes ad eam virtutem conatus,Nulla mercede virgines sint;

Dress and appearance of the Indian merchants, who are very cunning in their trade.
Banyans from Cambaia, very skilful in their knowledge of stones, writing, and calculating.
Brahmans, the popes or priests of the Indian idols.

The city and territory of Goa are inhabited by people of various descent: heathen, Moors, Jews, Indians from the surrounding areas, Arabs, Armenians, Persians, Banyans from Cambaia, and people from Gujarat and the Deccan. They adhere to various religions. Some worship idols that they call pagodas, several are Mohammedans, others observe the law of Moses, and yet others follow the Christian way of life. Generally speaking they are very adept in trade, good with figures, rich, and in possession of the most dazzling merchandise. There are also many magicians among them. They practise incantations and perform on stage with cheerful leaps. They are very skilful in mixing poisons and are ready for any crime.

The Banyans from Cambaia are known for their exact knowledge of pearls. They have their own street in the city with splendid shops. However, they have cunning and sophisticated minds. They surpass the Portuguese in adroitness and knowledge of merchandise. They do not eat or kill animals. This is connected with their belief that these animals embody human souls, an unmistakable influence of the Pythagorean notion of metempsychosis. For that reason they often redeem animals that have been destined to be killed by the Portuguese and native Christians. They regard that redemption as an act of charity. If you were to travel through Cambaia, you would often see urns filled with water and grain haphazardly strewn to feed the birds and animals. There are also many sanctuaries where they tend animals that have been wounded with particular care and use the customary means to cure them, which they regard as a laudable act of piety. They do not eat onions, garlic, radishes, or eggs and they are opposed to all red food as if it were the product of blood. They hate foreign food and keep away from meals of foreigners, and that is why when they are travelling they do not eat with the Portuguese or

people from other groups, no matter how hungry they are. They are olive-coloured in complexion and sometimes have a white skin. The women are even more beautiful than the Portuguese women. They have a European physique. They go about dressed simply in a white robe and cone-shaped red shoes. Their headgear is the same shape as that of the Brahmans, and they shave their beard like the Turks. They eat like the Moors, seated on mats and carpets. They take off their shoes when they go indoors. They are very keen on fresheners and scents.

The Brahmans are the most esteemed and highest-ranking among the Indians. They occupy virtually all of the top-ranking functions and are present in the ceremonies and service of the idols. They command great respect among the people. The king himself handles all matters on the basis of their opinion and recommendation. They are distinguished from the other Indians by a cord that hangs diagonally over their body from one shoulder. It is made of a fine thread and is obtained after a special oath. They will not abandon that token of honour for any money or threat. That is how strict the rule of that sect is. They go about naked except for a cotton loincloth covering their genitals. They cover their head with a white cloth and pay enormous attention to their hair. They wear golden earrings. They are vegetarians and animals are an abomination to them. Never, not even when they are very seriously ill, will they accede to bloodletting, but they treat every illness with sandalwood and aromas. Many of these priests are occupied with trade and shops. They have a fine nose for everything and are therefore very good at misleading the common people. They are also held to be prophets by the people and are considered very reliable and friends of the gods. The Brahmans also observe certain days of fasting when they eat nothing at all, sometimes for as many as four days, so that they rival the ancient gymnosophists.

PLATE 15

Habitus et facies Mercatorum Goensium Indorum,
qui mutandis mercibus valde industrij

Habýt en gedaente der Indiaensche Coopluýden
welcke in hare handel seer cloeck zyn

Banjanes e Cambaja populus æstimandis gemmis,
scribendo, supputandoque valde exercitatus.

Banjanen van Cambajen int kennen van gesteenten
schrijven en rekenen zeer geoeffent

Bramenes Idolorum in India Sacerdotes.

Bramenes der Indiaenscher affgoden Papen
ofte Priesters.

58 en 59

IN urbe ac territorio Goensi diversi generis homines habitãr, Ethnici, Mauri, Iudæi, Indi ex circũjacentib' terris, Arabes, Armenij, Persæ, Banianes ex Cãbaia, Gusarattes & Decanini. Hi diversas religiones affectãt; quidam enim Idola, quæ Pagodes vocant colunt, quidã Machometũ, alij Mosaicã legẽ custodiunt, alij & Christianas disciplinas observãt. In universũ sunt in mercatura peritissimi, in rationibus acutissimi, opulentj, splendidis instructi mercibus. Multi etiam inter hos magi, incantationibus vacant & ludicis saltationibus histrionicam agunt. Venefici peritissimi & in omne scelus parabiles, Banjanes ex Cãbaia cognitione gemmarũ certissima illustres sunt; ij plateã in urbe singularẽ habent, & instructas ibi officinas, omni e legantiæ genere sunt autẽ subtilis ingenij ac fallacis. Lusitanos ipsos arte & cognitione mercaturæ superant t. Animalia nõ comedũt, necq; occidũt; ita fert illorũ Religio; Esse quasdã animas hominũ in hisce animar tibus, certissimis Pythagoricæ opinionis de trãsmigratione animarũ vestigijs. Ideo à Lusitanis ac Christiar is animalia neci destinata crebro oblato precio redimunt, pro elemosyna hanc liberationẽ supputantes, Pas im in itineribus per Cambaiã urnas aqua plenas videres; & temere projectũ frumentũ, ad avium bestiarui q; sustentationẽ. Etiã Xenodochia sunt multa, in quibus singulari cura belluæ aliquo vulnere adtectæ ha   betur, & suetis artibus ad sanitatẽ perducuntur, memorabili ut existimant pietate. Cœpas, Porrum capitatu n, Raphanum, ova non comedũt, adversi omnibus cibis rubri coloris, quasi ex sanguine productis. Cibum alienæ mensæ in horrore habent, divisi à convivijs advenarum, ideoque vel fame extrema correpti, nec ex tinere

cum Lusitanis, aut cæteris exteræ nationis hominibus vescuntur. Colore sunt oliuastro, & aliquando albicante cute; Verum & mulieres forma ipsas Lusitanas superant. Corporis forma ut Europ hominibus, Veste alba tecti incedunt simpliciter, rubris turbinatis calceis, Capitis tegumentum gestant forma qua Bramenes, barba rasa ad Turcarum morem. Cibum capiunt ut Mauri, storeis ac tapetibus insidentes. Calceis exutis domum intrant; laxationibus ac odorib' amicissimi. Bramenes honestissimi ac dignissimi Indorũ, omnia fere supremæ dignitatis munera obeũt, immixti officijs & ministerijs Idolorũ; magnæ apud populũ authoritatis. Ipse Rex omnia negotia ex arbitrio & cõsilio horũ agitat, distincti etenim sunt à cæteris Indis, catena, que ex humero trãsversim corpus cingit. Ea ex filo tenuiter secto facta est, & certo cũ juramẽto suscipitur; nullo interim præmio aut metu insigne illud relichtur; nã ita hujus sectæ regula arctè fert. Nudi incedunt, pudenda tamẽ tegũt, & subinde corpus pallio gossypino. Caput albo linteamine velãt comam prolixè alunt. Inaures ex auro gestãt. Herbis victitant, animalia respuũt, Nunquã ad sanguinis missione etiã in acutissimis morbis perduci possunt, sed sandalo & aromatibus cõmuniter malũ tollunt, Multi ex hisce sacerdotibus etiã mercaturæ ac offic inis vacãt, ad singula subtili ingenio, ideoq; ad decipiendã plebẽ aptissimi. Vulgo etenim vates haben tur, ac summæ fidei & amici deorum. Jejunia quædã Bramenes stricta abstinentia custodiunt eamq; ad quatuor subinde dies sine cibo producunt, antiquorum fere Gymnosophistarum æmuli,

[85]

The manner of a wedding in the land of Ballagate behind Goa.

The Canarim and Deccans live in the Deccan region, popularly called Ballagate. Many of them live in Goa and have shops. They sell velvet, ordinary silk and half silk, damask, etc., and, after purchasing them wholesale from the Portuguese, also cotton robes, blankets, porcelain, and other noteworthy products from Cambaia, China, and Bengal, which they divide up into small portions for the benefit of the citizens. They make use of middlemen for the bargaining. They abstain from the meat of cattle, pigs, and oxen. These animals are held in particular veneration by them, because the people live under the same roof and eat the same food together with those animals. The Canarim also catch the excrement in their hands and cast it behind them, which they regard as particularly valuable.

Boys and girls are engaged at the age of seven or eight years, but the wedding is postponed until their twelfth year. At that age a solemn wedding ceremony can take place. The wedding is preceded by a celebration lasting around fourteen days. It is celebrated with an incredible din of drums and flutes that continues through the night. On the day of the wedding all the friends meet and, sitting on the ground in front of the hearth, they turn the fire seven times as a definitive ratification of the marriage. The girls do not bring the man a dowry, except for a few items of jewellery and earrings of little or practically no value. Inheritance is entirely in the male line, but the girls are kept by their brothers until their wedding day. The husband's dead body is cremated, and his widow is cremated along with him while she is still alive. No one seeks a profession outside that of his family, and marriages are concluded among members of the same professional group. Thus a cobbler marries the daughter of a cobbler. Families are distinguished from one another by their profession.

PLATE 16

Nuptiarum ritus, et epulæ in Provincia
Ballagatæ supra Goam.

Maniere van bruyloft int Lant van
Ballagate achter Goa gelegen.

58 en 59

Canaræ & Decanini incolunt Regionem Decan, vulgo Ballagattæ. Plurimum habitant in urbe Goa, officinis intenti. Vendunt enim holofericum, fericum, fubfericum, Damafcena, &c. ante empta à Lufitanis cumulatim, etiam goffipinas veftes, linteamina, porcellanas; & alia Cambaiæ, Chinæ, ac Bengalæ memoranda, quæ in partes ad ufum ciuium diftrahunt, ante empta à Portugallenfibus, paratis in iftas negotiationes proxenetis. A vaccæ, Porci & bubali carnibus tantum abftinent. Etfunt animalia hæc mirifico apud illos cultu obfervata, nam fub eodem tecto degunt, cibum eûdem capiunt homines cum hifce beftijs, etiam fimum Canaræ manibus excipiunt, ita poft proijcientes; fingulari (ut putant) merito.

Sponfalia feptem aut octo annorum pueri puellæque inter fe contrahunt, Nuptias vero ad annum duodecimum protrahunt, ea ætate folemne fit matrimonium. Ante ipfas nuptias profeftum aliquod eft quatuordecim fere dierum, id tympanorum tibiarumque maximo ac incredibili ftrepitu celebratur, nec per noctem ceffante clangore. Die nuptiarum amici omnes conveniunt, & ante focum humi fedentes ignem feptics vertunt, certa confirmatione matrimonij. Filiæ nullam dotê ad maritum adferunt, fi monilia quædam & inaures excipias, parui minimique valoris Filijs omnis hæreditas cedit, puellæ à fratribus aluntur ad tempus ufque matrimonij. Cadaver mariti crematur, cum eo fubinde uxor viva. Extra majorum artificium nemo quid tentat, & inter hos ejufdem generis artifices, ftata funt matrimonia, ita calcearius cum calcearij filia; &c. maritatur; familijs per opificia diftinctis.

The dead Brahman is cremated according to their law, and the wife
is burned alive with him out of love for her husband.

Among the Indians, in accordance with a very ancient tradition, the bodies of the priests, called Brahmans, are cremated in a circle of all their friends in a hollow pit, which they fill with wood and all kinds of other things. For the rich these are sandalwood, rice, grain, and oil, placed on the fire on which the corpse is laid to make it blaze more fiercely. The wife, however, is accompanied by loud music and by a crowd of friends who urge her not to hesitate to cheerfully perform the beautiful and excellent act of heroism of following her husband now that his life is complete, because that act, the supreme proof of faithfulness, wins her immortal fame. So she takes off her jewels and trinkets, distributes them among the relatives, and throws herself with a bright and cheerful countenance on the burning pyre, while the bystanders immediately assist in intensifying the blaze and suffocate the woman by throwing wood and oil on top of it. By mingling the ash of the husband and the wife they provide a signal example of marital fidelity, albeit by means of a cruel and barbaric ordeal. The woman who refuses to die like this (which happens only occasionally) receives the ineradicable stigma of dishonour and infidelity and is shaved bald and relegated to the lowest rank. Stripped of all her show and jewellery, she is exposed to scorn and derision. The bodies of all noblemen and of some merchants are cremated in more or less the same way. Their widows have their hair shorn and do not wear any jewellery as a mark of their sorrow.

There is an even deeper reason for that insane death of the women. Indians themselves say that housewives were once so terribly cruel that they killed their husbands by poisoning them (they are very skilled at mixing poisons) to make room for a new marriage and thereby to be able to give rein to their passion more easily and with greater pleasure. When the king heard of this crime, by which the kingdom was deprived of extremely distinguished notables to the detriment of the state through the wickedness of their wives, he decreed the law that a wife should be burned in the same fire as the body of her husband. With this the hope of more lasciviousness was dissipated, so that men's lives were made safer. This law applied to the noblemen and Brahmans. The common people merely swell the ranks of the slaves and do not carry any weapons. Later in the course of time the royal decree became a religious ritual, and wives willingly give up their lives as if from devotion and religious custom.

Girls of seven and boys of nine marry, but they do not speak to one another until the moment of the delivery of a child. The women go about dressed in a robe that covers them from top to toe. They have rings in their nostrils, and around their arms, toes, and neck, of silver or gold depending on their wealth, but commonly of glass, because that is the popular material for armbands and jewellery among the women of India.

PLATE 17

Bramenes cum mortuus est, secundum eorum legem crematur. uxor
autem ejus, præ amore, sese vivam in ignem cum illo conjicit.

De Bramene doot wesende wort nae haer wet verbrant, en zyn
vrouwe wt liefde haers mans, verbrant haer levendich met hem.

58 en 59

APud Indos, haud novo more corpora facerdotum, quos Bramenes vocāt, igne cremantur, congregata omnium amicorum turba, effoffo puteo, quem ligno & alijs rebus implent; ditiores fandalo, Oriza frumento & oleo ad nutrimentum violentioris flāmæ, cui cadaver tum ftatuitur. Verum ipfa uxor comitata magno muficies ftrepitu, ac amicorum multitudine ad pulchrum & excellens facinus exhortatium: ne metuat fata & maritum jam ante functum alacriter fequatur; Effe in ifto facto gloriam immortalem; fupremo fidelitatis teftimonio. Illa ergo monilia & elegantiora ornamenta deponit, inter cognatos diftribuit, ac læta hilarique facie in ardentem fe rogum conjicit, parato ftatim circumftantium minifterio, ad augendum ignem, refpiratione adempta mulieri, injectione lignorū ac olei, ita cineribus mariti mixti uxoris egregium implent conjugalis fidei exemplum; barbaro quidem & atroti experimento. Quæ mortem hanc recufat (quod raro contingit) certiffima infamiæ ac infidelitatis nota, in ordinem coma abfciffa penitus redigitur, ab omni ornamentorum fplēdore remota, contemptui & defpectui mancipatur. Nobilium omĭiū, ac etiam Mercatorum quorundam cadavera tali fere ritu cremantur. Sed & viduarum eft comam radere; ac fine ornamentis degere in teftimonium mæroris.

Altior fane caufa eft furiofæ iftius mulierum mortis. Ipfi Indi narrant; deteftabilem quondam fuiffe matronarum crudelitatem, in tollendis veneno (ut funt in veneficijs peritiffimæ) maritis; ut ita facto ad novas nuptias loco, libidini facilius ac majore cum voluptate indulgerent. Cæterum Rex comperto fcelere, in detrimētum totius Reip, fublatis uxorum malignitate præftantiffimis Regiæ principibus; Legem tulit: vt vivæ uxores eodem in igne arderent, qui cadaveribus maritōrum fupremus effet; ita fublata ulterioris Libidinis fpe Maritis vita contingeret fecurior. Valuit hæc lex duntaxat inter nobiles & Bramenes. Plebs enim vilis, manciporum tantum numerum implet, & inermis degit. Inde lapfu temporis in religionem fucceffg: edictum regium, & fponte vitam amittunt conjuges; velut pietatis ac cultus religiofi intuitu.

Connubium ftatuunt puellæ feptem annorum & juvenes novem, adempta facultate colloquij, ad tēpus ufque partus. Incedunt mulieres linteamine à vertice ufque ad talos tectæ, Annulos in naribus, brachijs, digitis pedum ac collo geftant, ex argento, deaurato, pro facultatibus; ex vitro communiter: Indiæ enim mulieribus vulgaris materia eft ad armillas ac monilia.

The dignity of the envoy of the King of Ballagate in Goa.

The kingdom of Deccan is also known as Ballagate, because of the mountains that they calls the Ghats. They are very high and are covered with clouds when viewed from the city of Goa. However, there is a flat and pleasant plateau on the tops of the mountains. That is why they are called Ballagate by the Indians, which means something like "On top of the mountains". The Portuguese use this name for the whole region. This is where the great king used to rule over the kingdoms of Deccan, Cuncam, and the Bengalese nobles. But after he was taken prisoner by the generals, whom he had previously bound to him with the greatest benefits and had subsequently put in charge of those parts, the very large kingdom, divided into small areas, had a large number of satraps. The one with the greatest authority was Hidalcam, who ruled the area in which the noble city of Goa was situated. After he had been driven out twice from Goa by the Portuguese, he lost the wonderful city. But the king of Bisnagar went to war against Hidalcam and defeated him and the other leaders of the kingdom and made them subservient to him. That is why they are still subject to the king of Bisnagar, in an everlasting succession of kingdoms. This print shows the dignity of the envoy of Hidalcam and his outfit. He is carried in this manner whenever he represents the king's interests in the city of Goa.

Another name that is given to King Hidalcam of Ballagate is Sabayo, because that is how they call their lord. There was a lord like that in the city of Goa when it was first taken by the Portuguese. His house is now in use by the Inquisition and the area between the main church and the building itself bears his name.

PLATE 18

Legati Regis Ballagatte in urbe Goa comitatus.

Die staet des Ambassateurs van den Coninck van Ballagatte binnen Goa

58 en 59

REgnum Decan, alio nomine Ballagattæ vocatur, id à montibus quibusdam deducitur, quos Guate vocant. Altissimi sunt & nubibus tecti conspicienti eos ex urbe Goa, planities tamen æqua & amœna in cacumine montium est, ideo Ballagattæ ab Indis dicuntur, quasi supra montes. Lusitani ita hinc totam Regionem indigitant. Solebat hic Rex maximus imperare, Regnis Decan, Cuncam & Bengalæ nobilis, sed eo à Ducibus, quos beneficijs ante maximis devinctos Regionibus præfecerat capto, imperium maximum in particulas divisum, plures satrapas sustinuit. Inter hos infinitæ authoritatis erat, Hidalcam, qui tractum istum regebat, in quo Goa urbs nobilis sita est. Hic bis à Lusitanis ex Goa ejectus amplissimum op-

pidum amisit. Sed Rex Bisnagar bellum Idalcamô intulit, eum, cæterosque Regni proceres devicit, sibique tributarios fecit. Ideo parent hodie Regi Bisnagar, vicissitudine imperiorum sempiterna. Imago hæc Legati. Hidalcami dignitatem demôstrat, ac habitum. Is ita gestatur, cum in urbe Goa Regis sui negotia agit.

Alio nomine Rex Ballagattæ Idalcamus, Sabayo vocatur, ita Dominum indigitant. Talis in urbe Goa erat, cum primum à Lusitanis caperetur. Ejus domus nunc conversa est in usum Inquisitionis, & obtinet locus nomen inter magnum templum & ipsas ædes.

An Indian farmer who cultivates the land, called a Canarim. Indian children wearing nothing but a thin linen cloth to cover their genitals, as is the land's custom. An Indian soldier, called a lascaryn. An Indian prostitute, who earns a living by dancing and singing.

The Canarim are farmers who cultivate the land, fish, and earn a living from the Indian palm that bears coconuts. There are also some who are exclusively occupied with the washing of clothes and linen. They are called Maynatti because of their peculiar profession. There are also Patamars who perform the function of messenger in winter, travelling over land because the stormy winter weather makes shipping impossible. The Canarim are the poorest among the Indians. They survive on a meagre diet and do not eat the meat of cattle, oxen, swine, or chickens. They observe the same religion as the Deccans and are to be found in more or less the same area. They go about naked except for a loincloth. The women wrap their bodies in a piece of linen that hangs from one shoulder, covering half of the bosom. Many of them have accepted the Christian religion, for they generally live close to the coast and the districts around Goa because the palms like the coast and the river banks. Rice also grows on low-lying land that is flooded in winter. That is the food of the Canarim. They take the chickens, eggs, fruits, milk, etc. to the market in the city. They live in straw houses with a simple, low door. The furniture is a mat to sleep on as a bed, a hollow to husk rice, and a pot to boil it in. That is how these most fertile of mortals live, for their houses are surprisingly full of children. These children go about entirely naked until the age of eight years, after which they cover their genital area. They receive a thorough and simple education, so that they often reach the age of one hundred years without any illness of note. The women give birth easily, on their own and without the presence of their menfolk or neighbours. They wash the child themselves and after undergoing the pangs of labour they do not at all mind resuming the other domestic work. Their education, in all its incomparable excellence, has provided them with a strong constitution and hardened them such that they pay no heed to pain. The Canarim shave their hair, but let a thick mat of hair grow on their crown. They are very good swimmers and excellent divers. This illustration shows a Canarim with his wife, children of India, a soldier from Ballagate, called lascaryn, and a danceress, called balhadeira. The latter earns a living with her body, appears at meals and parties, and entertains the guests with song and dance.

PLATE 19

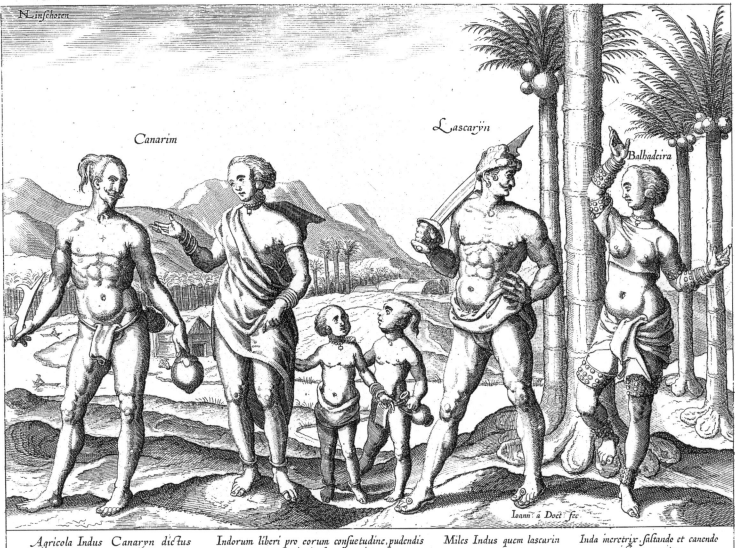

Canarim   Lascaryn   Balhadeira

Agricola Indus Canaryn dictus

Een Indiaens sant ofte bouwman
genaemt Canaryn.

*Indorum liberi pro eorum consuetudine, pudendis
tantum rariori tela contectis.*

Indiaensche kinderen als sſants manier is alleen die scha-
melheyt met een dun linnen doecksken bedeckt hebbende.

*Miles Indus quem lascarin
nominant*

Een Indiaens soldaet lascarin
geheeten.

*Inda meretrix saltando et canendo
victum queritans.*

Een Indiaensche lichte vrouwe met dan-
sen en singen haer cost winnende.

58 en 59

Canarini ruſtici ſunt,qui terram colunt,piſcantur & ex palma Indica, que Cocos ſert quæſtum aucupā-
tur,Etiam inter eos exiſtunt,qui operam dant tantum in lavandis veſtimetis ac Linteaminibus. Hi velut ſingularis artificij Maynatti vocantur. Sunt & Patamares qui tabellionum vicem implent, hyberno
tempore, terreſtri itinere, intercluſa ob tempeſtates navigatione. Cæterum miſerrimi Indorum Canarini,
exiguo victu corpus ſuſtinent,à Vaccæ,Bovis, Bubali, Porci ac Gallinæ carnibus abſtinent, eodem religionis
ritu cum Decaninis,& ſunt fere ejuſdem ſoli.Nudi incedunt, pudenda tamen pannis tegunt. Mulieres linteamine corpus cingunt, humeroque inijciunt;mediete papillarum contecta. Multi ex his Chriſtianam
fidem ſuſceperunt,habitant enim fere circa Littus maris;ac adjacentes Goæ terras.Nam palmę gaudent lit-
tore ac ripis fluminum;& Oriza quoque creſcit in depresſis agris, &hyberno tépore aqua merſis. Hic victus
eſt Canarinorum, Gallinas,Oua,fructus,Lac,&c,in urbem deferunt, ad forum. Habitāt in caſis ſtramineis
oſtio exiguo & humili ſuppellex eſt ſtorea ad ſommum,in lecti vicem, puteus Orizę tundendæ, olla ad Orizę
decoctionem; ita vivunt ſæcundiſſi;mi mortalium,nam ædes plenæ ſunt liberorum ad miraculum: ij uſque
ad octo annos prorſus nudi incedunt,poſt pudenda tegunt, firma ac plana educatione, ita ut ad ętatem centum ſubinde annorum pertingant, ſine ullo notabili morbo. Mulieres etiam ſolæ & in abſentia maritorum
aut vicinorum faciliter pariunt, infantem ipſę abluunt, ad cætera munera familiæ nequaquam ſegnes poſt
dolorem;ita educatio,incomparabili virtute,illas firmiore corporis ſtatu, ad dolores contemnendos firma-
vit.Canarini comam radunt,in vertice tamen capillorum cumulum alunt. Naradi ſunt peritiſſimi & ſum-
mi urinatores, Hæc figura Canarinum cum uxore oſtendit,Indiæ pueros, L, Lascarinum militem Ballagattæ,
& ſaltatricem,quam Balladeiram vocant,Hęc corpore quęſtum facit & convivijs epuliſque immixta, cantu
ac ſaltatione hoſpites recreat.

Boats that are used for fishing in Goa and Cochin, one hollowed out of a single piece of wood, another made from many branches bound together with ropes, the former called Almadias, the latter Tones and Paleguas, which are there in great number. They fill them with jars of fresh water to sell to the ships.

The Canarim use boats made from a tree trunk and traverse the rivers with them. Because of their lightness and small size (there is hardly room for one man) they often sink and are swamped by the river. But the Canarim, good swimmer as he is, often recovers the boot, bales out the water that has entered, and completes his intended journey. The boats are called Almadias and there are infinitely many of them.

The most miserable in this area are the farmers, who would even seize the food from the fire, in a manner of speaking. Because of the scanty food their limbs are thin and exhausted. They have a minimum of strength and are shy and are therefore vulnerable to injustice and have to endure the worst insults from the Portuguese. They are degenerate men and with the gauntness of their frame and sustenance they display a completely unmanly spirit. They have the same marriage ceremony as the Deccans and their religious ceremony is the same. When a man dies, a pyre is erected for the corpse. The woman is stripped of her hair and she breaks all her jewellery as a sign of her great grief. The jewellery, by the way, is of little value as it is of glass.

These people are dark in complexion and, as often among these Christians, of low intelligence and born to serve, as it were.

PLATE 20

Linschoten.

Cochin.

Palegua.

Tone de balheo, digo Banjleo.

Ioannes à Doetechum fecit.

Goa.

Almadia.

Almadia de Cangalha.

Scaphæ piscatoriæ Goensium et Cochinensium, alteræ ex solido trunco
excavatæ, alteræ, e pluribus funibus coagmentatæ, priores Almadias,
alteras Tones et Paleguas vocant, implent et hashydrijs aquæ recentis,
quam ad naves deferentes divendant, quarum magnus illic numerus.

Schuyten diemen te Goa, en Cochyn, gebruyckt om te visschen, d'eene wt een hout wtgeholt,
d'ander wt veel struycken, met coorden tsamen gebonden, d'eerste worden Almadias,
d'andere Tones, en Paleguas, genaemt, die daer in groot getal zyn, welcken verladen
met cruyeken vol soet waters daer in gestort, om aende schepen te vercoopen ____

58 en 59

CAnarini navigijs utuntur, ex trunco factis, iisque flumina transmittunt. Ob levi-
tatem ac exiguitatem (vix enim virum unum capiunt sæpe merguntur, & flumine opprimuntur. Verum Canarinus natandi peritus, navigium lapsum crebro, repo-
nit, aquam conceptam eijcit, & iter nihilominus susceptum perficit. Almadiæ vocãtur; & est infinitus numerus harum scapharum. Infælicissimi sane sunt agricolæ in
hoc tractu, qui (ut habet dictum) vel cibum ex flamma peterent. Parcissimo victu
macilentos ac exhaustos artus trahunt, minimarum virium, pusilli animi, ideo sub-
jecti injuriæ, ac à Lusitanis maximis contumelijs adficiuntur, degeneres viri & corporis victusque vilitate, animum haud virilem profitentes. In matrimonijs idem illis ritus qui Decaninis, & eadé religionis ratio. Viro mortuo rogus cadaveri extrui-
tur. Mulieri crines demuntur, & rumpit illa ornamenta omnia; velut in signú magni
luctus; quæ quidem exigua sunt; constant enim ex vitro.

Colore autem sunt hi homines fusco; & ut plurimum Christiani, humili ingenio
& velut ad servitutem nato.

Arabian sailors, whom the Portuguese entrust with the command of their ships, in which they usually live with their wives. Dress of the Abyssinians from the land of Pope John, who brand their faces instead of baptism.

The Arabs and Abyssinians are scattered over India in large numbers. The Arabs worship Mohammed, the Abyssinians for one part venerate Mohammed and for the other Christ, in accordance with the Ethiopian tradition, because they come from the kingdom of Pope John, which encompasses those parts of Africa that lie on the side of Mozambique, the Red Sea, and the sources of the Nile. Most of them, however, follow the tradition of the Moors and Mohammedans. They are the victims of supersitition and work as slaves in the East. The Christian Abyssinians brand their faces, in a remarkable rite of baptism, with four signs, each in the shape of a cross. The first cross is branded on the skin above the nose in the middle of the forehead, the second and third on either side of the eyes extending almost to the ears, and the fourth extending from the lower lip to the chin. This is the sign of Christianity for them, and this fire is in place of baptismal water. Those with the status of a free person practise the profession of seaman throughout India and are scattered among merchant vessels from Goa, China, Bengal, etc. The Arabs and the Abyssinians do their work on the ships for little pay and are prepared to carry out all kinds of services. They put up with the customary blows and stripes with amazing resignation and differ very little from slaves. They have virtually their whole family on these ships and live on their own diet of rice. There is usually one Portuguese among them with the title of captain, commander, and helmsman, and one Arab is the boatswain, called 'mocadon' in the language of that country. He gives orders to the other seamen like a master, and they are like servants to him.

He therefore makes a contract with the master and, after the number of seamen has been promised, he receives as it were the wage for them all, which he then divides among the Arab colleagues, with whom a wage has been agreed upon in an individual contract. The ships do not have casks to store water, except for a receptacle near the main mast that is thoroughly welded and closed, in which drinking water is kept.

These people are very willing to enter service and make natural slaves, as it were. If someone's hat or some other item of little value falls into the sea, even during the voyage, one of them immediately dives into the water and, with the art of swimming that they master very well, brings the lost object back. If the ship is in port and they all go on land together in a small rowing boat, one of them takes that rowing boat back to the ship and then swims after his companions. They are the most subservient of mortals, partly encouraged by those called mocadon, and thus they sometimes compete with one another for the position of servant, which one wants to perform before the other. They sing almost all the time they work, and a chorus leader determines the melody in harmony with those who sing after him, just as with real music. When they are free of work on the boat, they spend the whole day indulging in drink and share their constant drunkenness with their wives and children. That too is accompanied by an urge to sing, and the streets are filled with seamen who stagger about with foolish and carefree dance steps. The women also wear trousers like the Arabs and Mohammedans.

PLATE 21

Naute Arabes quibus naves suas regendas Lusitani committunt
in quibus cum uxoribus ut plurimum habitant.

Arabischer scheepluyden, welcke die Portugeesen, haer schepen vertrouwen
te regeren, in welcken sij oock met haer wyuen meest woonen.

Habitus Abissinorum quibus loco S. Baptismatis.
frons nutiritur

Habyten der Abissynen wt paep Ian slant welcke in plaets van
doop gebruycken brantmercken int aensicht.

61 en 62

Joannes à Doetechum fecit

ARabes & Abyssini magno numero per Indiam sparsi sunt, & sunt ipsi Arabes Machometi cultores; Abyssini autem partim Machometum adorant partim Christum more Æthiopico; sunt enim ex Imperio Præsbyteri Iohannis oriundi, quod eas partes Africæ, quę ad Mozambicque, rubrum Mare & Nili fontes jacent occupat, Plurimi autem Maurorum & Machometistarum cōsūetudine, hisce superstitionibus detinentur & servitutem in Oriente serviunt. Abyssini Christiani notabili Baptismatis genere faciem notis quatuor in formam Crucis inuruūt, Crux prima supra nasum ad mediam usque frontem cutem notat, secunda & tercia ad latera oculorum, tractu fere usque ad aures, quarta ab inferiore labro ad mentum usque. Ista nota illis pro Christianismo est, & supplet aquę vicem ignis, Cæterum qui ex his liberę conditionis sunt, in universa India nautarum fere munus præstant, distributi in naves mercatorias, Goę, Chinæ, Bengallæ, &c. Parvo sane pretio Arabes, sive Abyssini operas navales subeunt & sunt ad omnia ministeria paratissimi, flagra ac verbera sueta admirabili patiētia sustinent, vix tenui à mancipijs differentia. Familiam fere totam in hisce navigijs habent, proprio vivunt victu, Oriza nempe. Vnus fere Lusitanus inter hos titulo nauclerei, Ducis & gubernatoris gaudet; & alter Arabs celeustes, vocabulo istius terræ Mocadon dictus. Hic cæteris socijs velut Dominus imperat eosque passim in famulorum morem habet, Cum Domino ideo navigij cōtrahit,

& numero nautarum promisso, generalè velut stipendium accipit, quod tum inter Arabes socios dividit, quibus cum singulari contractu de mercede egerat. Vasa ad aquæ conservationem nō habentur in hisce navigijs, tantum ad majorem navis arborem Labrum est, studiose ferruminatum ac stipatum, in eo aqua servatur ad potum.
    Gens hæc ad familitium promptissima est ac velut in servitutem inclinata. Si cui vel capitis tegumentum vel aliud minoris etiam precij in mare decidat, etiam in cursu navigij, unus se statim in pelagum conijcit, & natandi peritia, qua pollent maxime, amissas res recuperat. Quando navis in portu est, si pariter omnes terram petant Acatio, unus illud ad navem reducit, ac natatu socios repetit. Officiosissimi mortalium, impelléte etiam eo, quē Mocadon vocant, itaq; sæpe de ministerio certant, quod alter ante alterum studet occupare. Cantantes omnem fere laborem implent, & modulatur præcedens subsequentium concordi strepitu, ad musices æmulationem. A marinis laboribus immunes totum diem potu terunt, assidua ebrietate, quam cum conjugibus & liberis exercent, comitante identidem cantandi studio, & impletis vicis discurrentium nautarum ridicula ac dissoluta saltatione. Fœminę etiam Braccas pro vestimento habent, more Arabum ac Machometistarum.

Moors from Mozambique and the surrounding countries, who are called Kaffirs.
Some are Christians, some heathen, and the majority are Mohammedans.

The Negroes, or Kaffirs, who inhabit the kingdom of Mozambique and the interior down to the Cape of Good Hope go about almost naked. However, the women who live in the region of Mozambique partially cover their bodies, in the manner of the Portuguese, for they use ivory and gold to buy cotton and linen from the parts of India. The others have the kind of clothing worn by the first human being in Paradise. They are very black in complexion and have scorched curly hair, a thin beard, a broad and flat upturned nose, and large thick lips, and their face is pierced in certain places. They insert ivory into the holes. They regard this as extremely elegant. They also apply a glowing iron to their body to produce stripes and holes, and thus their skin is marked by stigmata as among us the needle of the Phrygians marks the clothing. For these peoples this is a beautiful decoration, and they look down on our bodies, which seem monstrous because of their clothing and white colour. That is why the image of a white man covered with clothing is a representation of a demon or spirit to them. Some of them also file their teeth and shape them like needles. To sum up, they have the traditional view that Negroes surpass all men in beauty, colour, and way of life. The religion of some of them is the same as that of the Moors, especially in Abex, Melinde, and Mozambique, where enthusiasm for that very criminal sect grew very great through the sustained trade. There are also a few Chris-tians who have been converted by the Portuguese. The others live like animals without any fear of the gods or any ritual. However, they obey the kings, who are there in great numbers, because each village has one as its head. They are constantly engaged in war with one another and eat the flesh of their adversaries. They also take prisoners to the market and sell them to the Portuguese. The strongest are particularly highly esteemed. To demonstrate their virility they cut off the genitals of their enemies and, when they have been dried and cleaned, take them to the king, where, after first putting them in the mouth, they spit them out at their master's feet. He praises their courage and gives them the genitals back, but adds tokens of honour, which they regard as a sign of tremen-dous good fortune. Slaves of this people are on sale all over India; many prisoners are destined to be sold because of their numerous wars. Thus one man is worth two or three ducats, a small price for freedom. In times of famine parents offer their children as slaves and surrender them to that accursed way of life for six or seven measures of rice. And they are not molested by such a catastrophe, because they put the blame on fate and a stepmotherly treatment at the hands of fortune, and hope to be freed by their companions and friends who remain, as they claim, to avenge and rescue them.

PLATE 22

N. linschoten

Ioa: à Doe: fe:

Æthiopum e Moçambyque et conterminis regionibus icon
quarum alij Christiani alij Gentiles verum major
pars Mauritiñ Caffres vocant

Moerianen wt Moçambycke ēn die omliggende contreyen diemen
Caffres noemt sommighe zijn Christenen sommighe Heydenen
en t meestendeel Machometisten.

60 en 61

Nigritæ, sive Caffres, qui regnum Mosambicque & terras interiores usque ad Caput Bonę spei habitāt, nudi fere incedunt. Fœminę vero quæ circa Mosambicque degunt, consuetudine Lusitanorum tegunt corpus ex parte:nam pro Ebore & auro gossypium & linteamina ex Indiæ partibus comparant:Cęteri eodem vestimenti genere,quo protoplastus in Paradiso usus est degunt sunt autem nigerrimo colore.capillo crispo & adusto, barba rara,latis,planis & retusis naribus, magnis & crassis labijs, perforata in quibusdā partibus facie,& factis vulneribus,quæ ebore implent,singulari(ut existimant)decore. Etiam corpus ferro candenti,lineis & foraminibus lacerant,ita cutem stigmata notant; ut apud nos Phrygionum acus vestimenta. Pulchrum hoc ornamentum hisce populis est & contemnunt nostra corpora, vestimētis ac albo colore mōstris similia.Ideo etiam imago albi hominis & vestiimentis tecti,illis pro figura Dæmonis aut spectri est. Dentes etiam quidam lima terunt,& in aculeos formant.In summa Vetus est illis opinio. Nigritas præstare ante omnes homines,forma, colore ac ritu vivendi. Religio quibusdam eadem est quæ Mauris, in tractu nempe Abex,Melinde,& Mosambicque, ibi adsiduo commercio nefandissimæ sectæ studium invaluit,Pauci etiam Christiani sunt à Lusitanis ad fidem conversi. Cæteri vivunt belluino more nulle Deorum metu, nullo cultu,Regibus tamen parent, quos multos habent,singulis vicis præfectos. Continuis bellis afflicti inter se pugnant,& hostium carnibus vescuntur, etiam captivos ad forum trahunt ac Lusitanis vēdunt. fortissimus quisque in pretio est:& in testimonium virilitatis , hostium virilia detruncant , eaque ad regem siccata jam & à putre factione liberata deferunt,& ore primum assumpta ante pedes Domini expuunt,Is collaudate virtute restituit quidem membra, sed & honores addit;ac est illud ingentis fortunæ signum. Passim in India ex hac gente mancipia constant,crebris enim bellis multi capti venditioni fere exponuntur . Itaque vir unus duobus aut tribus Ducatis æstimatur, vili libertatis pretio. Etiam famis tempore parentes liberos ad servitutem trahunt,& Orizæ sex septemue modiolis damnatæ conditioni donant . Neque est illis dolori tanta calamitas,fatum accusantes & fortunam novercam,sperata interim libertate ex socijs & amicis, quos velut ultores & vindices adhuc restare prædicant.

The King of Cochin seated on an elephant, accompanied by his nobles, called Nayar.

The king of Cochin, who is a friend of the Portuguese and allied with them by a treaty, follows the practise of the kings of India in riding on an elephant, surrounded by his soldiers and noblemen. They are called Nayar and are the strongest people in the East. They always go about armed and ready to perform their services. Some of them carry a drawn sword in the right hand and a massive shield in the left. It is made of wood and covers the whole body. The Nayar beat the shield with the hilt of the sword to let the commoners know that the strongest men are approaching. Others carry a quiver with a bow and arrows, yet others rifles or muskets, which are extremely cleverly made and closely resemble ours. Thus are they ordered by their weapons, which they almost never remove. They are bachelors and are not allowed to marry, but they enter anyone's bedroom for promiscuous and licit intercourse. And there is no woman who refuses a Nayar the use of her body, so the doors are open. He lays down his weapons at the entrance and wages war with his Venus.

If a commoner touches a Nayar, it is punishable by death and the warrior is free to kill the rascal. That is why they shout as they proceed through the streets to announce their arrival. A Nayar who is impure from having touched a commoner is banned from associating with another Nayar until he has undergone a solemn and scrupulous washing. They make way for the Portuguese, however, because they were defeated in a duel between a Nayar and a Portuguese regarding supremacy in ranking and were forced to recognise the bravery of the Christians.

Thus had the king of Cochin wanted to prevent mutual rivalry from losing him the friendship that he had concluded with the Portuguese. Hence, nowadays a Nayar waits and gives way whenever a Portuguese passes.

The Nayar meticulously cultivate the growth of their fingernails. It is a sign of nobility, as if manual labour is thereby prohibited. But it also strengthens their fingers in wielding the sword, an idea that the Portuguese in those parts take seriously too. For they have long nails for the same reason. The highest-ranking among the Nayar wear gold or silver rings above their elbow as a sign of status, for they all go about naked among one another. They are certainly the strongest men, courageous soldiers, very disposed to exact vengeance, and able to withstand wounds. By law the daughters of the Nayar only sleep with Nayar, but they do not reject Christians and Portuguese and secretly allow them in, even at the risk of their lives, for a Nayar may punish this with death. They are very superstitious in washing. They wash their bodies in an artificial pool near their house, in putrid and dirty water, paying no heed to passersby. They do not allow river water and reject it as not being effective enough to purify the body. Sons do not inherit from their parents because they hold their womenfolk in common and the paternity of the children is therefore uncertain. But sisters' sons inherit, because even though the father is uncertain, the mother is certain.

PLATE 23

Cochini Rex elephante vectus, cum procerum comitatu, quos Nairos vocant.

Die Coninck van Cochin op een elephant geseeten verselschapt met sijn edelen diemen Nairos noemt

64 en 65

Rex Cochini Lusitanorum amicus & fœdere conjunctus, ad Indiæ Regum morem, Elephanto nehitur, militibus ac nobilibus ftipatus, Hos Nairos vocant, eftque in ijs potissimum robur oriétis. Armati semper incedunt, & parati ad servitium; quidam tenent evaginatum gladium dextra, & scutum ingens finiftra. Id ex ligno factum corpus totum tegit, & concutiunt id Nairi Capulo gladij, ut ita adventum tortissimorum virorum plebeius intelligat, alij Pharetram geftant & arcum ac fagittas, alij bombardas five muf-quettos, fabrefactos infigni arte, noftris maxime pares. Ita per arma divifi, nunquam fere illa deponunt. Cæ-libes funt, interdicto matrimonio, fed promiscuo & permisso concubitu omnium invadunt cubilia; neque eft quæ Nairo corporis ufam recufet, ita patent oftio pofitis ante fores armis Venerem fuam debellat.

Plebeius fi Nairum tangat mortis reus eft, permisfa facultate interficiendi temeratorem militi. Ideo per plateas incedunt vociferantes ac indicantes adventum. Etiam interdicta eft confuetudo cum cæteris Nairis huic polluto plebeij contactu, ante folemnem & fuperftitiofam lavationem. Lufitanis duntaxat cedunt, fingulari certamine Nairi & Lufitani de honoris gradu victi, & ad confessionem virtutis Chriftianorum deducti. Hoc enim Rex Cochini voluerat, ne ambitiofum certamen amicitiam quam cum Lufitano ftatuebat

averteret. Ideo hodie Nairus tranfeuntem Lufitanum operitur facto loco.

Vngues manuum Nairi ftudiofe nutriunt, id infigne nobilitatis eft; velut interdicto ita labore. Sed etiam fervit ad robur digitorum in gladijs tenendis, opinione in ijs partibus, vel Lufitanis non ridicula, qui eadem ratione ungues majores habent. Præcipui Nairorum annulos aureos five argenteos fupra cubitum oftétant, ad dignitatis difcrimen. Nudi enim omnes promifcue degunt: robuftissimi fane homines, animofi milites, vindictæ etiamnum cupidissimi, ac vulnerum patientes. Filiæ Nairorum non nifi cum Nairis ex lege concumbunt. Verum neque Chriftianū, neq; Lufitanum reijciunt, clam enim admittunt etiam manifefto vitæ difcrimine. Nam Nairus talem infamiam morte vindicat licenter. Superftitiofi valde in lavationibus, nam in ftagno quod ædibus efossum adjacet, corpus abluunt, aqua fœtida & fœda, fine ullo trâfeuntium refpectu. Fluvialem aquam non admittunt, & ut parum ad emundanda corpora efficacem refpuunt. Filij parentum ad hereditatem non admittuntur communes enim uxores funt, ideoque incerti liberi fororum tamen filij heredes funt, etfi enim pater incertus, mater tamen certa eft.

The Mohammedans of Cananor, deadly enemies of the Portuguese.
Inhabitants of Malabar, between Goa and Cochin on the coast where pepper grows.

The kingdom of Cananor in India in the province of Malabar is ruled by the Portuguese. It has a fortress to protect the city. A lot of pepper is harvested there. There is an open area near the fortress that is occupied by the Malabars. A large quantity of produce of all kinds is bought and sold there every day. Eggs, cheese, honey, butter, oil, and bananas, which are rated more highly here than in the rest of India, are displayed almost as they are in Holland. Here too the most wonderful ship's masts are sold, which are not inferior to those from Norway. The countryside is also very attractive, and with its many tall trees and the sweetness of the fruits it really is a joy to behold, as is this whole region of India. Numerous white Moors who adhere to the sect of Mohammed and trade on the Red Sea live among the Malabars. This trade is barely possible without the permission of the Portuguese. They have to request a document from the Portuguese; otherwise they become a booty. When the viceroy's fleet, which guards the coast and sea in the normal season, encounters people who are sailing the Red Sea without the governor's permit, they are carried off as prisoners. The Moors of Cananor are regarded as friends of the Portuguese, but in secret they are their foes, for they assist the other Malabars, who are enemies of the Portuguese, with silver and gold and incite them to war. The other inhabitants are very skilled in the art of warfare and are the most bitter opponents of the Christians. They are encouraged in this by the Moors, who resist the Christian belief with extremely wicked and intolerant scheming and prevent the natives from reconciling themselves to it. In short, they leave no stone unturned to sow the seeds of tumult and upheaval.

PLATE 24

Hinschoten

Joannes à Doetechum fecit.

Inquilini e Cananor Mahometani infectiff.
Lufitanorum hoftes
Die Machometiften van Cananor en doot
vianden vande Portugeefen

Incolę Malabarę maritimi inter Goam et Cochina
apud quos piper nafcitur.
Jnwoonders van Malabar tuffchen Goa en Cochÿn
aende Zeecant daer die peeper waft

64 en 65

CAnanor Indiæ Regnum in provincia Malabar à Lufitanis tenetur, arce ad confervationē vrbisinftructa. Multum hic Piperis colligitur, & eft locus patens apud arcem à Malabarenfibus occupatus; ibi quotidiana eft omnium rerum ad emptionem venditionemque celebritas, Batavo fere ritu, expofitis Ovis, Cafeo, Melle, Butyro, Oleo & Ficubus, quibus in hifce partibus majus nomen eft, quam in univerfa India. Etiam arbores navium pulcherrimæ hic venduntur, ut nec Norvegia meliores habeat. Ipfa terræ crufta amæniffima eft, multis altifque arboribus, fructuum fuavitate, fpectatu prorfus jucunda, ut etiam omnis hic Indiæ tractus. Inter Malabarenfes habitant multi Mauri albi, qui Machometi fectam fequuntur & mercatu-

ram agunt per mare rubrum. Cęterum fine licentia Lufitanorum commercij ifta facultas vix conceditur. Diploma ab ijs exigere debent, alioquin in prædam cedunt & Claffis Proregis, quæ littus ac mare fueto tempore cuftodit, fi in hofce incidat, qui fine licentia Præfecti Rubrum mare petunt captivos abducit. Mauri Cananor amici Lufitanorum habentur, fed tecti funt hoftes; nam argento ac auro Malabarenfes cæteros Portugallenfium inimicos adjuvant, & ad bellum hortantur. Cæteri incolę periti funt artis militaris, & hoftes certiffimi Chriftianorum, incitantibus Mauris; qui peffimo & afperrimo ftudio fidem Chrifti impediunt, indigenas à cōcordia deterrēt; in fumma omnē lapidē movent ad turbas ac feditiones feminandas.

A native of Pegu, where copious gold, diamonds, and rubies are found and where lacquer is made.
An inhabitant of the islands of the Moluccas, where nutmeg grows in abundance, whose clothing is of straw.
Of the Penequais family of Saint Thomas, all accursed, as the Indians say.

The inhabitants of the kingdom of Pegu have more or less the same features as the Chinese, but they are darker in colour, while the Chinese are lighter-skinned. They have a remarkable tradition for receiving a guest. First they ask him how much time he intends to spend in the region for trade, then they present him with a large number of their daughters to choose from, to take one to his home after a bargain has been struck on the price. During that period he possesses her as a servant and wife, but is strictly prohibited from contact with another man's wife. When the period draws to a close, he pays the price to the parents or friends and gives the concubine back. She returns home and waits for another relationship, without her honour having been damaged. And when a marriage is made later, but the first guest returns and claims her as his wife, she submits to his authority and leaves the new husband. And when a member of the nobility marries a woman, he seeks out a stranger and requests that he deflower the bride, a very enjoyable and very honourable service.

Many of the people of Pegu have a little bell attached to their prepuce to prevent illicit intercourse. They sew up a girl's genitals, and when she becomes a bride they cut it open again to suit the wishes of the husband, while doctors and physicians stand at the ready.

The islands of the Moluccas that are very famous for their vast quantity of nutmeg are inhabited by people who exchange it with the other peoples of India to obtain everything necessary for their subsistence, for the islands produce nothing except nutmeg. They obtain meat and fish, rice, grain, leeks, etc. from elsewhere. The ground itself is parched and has volcanic mountains that demonstrate the heat of its interior. They wear clothing made from straw or plants, which is woven with great care and skill. The so-called bird of paradise is found on these islands, and has a curious nature and an unusual appearance.

Among the Malabars live the Saint Thomas Christians too, who are born with a swollen foot and, according to the story, are accursed by Saint Thomas in perpetuity. The illustration here shows their deformation and the appearance of the peoples of the Moluccas and of Pegu.

PLATE 25

N.linschoten.

Joannes à Doetechum fecit.

Provinciæ Pegu incola, auri adamantum et rubinorum ferax, undelacca sigillatoria advehitur.	Incola ex Insulis Moluco, ubi Caryophylla magnâ copiâ crescunt, quorum vestes e stramine sunt factæ.	Penequais familiæ, a Divo Thoma execratæ, intotam (ut Indi referunt) pro-geniem
Een uut Pegu, waer veel gout diamanter ēn robynen gevonden ēn het zegellack, gemaeckt woort	Een inwoonder uut die Eylanden van Moluco, daer die Garyophyl. nagelen overvloedich groyen, welcks cleederen van stroy zyn	Van penekays geslachten van S. Thomas als die Indianen seggen gantselicken verulceckt.

64. en 65

IN Regno Pegu incolæ eodem sunt fere vultu quo Chinenses, verum colore fusco, qui Chinensibus candidior est. Morem habent in suscipiendo hospitæ memorabilem. Nam ex eo primum quærunt tēpus, quod in ista provincia terere mercaturæ gratia velit, inde multos illi filias statuunt, ex quibus unam eligat, & pretio conventione inita domum deducat; hanc ut famulam & uxorem illo spacio habet, interdicta tamen arctè cōsuetudine cum aliena. Finito tempore pretium parentibus sive amicis numerat, Concubinam restituit, illa domum reversa, nullo pudicitiæ detrimento aliud commercium exspectat. Et contracto postea matrimonio, si prior hospes revertatur, postuletque coniugem, recedit illa in potestatem relicto novo marito. Etiam qui ex nobilitate uxorem ducit, aliquem advenam diligenter investigat, eumque rogat ut sponsæ virginitatem eripiat; gratisimo & honorifico facto.

Multi ex Peguensibus nolas affixas præputio habent ad avertendum usum præposteræ ve-

neris. Puellis muliebre membrum filo contrahunt, & sponsæ jam pro arbitrio mariti sectione aperiunt, paratis ad tale vulnus medicis & remedijs.

Insulæ Moluccæ Caryophyllorum immensa copia celeberrimè, incolas habent, qui ex istis cum cæteris Indis facta permutatione, omnia ad victum necessaria conquirunt; nam Insulæ hæ nihil ferunt, præter Caryophylla, Carnem & Piscem, Orizam, frumentum, porrum, &c. aliunde accipiunt. Terra ipsa arida est & habet mōtes flammiuomos, in testimonium interioris caliditatis. Vestimentum incolis est ex stramine, aut herbis, magna cura & arte contextū. Avis, quam Paradisi vocant in hisce Insulis reperitur, rara natura & specie insolita.

Inter Malabarenses habitant & Christiani quidam S. Thomæ, crasso pede nati, & ut fertur à Divo Thoma in totam progeniem execrati, Præsens figura formam ostendit, & incolarum ex Moluccis ac Pegu habitum demonstrat.

Terrible images of the Indian idols, called Pagodas, are placed at every street corner, where they make their offerings and their popes the Brahmans (who are held to be very wise there) worship them in great devotion. Mosque, or temple of the Mohammedan Indians, whose sect has penetrated almost the whole of the Orient.

The Indians believe in one God who is obeyed by all. All the same, they have a number of gods, who were formerly humans and were held in high esteem for their piety and holiness, but have now been included in the pantheon and have made themselves an object of adoration by other men through particular miracles. They are venerated with a gigantic and awesome image because, so they say, the deity wishes it. Everywhere by the roadside and at crossroads you can see diabolical statues, a repulsive disgrace to every right-minded person, with long teeth, a terrible face, a gaping mouth, long ears, and a belly divided by various lines. In the temples too are terrifying statues that they called Pagodas and which were worshipped for the most foolish reasons before the Portuguese came to Goa. Nowadays this idolatry still flourishes in the interior of India. And on the island of Ceylon they worship a monkey's tooth with great honours in the most solemn ceremony that you can imagine. In the hope of larger profit, the Portuguese had taken this with them, hidden in a chest encrusted with pearls and gold. This greatly dismayed all the kings, who sent envoys to the Portuguese with an offer of seven thousand ducats to buy back the tooth. But the archbishop prevented it, stating that it was not right for Christians to support a horrible cult in exchange for money. So the tooth was cast into the fire and, to the sound of loud lamentations from the envoys, it was transmuted into ash. However, a cunning Banyan (for they are almost all cunning there) obtained another

tooth and offered it to the king of Bisnagar, as if the tooth had been rescued by a miracle and the pagoda had revealed its whereabouts to him. He was amply rewarded for it. And that tooth was then honoured with the same devotion and ceremony.

This illustration also shows the mosques, the temples of the Moors, in which they say their prayers. Floors and small buildings have been added above the temple, where they instruct the children in religion and teach them the catechism, as it were. They wash their feet, and there is a receptacle full of water in front of the temple entrance to wash their feet. They take off their shoes when they enter the shrine, fall on their faces in adoration, with demonstrative gestures and ridiculous movements of their body. These temples do not contain a single statue but only certain stones with Chaldean inscriptions. They worship God in the heavens and spurn all idols as useless. That is contained in their religion. The Pagodas, which, as we said, are honoured and worshipped by the Indians, are scattered all over the country. The idol that is paid the highest respects is on the island of Pory. The Portuguese call it the Elephant Statue. In this temple there are statues of lions, elephants, etc., crafted with the greatest artistic skill. It has been claimed that the Chinese were once in control of these lands through trade and that they made the images and sculptures with their wonderful craftsmanship. The great prestige and respect paid to that handiwork continued afterwards.

PLATE 26

Horrendæ Idolorum effigies, quæ in omnibus viarum angulis obuia Indi proftrati paffim adorant
et donarijs profequuntur, a Bramenis facerdotibus, ob fapientiæ opinionem, apud
illos magni habitis, Pagodes dicta.

Scrickelicke beeldeniffe der Indiaenfche affgoden geftelt op alle hoecken van de weegen welcke fij haer
offerhande doen en feer de voetelicken aenbidden van haer papen Bramenes (die
om opinie van wyfheyt daer feer geacht fijn) Pagodes genaemt

Mefquita feu templum Indorum Mahometiftarum quæ fecta
totum fere, orientem pervafit.

Mefquita ofte tempel der Machometifche Indianen welcke
feckte bynaer geheel Orienten doordrongen heeft

66 en 67

Bapt: a Doet: fe:

INdi unum Deum, Regem cui omnia parent fatetur, quofdam tamen Divos habent, olim quidem homines ac pietatis fanctitatifque opinione clariffimos, nunc vero in divorum numerum relatos, & hominibus
cæteris certis apparitionibus ad venerationem manifeftatos. Colunt aute hos figura enormi & immani,
ita (ut aiunt)volente numine:paffim in vijs & compitis diabolicæ imagines,omni ingenio ad turpitudinem
ac terriculamentum,longis dentibus facie fœda,ore fparfo, auriculis longioribus, ventre divifo per varias
lineas effictæ, oftenduntur.In templis quoque horrendæ imagines;quas Pagodes vocant, & colebatur ftul-
tiffima opinione,ante adventum Lufitanorum circa Goam,Nunc in partibus Indiæ interioribus adhuc hæc
floret idololatria;& fuit in Infula Zeilan honorifice cultus dens fimiæ, tanta folemnitate;ut nihil fupra.Huc
Lufitani fpe majoris lucri abftulerant,inclufum Ciftæ gemmis & auro ornatæ,magno omnium Regum do-
lore,qui ad Lufitanos legatos mifere,cum oblatione 7000.ducatorum,pro redemptione dentis. Cæterum
impedivit Archiepifcopus;non convenire Chriftianis accepto pretio nutrimentum deteftabilis cultus dicti-
tans. Itaque injectus dens igni, magna legatorum commiferatione in cineres abijt. Sed Banianes quidam
fubdolus(ut funt ifti homines fere)alium dentem comparavit,eumque velut miraculo ereptum & fibi à Pa-

gode idolo revelatum Regi Bifnagar obtulit;magnis inde affectus præmijs. Eftque is tunc in honore habitus
pari veneratione & obfervantia.

Mefkytas,Maurorum templa etiam hęc figura oftendit,ibi preces fundunt.Templo fuperftructa funt ta-
bulata & ædificia, ibi pueri religionis femenia imbuuntur & velut ad Catechifmum tenentur.Lavant pedes;
& eft vas aqua plenum ante fores templi,ad ufum lavandi. Calceos intrates ædem facram exuunt, in faciem
adorantes procidunt,multis manuum jactationibus;& quadam motione corporis ridicula. Nulla in hifce
templis imago eft;tantum lapides quidam literis notati Chaldaicis.Deum in Cœlis venerantur,figuras omnes ut inanes reijciunt.Ita fert horum religio,Pagodes autem quos ab Indis in honore ac veneratione habi-
tos diximus,per totam Regionem fparfi funt. In Infula vero Pory fummæ religionis idolum eft, quod Ele-
phantis,Lufitanis vocatur.In templo hoc figuræ Leonum, Elephantum, &c,oftenduntur,fumma arte laboratæ;Creditum eft Chinenfes aliquando has terras mercaturæ ftudio tenuiffe, qui ingeniofis operibus figu-
ras & fculpturas perfecerint, Inde manfit honos ac operis veneratio.

The fruits that grow in India and are very pleasant to eat are the mangos, cajus, jambos, jacks, and pineapples, with the ginger, which is held in little esteem because it is so plentiful, copied from life as they stand and grow.

The palm of victory among the fruits of India is owed to the pineapple, which was first imported into these parts from Brazil. They ripen during Lent and have a delicious flavour. They are the size of a melon, shaped like a distaff at the top, with the outward appearance of a pinecone, and they are red and green in colour. The plants grow to the height of an ell and resemble thistles. They are evergreens. The pineapple is cut into rings and has the colour of a ripe peach. They are warm, and if someone plunges his knife in and leaves it there for half an hour, the knife itself is consumed. That is why the ill are not allowed to eat it. They are not so harmful for healthy people, unless eaten to excess.

The jacks are of an extraordinary nature. They grow on the trunk of a very tall tree beside the coast. When the tree produces leaves and branches, it does not produce fruit. They have the size and shape of melons and resemble the pineapple, but they are light green in colour. The inside is divided into parts by fibres and is whitish-yellow in colour. The pits taste like honey. A single fruit contains around one hundred such pits. There are two kinds. The best is called Girasal, the plainer one Chambasal. The trees and fruits have the same shape, but differ in sweetness of taste.

The mangos hang from the trees, just like the jackfruit. They are as big as a peach and the colour is green to red. They have a large pit that is not edible. The colour of the inside is yellowish. They are much used in India, like olives in Spain. They are very sweet-tasting, though less

so than the pineapple. People boil rice with these fruits and they are the daily fare of the servants. They ripen between Lent and August. They are found everywhere in abundance and are extremely cheap.

There is a tree in India that resembles an apple tree. Its fruits are the size of a pear, yellow, tapering at the back and rounded at the front. If they are ripe, they are soft to the touch and have a shape very different from an apple. For while the apple hangs by a stalk on its rounded side from the tree, these fruits (called Cajus) have a chestnut, which is sweet if you open it with a knife and place it in the fire. The Cajus apple itself has a sharp taste and irritates the throat somewhat, but it tastes better with a little salt. It is found everywhere but is less esteemed than the mangos and pineapples.

India also produces jambos, very sweet apples, with a wonderful flavour, scent, and colour. The tree, which looks like a plum tree, bears fruit three to four times in India and while ripe fruits constantly drop from one part of the tree, in another part they are still green and still produce new leaves. So they can be picked all year round in an enjoyable succession. The colour is of a red and white that no brush can imitate. The scent is like rosewater. On the inside they are white. The pulp is moist and watery. The sick are allowed them because they have absolutely no negative effects. They have a pit, like the fruit of the cypress. These are the best fruits of India. The rest are held of little account. Common ginger is to be found in abundance and is therefore looked down upon.

PLATE 27

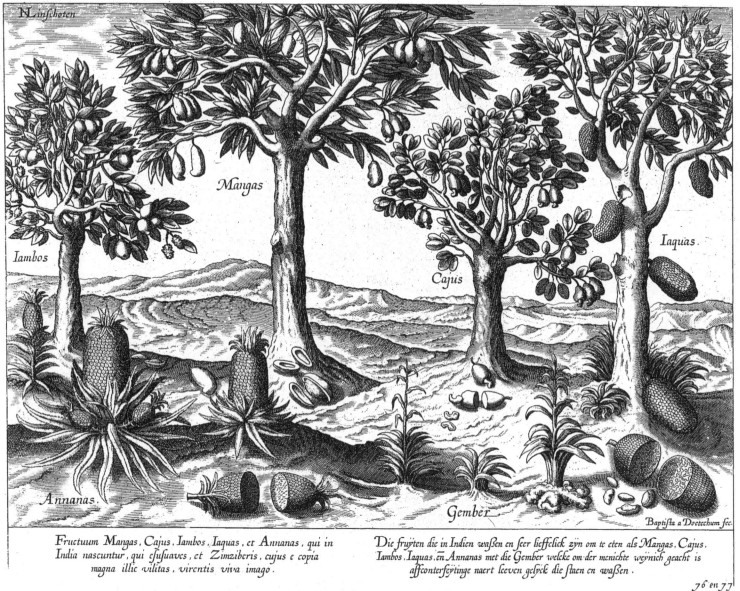

Fructuum Mangas, Cajus, Iambos, Iaquas, et Annanas, qui in India nascuntur, qui essuaves, et Zimziberis, cujus e copia magna illic vilitas, virentis viva imago.

Die fruyten die in Indien wassen en seer lieffelick zijn om te eten als Mangas, Cajus, Iambos, Iaquas, en Annanas met die Gember welcke om der menichte weynich geacht is affconterfeytinge naert leeven gelyck die staen en wassen.

76 en 77

Baptista a Doetechum fec.

INter fructus Indiæ, saporis gratia palmam fere obtinent Anane, ex Brasilia primum ad Orientales partes tráslatæ.Quadragesimę tempore ad maturitatem perductæ, optimo gustu sunt, magnitudine Melopeponis,forma ad caput coli, specie Nucis pineæ, colore rubro & viridi;excrescunt altitudine cubiti ad formam Carduorum;folia sunt ut semper-viuæ, Pomum scindût orbiculatim, & est color ut Persico maturo. Calidæ sunt; ac si quis cultrum per horæ dimidiatę spacium, pomo infixum habeat, eo spacio fere ferrum ipsum cōsumptum erit, Ideo esus infirmis interdicitur;sanis non ita nocet, nisi abundanter & supra modū sumātur.

Iaccæ mirabili natura ex trunco altissimæ arboris nascútur,ad Littus maris: Vbi arbor in folia & ramos se fundit nulli sunt fructus. Magnitudine autem & forma Melopeponis fere sunt,ad Ananas accedunt,colore tamen subviridi. Tunicis autem distinctus est interior nucleus, colore inter albedinem & flauedinem; sapore mellis.Tales fere tunicę centum numero in uno pomo reperiuntur. Est autem duplex genus: Optimum vocatur Girasal;illud quod simplicius est Chambasal. Arboribus & fructibus eadem forma est; Sed ex gustus suavitate discernuntur.

Mangæ ex arboribus dependēt,ad similitudinem arborum Iaccæ,magnitudine Persici sunt,colore viridi, & ad ruborem accedente.Osficulum habent maius;sed ad esum nullo usu. Interior Mangæ color ad flauedi-

nem accedit,magni in India usus;ut Olivarum in Hispania;Post Ananas gustu sunt maxime suavi,Orizam cum hisce fructibus coquunt.estque quotidianus mancipiorum cibus.Maturitatis tempus à Quadragesima illis ad Augustum durat;ingenti passim numero & vili pretio.

Arbor in India ad mali formam fructus fert Piri magnitudine,flavo colore, posteriore parte acuta,& anteriore crassa, molli tactu sunt maturi & contraria plane forma pomis. Cum enim poma pediculo in crassiori parte arbori adhereant,hi fructus(quosCaius vocant)Castaneam habent,quę culto discissa;& igni admota suavis est,Ipsum pomum Cajus,acidi saporis est & in gutture aliquantulum arctat ; sale tamen addito melioris saporis est.Passim habetur ac in minori æstimatione est post Mangas & Ananas.

Iambos etiam fert India;poma sane suavissima & excellentis saporis, odoris ac coloris . Arbor ut Prunus per Indiam ter quateruę fructus fert,& in una parte subinde maturos cadentibus folijs,in altera adhuc virides folijs nascentibus.Ita per universum anni tempus grata vicissitudine carpuntur. Color rubicúdus est & albus nullo penicillo exprimēdus;Odor ut Aquæ ex Rosis, interior color albus est,succus humidus & aquosis,infirmis non interdicitur;est enim haud noxiæ virtutis. Osficulum habēt;ut fructus Cyparissi , suntq; hi fructus Indiæ præstantissimi,cæteri parvo sunt in honore; Zingiberis vulgaris copia est & cōtempta idea.

Indian nuts or palm trees, which produce a lot in India because they provide sweet food and drink, and material for ships, sails, and ropes, and are loaded into the same ships and nourish the mariners. A plant that bears fruit all year round, called the Indian fig, highly nourishing, and a staple of the Indian's daily diet. Fruits called Areca or Faufel and betel leaves, which the Indians mix with a little chalk and chew all day long. They extract the sap as a purgative and for its other properties. Oriental pepper grows like ivy.

India has a tree that possesses many qualities and lends itself for a variety of uses. It is known as the palm. Thanks to the copious generosity of nature it bears fruits which stand out for their utility for an almost infinite number of purposes. The Portuguese call these fruits coconuts, and they are also mentioned by Avicenna. The tree itself is slender and has no branches except at the top. The nuts grow beneath the leaves, attached to the tree itself. The wood is spongy and the roots short but strong, which is surprising in view of its great height. The Canarim climb this height at a tremendous pace, to the alarm of spectators, and have made incisions in the bark to make it easier to climb. Although the wood is spongy, the natives of the Maldives use it to make boats, without any iron to hold it together. They fasten the timbers with a cord that they produce from the nuts. The ropes and anchor cables are made of the same cord. The sail is made from the leaves, which they call Olas, and which are also used to roof the houses of the Canarim, as mats for the palanquins, and as sun helmets. They are very popular. Some cultivate this tree for the fruits, others for the wine. The coconut itself is the size of an ostrich egg and is covered with a green husk or bark, just like our nuts. This husk, which is hairy, is used to make all the ropes in India for seafaring. They are well able to withstand saltwater but rot in the rain. When the fruits start to ripen they are called Lanha, and they contain water that changes after a while into a pit or apple with a very pleasant taste. When the husk has been removed, the shell is used as a beaker and spoon, which is very convenient. The pit, however, is the fare of the servants and is exported to every part of India. They also use this fruit to make oil and water as a healthy drink, and even vinegar, wine, and sugar. The Indians make paper from the pith of the tree, and all the books in India are made of this material, while nature produces folds in the tree itself to separate the pages.

The banana tree in India is splendid. It grows to a man's height and has amazingly long leaves, which are very useful for disparate purposes. It bears a large crop of fruits just like grapes, which are the size of a cucumber and which hang from the tree, provided each tree is pruned after producing a shoot with a bunch of fruit. Immediately afterward it grows back again very quickly and produces new fruits. It is the staple diet of the Indians. The best come from Cananor. Sometimes a bunch calls for the strength of two men, as the Holy Bible also mentions [Numbers 13:24].

Indian women constantly chew betel and areca. Betel grows like pepper and ivy, areca in the shape of the palm tree. The habit of chewing these fruits for the digestion and for clean breath is universal among the Indians. Pepper climbs around the tree just like ivy. This illustration shows how it does so.

PLATE 28

Nuces Indicæ, magni in India usus et questuosæ, cibum et potum homi: nibus suaves et navibus materiam præbent idoneam quibus e eadem et onerantur et aluntur nautæ.	Ficus Indicą per totum annum ferens fructus copiosé nutrientes quotidianam mul: torum escam.	Fructuum icon quos Arrecca sive Faufel vocant, et Bettelle folia, quos pauco calcis subactos integrum diem masticant, suc: cum deglutientes ad corporis purgationem aliasq; utilitates.	Piperis frutex hæderæ non absimilis.
Indiaensche nooten ofte Palmboomen welcke in Indien veel opbren: gen want geven soete spijs en dranck stoff tot scheepen, seylen en touwen en daer die selffse scheepen met geladen en die schip: luyden mede gevoet werden	Een plante draegende het geheele Iaer vruchten, diemen Indiaensche vygen noemt, seer voedende en een daegelickse spijse der Indianen.	Fruyten diemen Arrecca ofte Faufel noemt en die bladen Bet: telle, welcke met wat calcks vermengt die Indianen een gant: schen dach kauwen het sap doorswelgen om t'lichaem te purge: ren en ander haerder crachten.	Orientaelsche Peeper wasschen: de t'muer cryvt niet ongelyck.

80 en 81.

Habet India arborem multæ virtutis; multique usus, quæ Palmæ quidem nomine nota est, verum fructus fert prodiga naturę liberalitate in infinitas pene res utilitate præstantes. Hos Lusitani Coquo vocãt; & sunt Avicennæ etiam noti. Arbor ipsa procera, ramos nullos præterquam in summitate producit. Nuces sub folijs crescunt, ad ipsam arborem fixæ. Lignum spongiosum est & radice minuta verum firma, quod mireris, insigni altitudine, quam Canarini eximia velocitate superant, cum horrore spectantium, & sunt scissuræ in cortice laboratæ, ad faciliorem ascensum, Ex Ligno autem, licet spongioso, incolæ Maldivat naves conficiunt, nulla ex ferro junctura sed enim filo contexunt, quod ex nucibus paratur. Itaque Rudentes & anchoralia ex eodem filo sunt, Velum autem ex folijs, quæ Olas vocant, & serviunt illa etiam ad tegumentum ædium Canarinorum, storeas Pallanquinorum, Galeros ad arcendum solem, multa æstimatione. Quidam autem hanc arborem colunt fructuum gratia, quidam vini. Nux ipsa coquos ad magnitudinẽ Ovi Struthionis, cortice sive culleola tegitur viridi, ut nostrę nuces, Ex cortice, est enim pilosus, omnes Indiæ rudentes conficiuntur, ad usum marinum, & aquam salsam amant, cælesti putredinem adsciscunt. Fructus ad maturitatem accedentes Lanha vocantur, & intus aquam habent, quę temporis tractu in nucleum muta-

tur, vel potum saporis gratissimi. Cortice dempto exterior: tunica ad calices & cochlearia servit, commodissimo usu. Nucleus autem famulorum cibus est, & per omnes Indiæ partes distrahitur. Oleum ex hoc fructu etiam conficiunt, & aquam ad potum salubrem, etiam acerum, Vinum & Saccarum. Ex interiori medulla Arboris Chartam Indi habent, suntque omnes Libri Indię ex hac materia, natura producente in ipsa arbore Plicas, ad distinctionem foliorum.

Ficus Indiæ præstantissima, ad hominis magnitudinem crescit, folijs longis ad stuporem & in varios usus commodissimis. Fructus uvarum specie in magnitudinem Cucumeris multiplices, ealibus adhærent Racemum duntaxat unum quæque arbor fert, & detruncatur tum arbor, quæ continuo brevi spacio excrescit, & novos fert fructus, communis Indorum cibus & sunt præstantissimæ ex Canonor. Racemus aliquando duorum virorum vires implet, ut & S. scriptura testatur.

Bettelam & Areccam Indice mulieres omni tempore mandunt. Bettela crescit in formam Piperis, & Hederæ. Arecca in formam Palmæ, estque hic mos vulgaris apud Indos ore terere hos fructus ad stomachu & boni halitus gratiam, Piper ut Hedera arbores amplectitur & ostendit præsens figura formam.

Indian reed that grows to the thickness of a man's thigh or leg. A wondrous tree whose branches reach downward, and extending so much at the roots as to provide enough room for a whole army to rest beneath it. The fruits called durians, praised above all others for their taste and sweetness, grow only in Malacca.

Malacca produces durians, fruits of an incomparable sweetness with the shape of a melon, just like the jackfruit but the husk contains more thorns. For anyone not used to it, the scent is unbearable, but the flavour is very refreshing without the sweetness ever becoming tiresome. They are therefore very esteemed among the inhabitants, even though they cost little, and people write epigrams and songs to them. They have remarkable qualities as a dish called *mangiar blanco,* which ranks among the delicacies of the meal. There is a sort of natural antipathy between betel and durian, for if betel is placed besides the durians, they die, and if the stomach is burdened by excessive consumption of durians, it is relieved with the assistance of betel, a tried and tested remedy for every overindulgence.

The root tree of India is also famous everywhere. It has branches that extend so far on all sides that two hundred men can stand beneath them, and roots hang down which, because they reach the ground, give the tree the appearance of a multiple trunk with widely extending branches that keep on forming new trees. They do not bear edible fruit.

The Coromandel region produces reeds as thick as a thighbone. The Portuguese call it bamboo. It contains a white material that is very effective as a remedy and very much sought by Arabs and Persians. They call it tabaxyr and pay gold and silver for it. The Indians use it for wounds to the testicles and penis, and it also helps against choleric afflictions and dysentery. The reeds are shaped and bent for the palanquins by making them into a sort of stake. The Indians also make boats from them, which they use on the river Cranganor, and they claim that crocodiles make way for these boats, attacking the other boats but never throwing themselves upon the bamboo boats.

There are other, enormously thick trees in the Orient from which boats are made. Near Cochin there is a tree called angelina. It is used to make boats called tonis, which consist of an entire tree trunk, with an incredible capacity. And it is very hard, hard enough to cause damage to iron. These boats do not have any seams, because the dugout trunk simply floats on the water.

Behold, the Indian tree extends wide with its dark and widely extending branches, such that it offers pleasant shade for entire armies. To produce new branches and to drive them toward the open air, it has large hanging branches with their seeds. P. HOOGERBEETS

PLATE 29

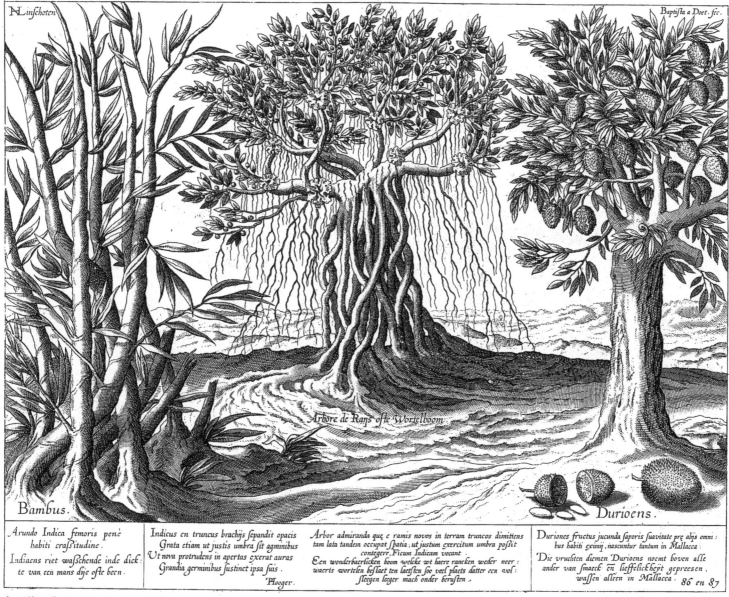

Linschoten   Baptista a Doet. fec.

Arbore de Rays ofte Wortelboom

Bambus.   Durioens.

| Arundo Indica femoris penè habiti crassitudine. Indiaens riet wasschende inde dick: te van een mans dije ofte been. | Indicus en truncus brachijs separdit opacis Grata etiam ut justis umbra sit agminibus Ut nova protrudens in apertas exerat auras Grandia germinibus sustinet ipsa suis. Plooger. | Arbor admiranda quæ e ramis novos in terram truncos dimittens tam lata tandem occupat spatia, ut justum exercitum umbra possit contegere, Ficum Indicam vocant. Een wonderbaerlicken boom welcke wt haere rancken weder neer: waerts wortelen beslaet ten laetsten soo veel plaets datter een vol: sleegen leeger mach onder berusten. | Duriones fructus jucunda saporis suavitate præ alijs omni: bus habiti exinij, nascuntur tantum in Mallacca. Die vruchten diemen Durioens noemt boven alle ander van smaeck en lieffelickheyt gepreesen, wassen alleen in Mallacca. 86 en 87 |

Malacca Duriones fert, incomparabili suavitate fructus, in formam Melonis, ut Iaccæ, sed cortice spinosiore, tetro odore insolitis sunt, sed gustu amænissimo, satietate nulla ob dulcedinem. Ab incolis ideo celebrantur quamvis vili pretio, inde etiam epigrammata & rythmos in honorem con: cinnant. Et est sane insignis præstantia; ut cibi quem mangiar blanco vocant, honorifico inter delitias mense nomine. Inter Bettelam & Duriones quædam contrarietas naturarum est, nam si Bettela Durioni: bus apponatur pereunt Duriones, & stomachus gravatus nimio esu Duriorum Bettellæ adjumento libera: tur, certissimo remedio ad omne fastidium.

Arbor radicum Indiæ quoque notissima est; ea fundit ramos patentes ad capacitatem ducentorum ferè hominum, & dependent radices quæ in terram iterum infixæ longa serie arborem hanc ostendunt patulis ramis & ad novos fœtus semper efficacibus, Fructus non fert esui commodos.

Arundines fert Regio Charundel fæmoris crassitudine, quas Lusitani Bambu vocant. Est interior Arun:

dinum materia alba, & ad usus medecinæ aptissima, ab Arabibus & Persis summo studio quæsita; Tabaxyr vocant, & auro ac argento ponderatur. Indi ad vulnera testiculorum & virgæ utuntur, valet etiam contra colericas passiones & Dysenteriam. Formantur autem Arundines & incurvantur ad usum Pallanquino: rum, nam ex ijs conficiuntur veluti stipites. Naves quoque Indi conficiunt quibus in flumine Cranganor, utuntur, & existimāt Crocodilos ab hisce navigijs abhorrere, nam cum cætera sæpe invadant, arundineum Acatium nunquam adoriuntur.

Aliæ in Oriente Arbores sunt, crassitudine mirabiles, ex quibus etiam navigia conficiuntur. Circa Co: chinum Arbor est quam Angelinam vocāt, ex ea naves ædificantur, quas Tones nominant, integro trunco, capacissimo & durissimo; nam & ferrum duritie sua rodit; Nullæ in hisce navigijs commissuræ, ita excauata tum duntaxat lignum pelago innatat.

A tree known only in India, which produces many sweet-scented blossoms at sunset,
which all fall when the sun rises, the whole year round.

The tree known as the tree of melancholy is said by its wonderful nature to have stirred the pens of resourceful minds to noteworthy stories and poems. The Indians too tell a story about its origin, which is worthy of songs and poetic ecstasy. A nobleman called Parisatico had a very beautiful daughter. Fired by love for her, the sun dallied with the girl. In her joy at such an exceptional suitor, the girl exchanged her virginity for the deity's love, until he, with the fickleness that is a characteristic of the gods, turned his flames of love upon another woman. Then the disconsolate girl ended her life on the spot. Placed on the fire and transformed into ash, she made the site of the pyre fertile to produce this tree. So whenever the sun shines, the tree hides the beauty of its flowers and folds its leaves as a sign of its justified wrath, but after the sun has gone down it is ablaze with blossoms and delights mortals with the most pleasant scent. That is the Indian story. And indeed, this alternation takes place all year round and the tree sheds its blossoms after sunrise and reveals them again after sunset. A wonderful symbolism. The tree is the size of a plum tree and stands besides entrances as an adornment and a pleasure. It has an exceptional growing force, for even if it is chopped down, it easily triumphs over its fate with a new crop of blossoms. It is only at home in India, for numerous experiments have shown that it does not grow in Portugal. Like the Assyrian apple tree, it bears blossoms with a delightful scent, which disappears, however, at a touch. These blossoms produce a very pure and aromatic water. Clusius considers that the sap of the tree cannot withstand the heat of the sun and that the blossoms therefore fall from lack of nutriment. For trees on which the sun shines less mercilessly blossom for a much longer period.

Behold a branch that is enriched with sweetnesses in the dark of night. When it is enriched, the mild day strips it of its blossoms. To make this jewel become strong and weak in the same hour, night and day alternate permanently. To that it owes the epithet 'the melancholy', since it is a bare trunk once the rays of the golden sun shine over the red world. Just so the renewed light of the truth produces the conviction that what is beautiful in our perception is merely smoke.
P. HOOGERBEETS

PLATE 30

Arbore triste de dia. *Arbore triste de noite.*

Fule.

Pim.ta Peeper *Arecca Faufel.*

Ecce tibi ramum nigra quem nox fuavibus ornat
Exuit ornatum floribus alma dies
Ut decus hoc una augeatque et defluat hora
Continuas obeunt illa diefque vices

Traxit et hinc nomen tristi quod fqualido trunco
Auricomum rutilo cum nitet orbe jubar
Haud fecus et noftro que fenfu fplendida fumos
Effe, fidem veri lux rediuiua facit
Plooger

Arbor foli Indiæ nota, cui per totum annum occidente fole flores, gignuntur multi, et
odoratu suaves, oriente defluunt, unde tristi illi nomen.

Een boom welcke in Indien alleen bekent is, int ondergaen vande Son voort,
brengende veel welrieckende bloemen, welcke alle int opgaen vande felve
weder af vallen, en dat het gantfche Iaer door.
86 en 87

ARbor, quam Triftem vocant, mirabili natura, olim fplendidorum ingeniorum ftylum mirificis fabulis & lufibus excitaffet. Etiam Indi originem narrant, Carmine ac furore Poetico dignam Nobilis quidam Parifatico dictus, filiam domi habebat pulcherrimam. Ejus in amorem fol raptus, Virgini ftuprum intulit. Illa gaudens tanto amatore, virginitatis pretium in numinis adfectu ponebat, donec fueta Deorum leuitate in aliam flammas fuas vertit. Ibi tum filia defperatione vitam finivit, & igni impofita in cineres verfa, locū rogi, hujus arboris proventu fæcundum fecit. Ea velut in teftimonium Iuftæ iræ fole fplendente pulchri-gudinem florum occultat & folia claudit, poft occafum floribus paffim exornata, gratiffimo odore mortales adficit. Ita Indi. Et fane omni anni tempore hæc viciffitudo, & flores ad diei exortum abjicit & ad occafum producit; infigni Emblemate. Arbor ipfa magnitudine pruni eft & fervit ante fores velut ad delectationem, largiffimis incrementis; nam etiam detruncata facile fortunam nouo florum proventu fuperat, foli Indiæ familiaris, nam in Lufitania, ut experimentis multis compertum eft, non crefcit. Flores fert ut malus Affyrica, eximio odore, qui tamen attactu perit. Aqua ex hifce floribus amæniffima eft, & odorifera. Clufius exifti-mat fuccum arboris non ferre folis ardorem, ideoque velut deficiente alimento, decidere fo-lia: nam quibus fol non ita infeftus eft diuturniore flore perfeverant.

Index

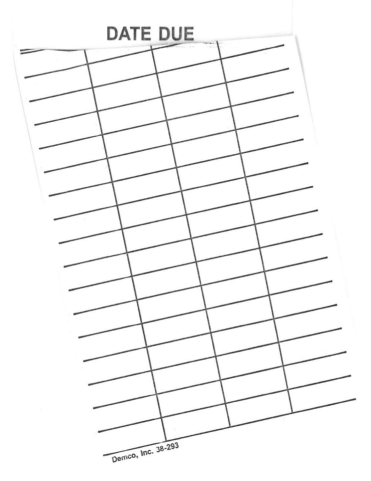

DATE DUE

Demco, Inc. J8-293